Law-Finders and
Law-Makers

IN MEDIEVAL ENGLAND

COLLECTED STUDIES IN
LEGAL AND CONSTITUTIONAL HISTORY

Helen Cam

New York

BARNES & NOBLE Inc

First published in 1963 by
BARNES AND NOBLE INC
105 Fifth Avenue, New York 3, N.Y.

Printed in England

TO
The Historians of Harvard
My Friends and Fellow-workers 1948-1954

Contents

Prefatory Note

THE CONTENTS of this book have for the most part appeared in various contexts in the last eighteen years. They are reprinted with only a few necessary corrections and additions. The place where each article originally appeared is stated as a footnote.

H.M.C.

Introduction: The Rule of Law
in English History

IN THE seventy-five years that have elapsed since Dicey gave us the phrase "The Rule of Law" has become almost a catchword. To him it was one of the two permanent features of English political institutions, and although we do not today take it for granted that the English system of government is a model for the whole world, "The Rule of Law" is still used as a criterion by which the merits or defects of other governments may be judged. Their law may not be our law, and our law may not provide that equality of all men, including the agents of the government, before the law that Dicey ascribed to it in 1885, but the distinction between fixed rules and arbitrary options underlies our conception of the liberty of the subject. There is certainly no idea of the equality of all men before the law in Magna Carta, which is so largely concerned with the rights and interests of one class, yet its legendary reputation is founded on fact. "In brief it means", said Maitland, "that the king is and shall be below the law." In 1215 the king was the chief executive, and the Charter says that he may not imprison any man save by the law of the land, and that his agents, the men who act for him in the shires and villages, are to know the law of the realm—a law which includes old custom, and feudal practice, and the new legal devices of the king's court. And the king owes justice to all men, not only to the great men of Runnymede.

In 1215 Magna Carta was a banner of revolt, condemned as such by the pope. Its last clause was in effect a programme for civil war, and it led to civil war. Yet John was scarcely in his grave when the charter was reissued in his son's name, and the final revised version of 1225 was to become the first statute on the statute book. It was in itself the first and most dramatic answer to

the question "Who makes the laws of England?"[1] The Great
Charter that is still law, and has been cited in the courts as
recently as 1920, was not the work of one inspired patriot. True,
it was an "obvious artefact" and not simply written custom,
but what was behind it? Not only the coronation charter of John's
great grandfather, but lesser local charters granted by magnates
as well as kings had set precedents; not only the terms of the
revivified coronation oath administered by Stephen Langton to
John in 1213, but the doctrines of the unknown commentator on
the fictitious "laws of Edward the Confessor", preserved with
Henry I's Charter at the Guildhall; not only the rebellious
"Northerners" but the loyal supporters of John and his son; not
only the feudal magnates but the legal experts who helped to
draft it had their share in assuring the perdurable worth of Magna
Carta.[2] Then as now the laws of England had many makers.

The essays in this volume are concerned with the law that ruled
England in the Middle Ages. Where did it come from, and how
was it made? For the English who came to England some 700
years before Magna Carta law was not made—it was there to be
found. They had, in fact, brought it with them across the North
Sea, for it was the custom of the folk. The laws of the Kentish
men, the Northumbrians, the Mercians, the North folk and South
folk of East Anglia, the East, the West and the Middle Saxons was
the possession of the people, preserved in the memory of men who
for the most part neither wrote nor read. It was declared by them
in their local assemblies where they did justice one to the other,
finding the custom that applied to the case and adjusting it at
need.

Almost certainly the law was older than kingship. When
Bracton said "The king should be subject to God and the law,
for it is the law that makes him king", and the poet of Lewes
wrote "The law says, by me kings reign", they were translating
into abstract terms the position of the earliest tribal rulers. "The
law was what the people had established", as a Roman lawyer
had said in the days of Marcus Aurelius, and when kings came on

[1] pp. 135-136.
[2] For all this see the writings of F. M. Powicke and J. C. Holt.

the scene it was their duty to preserve it. But when new conditions called for a new definition of men's rights, as when the newly converted king of Kent had to make a place for priests and deacons in Kentish society, or when the king of Wessex, having annexed Devon and Cornwall, had acquired Celtic subjects, or later still, when the legal status of Danes under English rule and English under Danish rule had to be defined, there was need of deliberate addition to the laws. Moreover, the missionaries taught the king of Kent that laws should be written down "after the example of the Romans," and from the beginning of the seventh century there are a succession of old English codes. These written laws represent only a fraction of the laws men lived by. They register changes; they select from rival customs; many of them, as time goes on, express the king's endeavour to protect life and property and enforce order, so that the law may take effect, for the wars that had made the kings necessary as army leaders created conditions that made them necessary as guardians of the peace. The kings do not see themselves as departing from custom or acting on their sole authority. When they issue decrees it is with the counsel of their wise men who speak for the people. Alfred "dares not thrust himself forward, not knowing how that will please those who will come after him".[1] Nor are they the sole agents in enforcing the law. Alfred's son calls on his councillors to be of his fellowship in seeing that the peace is kept, and the profitable royal privileges and perquisites bestowed on churchmen and magnates entail the sharing of royal responsibilities.[2]

Both the interests and the ideals of the Church made the clergy upholders of the law. Churchmen were the king's counsellors and clerks and helped to draft as well as record his decrees. But more than that, to them is largely due the lasting association of the royal office with the maintenance of justice and the protection of property. The first version of the coronation oath administered to Edgar by Dunstan in 973 includes the promise to prevent robbery and to see that justice and mercy be observed in all judgements. It it in judging that king and people declare and preserve and, indeed, make law. In the local moots, which according to Edgar's

[1] p. 184.　　　　　　　　　[2] pp. 27-30, 60-61.

laws, were those of the shire, the hundred and the borough, judgements were found by the men who attended the courts. And it seems certain that the same procedure obtained in the courts held by magnates for their dependents.[1] In all these courts, the unwritten as well as the written laws were evoked and applied; and, in the shire-moot above all, legal transactions were witnessed and so authenticated.[2] Though in difficult cases men could apply to the king, most of the decisions as to property and persons were made in the local courts where, whether the presiding official represented the king or a bishop or a lay magnate,[3] the men of the hundred or the shire found the judgements and so built up the law.[4]

How closely the law and the communities were linked appears in the persistence of local legal customs, even when a law common to all England had come into being. The boroughs, which owed their special position in part to military, in part to economic needs, retained their own customs intact, some of a very archaic nature. A succession of charters, from William the Conqueror's onward, guaranteed to the City of London her peculiar rights; for almost all civil litigation she could contract out of the national system throughout the Middle Ages.[5] The royal justices of the twelfth and thirteenth century, as Glanvill and Bracton taught, accepted and enforced not only the customs of London but the laws of Cheshire, of Norfolk, of Wiltshire, of Pickering,[6] and the men of Devon and Somerset under John, like those of Lincolnshire under his son,[7] successfully vindicated their local custom against the royal sheriffs. "What usage has approved becomes law without writing," said Bracton, with his long experience of doing justice in the shires. Only when a custom actually conflicted with the common law, or later with statute law, did the justices refuse to allow it. Even the smallest community, that of the vill, had its own by-laws, concerning agriculture rather than litigation. And in the thirteenth century the vill had a legal status, and could sue

[1] p. 26. [2] pp. 117-123, 170-172. Ch. 9, pp. 21 f.
[3] pp. 26, 60-62. [4] p. 24.
[5] pp. 87-94, 105.
[6] See J. C. Holt in Eng. Hist. Rev., 1955, p. 11. Henceforth cited as E.H.R.
[7] pp. 170, 171.

and be sued in the courts—a right that came to be the hallmark of the corporate borough.[1]

It was these legal customs, general and particular, rather than any specific enactments, that William the Conqueror promised to maintain when he said that he would observe the laws of Edward the Confessor. The English he ruled were to have their own law, as the French were promised theirs when England conquered Canada. But William, like his Anglo-Saxon predecessors, made additions to them "for the good of the English people". In effect, a whole body of new customs came in with the Norman fief.[2] Feudal custom gave the tenant the right and duty of counselling his lord, and thus the Norman tenants-in-chief stepped into the shoes of the Anglo-Saxon Witan. William and his successors issued their decrees with the counsel of their barons. Their share in legislation is assumed by Grosseteste,[3] by Bracton and by Edward I himself. "Laws cannot be amended or repealed without the common assent of those by whose counsel and consent they were promulgated." Feudal custom, moreover, gave the vassal the right of resistance if his fellow vassals backed him up in declaring their lord had broken his contract with them and thus legalized the revolts of 1215 and 1264.[4] An American historian has seen in feudalism "the origin of the English constitution". And whilst the king's vassals fulfilled their responsibilities and vindicated their rights in his court, all over England their own sub-vassals, the "barons' barons", were acting as judges in their lords' courts, and helping to adjust the conflicting claims of the old and new tenants of the honour and the manor. Their contribution to law making in the century after the Conquest has been attested by Sir Frank Stenton.

But the king of England was not only the apex of the feudal pyramid. He inherited from his Anglo-Saxon predecessors rights and duties towards all his people, and not least of these was the duty of safeguarding their property rights. William had promised the citizens of London that every man's rights of inheritance should be safe; he had promised that all men should enjoy the laws of

[1] pp. 71-84.   [2] pp. 46-48.
[3] p. 137.   [4] p. 48.

Edward in their lands and other goods; he had called in the men of the shire, the hundred and the vill to declare on oath what were the customary rights which Norman bishops and magnates had taken over from their English predecessors, and had in the Domesday inquest made the shire and the hundred arbiters in disputed claims. But when William's son, the Lion of Justice, was succeeded by William's incompetent grandson, the king failed to keep his vow to forbid robbery and do justice. In the anarchy of Stephen's reign, no man could count his person or his property safe, and the first task of Henry II was to restore some sort of security. It is doubtful if any legal device has had more far-reaching effects than Henry's assize of Novel Disseisin.[1] It provided that self help could not give a man a title to his land; he must seek a lawful judgement in a court if he wished to recover what he claimed as his right. And in the second place, the facts in the case were to be determined by the sworn statement of his neighbours. A jury of the neighbourhood, as in 1086,[2] was to co-operate with the king in doing justice, but this time the "royal benefit" of the jury was to be available to any free man who asked for it. The king's justices carried the procedures round the shires, where they were eagerly used by great and small, and the law of the king's court became the law of all England.

If the possessory assizes made the monarchy, politically speaking, the ally of all land-owners, they were, legally speaking, the starting point of a rich proliferation of other legal devices, and, administratively speaking, their popularity called into existence that great body of legal experts who watched over the growth of the common law. From the time of Ranulf Glanvill, the chief justice of Henry II, who in his great book maintained the dignity of the unwritten laws of England, the *jura et consuetudines regnae*, and who used his knowledge of Roman law to systematize in writing Henry's legal innovations, down to those of Sir John Fortescue[3] the chief justice of Henry VI, who sang the praises of the laws of England and gave us the first account of the English

[1] pp. 95-105.
[2] p. 169.
[3] p. 208.

constitution in the mother tongue, these great judges stand first among the law makers of medieval England. They made law by their judgements in the courts; they made law in framing the statutes of Parliament, which by the end of the Middle Ages had an authority even greater than the common law of which they were the champions. They had the pride and the *esprit de corps* of the professional; as early as 1219 they are found upholding the law against the royal authority that had given them their offices.[1] Not for such justices was the saying "Kings dispense with laws themselves have made." When in the fifteenth century a pseudo-feudalism was terrorizing juries, and turning the justices of the peace into tools of the local magnates, and making the king's Council the accomplice of criminals, so that a demagogue could say "the law serveth for nought but to do wrong",[2] even then the Benches at Westminster preserved their integrity and were able to hand on to the next generation a tradition of the law which the Tudors were glad to rely on.

The local communities with their customs, the kings with their decrees, the barons with their counsels and the judges with their expertise all found a meeting-place in what was to become the supreme legislative organ of England—parliament. Since Maitland,[3] no one is likely to forget that parliaments were originally sessions of the king's highest court, where the king did justice to all, and where men of the law and feudal magnates adjudicated in cases that involved new legal issues or high political personalities, and so made law by their decisions. As late as Elizabeth's reign a statute could be described as a judgement given in parliament. Possibly less familiar is the judicial provenance of the expression *in pleno*. It was a formula for expressing the publicity and formality of proceedings in a court, whether a shire court, a church court or a town court,[4] and thus *in pleno parliamento* comes to be used of transactions in the king's court assembled for parleyings with people of importance. At these sessions or parliaments the king's great officials discussed administrative business, the king held counsel with his magnates on political matters, as feudal

[1] p. 183.
[2] pp. 52-58.
[3] pp. 218-223.
[4] pp. 106-131.

action prescribed, and, as feudal custom also prescribed, sought their consent for extraordinary taxes.

There was nothing popular in such assemblies. The "community of the realm", who, according to the rules laid down at Oxford in 1258, were to attend the three parliaments of the year, were purely baronial. But social and economic facts drove both king and barons to consider the people who would have to supply military and financial resources in time of need—the knights of the shire and the burgesses of the towns. And so Maitland's high court of Parliament has to be reinforced by Stubbs' "concentration of local communities", and "assembly of estates".[1] Representation has a history of its own,[2] and the extension of the principle of consent to taxation from the feudal to the non-feudal classes is of the first importance in assuring the presence of the plenipotentiary representatives of the local communities. But the involvement of the commons in the processes of law making is bound up with the original character of the parliaments. Had parliaments been for them merely what the French-Canadians called them—"a machine for taxing us"—they might well have remained unpopular. But when a parliament was held, all men were invited to bring their petitions.[3] A parliament meant a direct contact between the king and all those folk who had a personal request to make or a local grievance to air. Such "singular" petitions soon came to be passed on to another authority for answer; but the "common" petition that concerned the general welfare, if it was granted, issued in a statute. In the thirteenth century, the king's judges and councillors had initiated laws; in the fourteenth most statutes originated in such petitions, often backed by the Commons as a body.[4] By 1414 they were claiming to be "assenters as well as petitioners" and asserting that "it had ever been their liberty and freedom that no statute or law be made unless with their consent". By the middle of the fifteenth century a statute can be defined as a law which has been made by the king with the advice and assent of the lords and commons and by authority of parliament. Fortescue, contrasting French and

---

[1] pp. 174, 195-198. [2] pp. 159-175.
[3] pp. 198, 219, 222. [4] pp. 144-149.

English systems of law making, said "Statutes are made by the assent of the whole realm, and by the device not of one man alone but of three hundred chosen men." And in the courts, where both common law and statute law were administered, it was held that statutes could "abrogate old law and make new law".

How far the commons in parliament spoke for those who elected them, and how far they were used by king or magnates is a matter of controversy. But they cannot be left out of account. Well before they had an established place in the parliaments it is evident that the law makers who framed the statutes were influenced by voices from the outer world,[1] and as their presence became the rule and not the exception there are signs that parliaments may be platforms for royal or baronial propaganda.[2] Most significant is the evolution of the device of impeachment, when the lords were prayed to judge the men whom the commons charged with offences against the king and the community. The impeachments were the forerunners of the deposition of a king, if not in parliament, yet with the backing of representatives elected for a parliament.[3] And the charges brought against Richard II reflect the concern of the common man for his rights at law. Richard, it was alleged, had declared that the law was in his own mouth and even, at times, in his own breast: he had been toying with the Roman doctrine that what pleases the king has the force of law. Further, he had frequently said and affirmed that the life of everyone of his subjects and their lands, goods and chattels were at his disposal, "which is altogether against the laws and customs of the realm". The common man might not be concerned with the political intrigues of the magnates, but when Henry of Bolingbroke averred that he came only to claim his father's lands —the lawful inheritance that Richard had seized—the common man felt that his own property might be snatched from him. His common law rights meant more to him than his share in the doings of parliaments.[4]

A century later, Tudor rule was welcomed as affording that

[1] pp. 143-144.
[2] p. 197.
[3] pp. 173-174.
[4] p. 208.

security for person and property which the Lancastrians had failed to provide. Governance, as Sir John Fortescue had preached, was what England needed, and in supplying governance the Tudors supplemented the common law with new laws and new courts, whose authority derived from the king's prerogative of seeing that justice was done. Their efficacy made them welcome, and though the subject was deprived of some of his old common law procedural rights, their power did not extend to deprive him of his life or his freehold. He still "enjoyed the inheritance of the common law and the acts of parliament" as the Lord Chancellor said in 1547. "The medieval doctrine of the supremacy of the law was adapted to the needs of a modern state."[1]

When, however, the emergencies of the sixteenth century were past, and the Stuarts repeated Richard II's mistake, and theorized as to the nature of those powers which the Tudors had tacitly exercised, conflict was inevitable. They claimed, in effect, that the king was above the law, and if the common law rights of the subject were at variance with royal authority, the subject must give way. Against this doctrine the historians, the common lawyers and the parliamentarians deployed their forces. "The common law hath no controller in any part of it but the high court of parliament," said Coke. But there were precedents going both ways. The limits of the king's rights as supreme executive had never been defined. The dilemma was stated by the Scottish lawyer who said "Government is the King's, and Property is the Subject's birthright." In 1637 the issue of the indefeasible rights of government versus the imprescriptible rights of property was tried in the case of Shipmoney. The king could not take the subject's property without his consent; the subject could not question the king's discretionary right to provide for the defence of the realm. The judges divided seven and five; and it took a civil war and two revolutions to settle the question. Parliament abolished the prerogative courts and declared shipmoney illegal in 1641, but only in 1689 was the issue determined. Parliament was to have the last word in law making; parliamentary statutes were not to be suspended by royal decree.

[1] Holdsworth, *History of English Law*, IV. 188.

The judges, the guardians of the common law, were to hold their posts not at the king's good pleasure, but by that of parliament. The Rule of Law was re-established.

The story does not end there. No story can end, in history. Twelve years after the Bill of Rights had laid down that "subjects have a right to petition the king" five Kentish gentlemen were sent to prison for presenting to parliament a petition imploring the commons "to have regard to the voice of the people". Parliaments as well as kings could be tyrannous. Public associations and the press did something to fill the gap between the sovereign law makers and the common man, but not until 1928 could it be said that the English citizen was adequately represented in the Commons. Nor were the law finders much nearer to the people. "Laws are they not which public approbation hath not made so," and the laws of the eighteenth century were very far from having public approval. "The law is an ass," said Dickens' Mr. Bumble, and want of faith in the courts is a recurrent motif in his novels. The juries who refused to convict those who had infringed the terrible criminal code of the early nineteenth century showed clearly how much needed to be done to bring the law into line with public opinion. But in the long run respect for the law has been preserved, and as of old its guardians keep their eye on the actions of an executive which today has so great a part in the making of the law. The old lady who asserted "The law would never permit the government to pass such an act" was no expert in legal matters, but she expressed a common faith in the protection afforded today by the rule of law.

And even amongst the incessant output of parliamentary statutes and statutory orders some vestiges still remain of the old customary law—of what Maurice Hewlett called "Saint Use". Common law is, if only very occasionally, called in to supplement statute law in the courts. The word "Cow" has three different meanings at law, depending on the custom of the country. And who made the rule of the road?

I

The Evolution of the Medieval
English Franchise[1]

"*Primo explicuit socnam*—he shed his life blood for the sublime truths of sac and soc." So, thirty years later, Henry Adams sardonically described the struggles of that pioneer Harvard seminar which issued in September 1876 in the volume *Essays in Anglo-Saxon Law*. The Adams of 1876 called it "a really satisfactory piece of work," and it has a secure niche in any bibliography of the subject. The Adams of 1905 derided it as the fruit of wasted energy.[2] The clue to the meaning of the Middle Ages was for him rather to be found among the pillars of Chartres than in the barren fields of law books.

Those who today re-read the essays of Adams and his pupils will indeed realize how much our attitude to the Anglo-Saxon period has changed since 1876. A purely legalistic approach seems almost fantastically inadequate. Today we are aware of a living society whose economic and social conditions have been explored by a succession of scholars drawing upon linguistic, literary, graphical, archaeological and topographical sources. It is in this setting that we study the laws, charters and writs of the Anglo-Saxon period, and it is by their aid that we attempt to solve or to re-state the problems posed by Sohm and Maine and Henry Adams.

If any one writer can be held responsible for this change it is undoubtedly Maitland. He never allows us to forget that laws are concerned with human beings whose habits and ideas are of

[1] Reprinted from *Speculum*, 1957, pp. 427-442, by permission of the Mediaeval Academy of America, to whom this paper was read in its first form in 1952. Of the many friends who have been good enough to discuss it with me I should like especially to thank Sir Maurice Powicke, Professor T. F. T. Plucknett and Professor A. J. Otway-Ruthven.

[2] See below, pp. 177, 179.

necessity related to their environment. In *Domesday Book and Beyond*, a work apparently unknown to Henry Adams[1] he expounded more forcibly than anywhere else the danger of applying the measuring rods of later centuries to the words and ways of primitive times, and set before historians, above all, legal historians, the ideal of thinking the thoughts of a past age.[2] He did his work so well that we are unaware of the debt we owe him. We even use the weapons with which he armed us to attack him— as he would undoubtedly have wished. This article is an attempt to apply his principles in a field in which, as it seems to me, he failed to live up to them. To read *Domesday Book and Beyond* for the first time, in 1905, was an experience as exciting as it was educative; but it is worthy of note that he himself was not wholly happy about the book. Three years after its publication he wrote to R. L. Poole, "Of all that I have written that (my Domesday) makes me most uncomfortable. I try to cheer myself by saying that I have given others a lot to contradict."[3] but he continues, "What I am most inclined to stick to is the king's 'alienable superiority;' " and it is precisely there that some qualification of his position seems to me desirable. What exactly was this alienable superiority? or, again in Maitland's own words, "What had the king to give?"[4]

It is not disputed that the basic purpose of a royal grant by charter or book was financial: to bestow wealth on the beneficiary. The Anglo-Saxon rulers, in the days of the earliest land-books, had material resources of various kinds but not much actual ready money. They had lands whose produce supported them and their court officials; they had rights to service, to entertainment and to tribute, in kind and in cash; they had the right to toll and custom, and they had a share in the financial penalties arising from the judgements found by the doomsmen in the moots. Maitland classifies these rights roughly as "fiscal" and

[1] But Maitland cited Adams' "learned and spirited essay," in *Domesday Book and Beyond*, p. 258, n. 1.

[2] *Ibid.*, pp. 9, 356, 520. The point has been admirably developed in R. L. Schuyler's article, "The Historical Spirit Incarnate, F. W. Maitland," *American Historical Review*, LVII. 2 (January 1952), 303–322.

[3] *Cambridge Historical Journal*, 1952, pp. 329 f.

[4] *Domesday Book and Beyond*, p. 234 (margin).

"justiciary,"[1] though noting that long after these days "the right to hold a court was after all rather a fiscal than a jurisdictional right".[2] The grant could take a negative or a positive form; exemption from rendering royal dues, or the right to receive royal dues from other men. Would such a grant involve the delegation of governmental functions to the grantee?

The Anglo-Saxon landbooks run from the seventh to the eleventh century, and Maitland has warned us against reading the legal ideas of a later age into deeds couched in a foreign tongue and in the terminology of an alien system.[3] But the historian who has reminded us that jurisdiction was not in those days a right of *jus dicendi*,[4] and that whoever presided in an Anglo-Saxon court it was the suitors who made the judgements, gives way to the lawyer who, forgetting his own precepts, applies to the Heptarchic rulers concepts and attributes which derive ultimately from imperial Rome. From the point of view of universal history, he says, there is retrogression. "Lines that have been traced with precision are smudged out and then they must be traced once more."[5] And in spite of his disclaimers we are left with the impression that from the point of view of English history the Anglo-Saxon kings were blameworthy in not living by foreign standards. Not proprietary rights but superiority is being granted in the landbook: "something political" is entering into it, when the king grants sake and soke and toll and team and infangthief; and the Anglo-Saxon kings are "guilty" of delegating or appropriating justice and of "abandoning" its administration to others.[6] "The state has been very weak; the national scheme of justice has been torn to shreds;" and the outcome is "stupendous failure".[7]

Did the Anglo-Saxon kings actually possess the powers and duties which, it seems, they are charged with relinquishing? We cannot, says Maitland, consider the question in isolation from the Continent.[8] But the Frankish kings took over more than terminology from their Roman predecessors. They inherited actual assets and a framework of administration. The character of a

---

[1] *Ibid.*, p. 234. [2] *Ibid.*, p. 277. [3] *Ibid.*, p. 225.
[4] *Ibid.*, p. 278. [5] *Ibid.*, p. 224.
[6] *Ibid.*, pp. 234, 251, 260. [7] *Ibid.*, pp. 101, 103. [8] *Ibid.*, p. 278.

privilege must depend on the system from which exemption is granted, and the Frankish immunity implied a system of comprehensive and centralized control, however decadent, for which there is no parallel in England. To speak of "the state" or of "a national scheme of justice" in Anglo-Saxon England, even to use the term "political," suggests the existence of categories not yet established there.

If we ask what system lay behind the Anglo-Saxon landbooks we recognize at once that no answer will be equally applicable to the seventh and the eleventh century.[1] Maitland points out in one passage that "every increase in the needs of the state, in the power or the state, gives the king new rights in the land, consolidates his seignory;" in fact gives him "a new immunity for sale".[2] We are following up lines indicated by himself, then, if we ask at each stage in the evolution of the English franchise, "What had the king to give?" linked with the further question, "Why does he wish to give it?" Vinogradoff answers the second question by saying that bookland proceeds "from the wish to place the fighting and praying portions of the community in a privileged position".[3] What privileges did the book convey?

As to the "fiscal" privileges—exemptions from toll and feorm and geld and so forth—there is no controversy, though there is ample room for elucidation.[4] It is over the grants of the profits of justice, the royal dues arising in the courts, covered by phrases like soke and sake, *infangenetheof, fihtwite, hamsokne* and so forth that lances have been broken by a succession of writers from Adams and Maitland down to J. Goebel and N. Hurnard. Where did these profits arise—in the folk moots, the *popularia concilia*, or in a court held by the grantee? Did the grant convey the right to hold a court? From the silence of the landbooks we might suppose, as Maitland says,[5] that this was not so important a matter to grantor or grantee as it has seemed to legal historians. By Maitland's

---

[1] For the evolution of the landbook see F. M. Stenton, *Anglo-Saxon England* (1943), pp. 302-309; *The Latin Charters of the Anglo-Saxon Period* (1955).

[2] *Domesday Book and Beyond*, p 240

[3] *English Society in the Eleventh Century* (1908), p 196.

[4] The records of Bury St. Edmunds, as investigated by Mr. R. H. C. Davis, contribute valuable evidence See *The Kalendar of Abbot Samson* (C. S. 3rd Ser., LXXXIV), 1954.

[5] *Domesday Book and Beyond*, p. 279.

definition the only difference between "jurisdiction" and "the profits of jurisdiction" is the right to appoint the president of the court;[1] the equivalent, that is, of the king's reeve who from the days of Alfred, at least, was presiding in moots and levying dues.[2] But the earliest reference to action by the grantee's officials seems to be in Cnut's famous writ of 1020 to Christchurch, Canterbury; "I forbid anyone to take anything therefrom except him (the archbishop) and his officers (*wicneras*),"[3] and it seems highly improbable that this grant set up a court that had not previously existed. Maitland's belief that in the Confessor's day "justiciary rights could only be claimed by virtue of royal grants"[4] is hard to reconcile with his statement that "we have no warrant for the supposition that royal diplomata have perished by the hundred and left no trace behind."[5] He took no note of the evidence that has led Stenton to believe that from at least the time of Alfred lords were holding courts and hanging thieves by virtue not of written grants but of custom reinforced by the laws.[6] Maitland himself observes that the phraseology of the grants suggests something that "has long been fashioning itself in the minds and mouths of the people and is no piece of new-fangled chancery style."[7] When, in the second half of the tenth century, the grants of sake and soke began,[8] it seems almost certain that long established practices were being explicitly recognized, and the question arises, why? Under Edward the Confessor, we are told, the necessity arose for showing title-deeds for rights actually exercised —it may well be from remote antiquity.[9] Did this indicate weakness or strength in the monarchy? It was surely the accession of

[1] *Domesday Book and Beyond*, pp. 96 f., 101 f., 278.

[2] W. A. Morris, *The Mediaeval English Sheriff*, pp. 4-16.

[3] F. E. Harmer, *Anglo-Saxon Writs*, p. 183.

[4] *Domesday Book and Beyond*, p. 89.

[5] *Ibid.*, p. 289.

[6] Stenton, *Anglo-Saxon England*, pp. 486-487, 493.

[7] *Domesday Book and Beyond*, p. 266. Cf. Stenton, *op. cit.*, p. 490, "Taken over by the king's writing officers from the speech of common men," and Harmer, *Anglo-Saxon Writs*, pp. 85-92.

[8] The oldest authentic grant of "sake and soke" is dated 956, and the first instance of the complete formula "sake and soke, toll, team and infangthief" is found 1042-1066. Harmer, *Anglo-Saxon Writs*, pp. 73, 75.

[9] V. H. Galbraith, in *E.H.R.*, 1920, p. 382.

more power to the crown, the evolution of more effective governmental machinery, that made it desirable for prescriptive practices to be sanctioned by written statements. It was not the kings, as Maitland suggests in his famous comment on II Cnut 12-15,[1] who were attempting to recover what their predecessors has been losing; rather it was the subjects, who in the past had relied on immemorial custom or on some ancient charter couched in general terms and were now feeling the need of stronger assurance. But it may be doubted whether every man who had sake and soke on the eve of the Norman conquest could show a charter to warrant it. Stenton thinks we are more likely to underestimate than to overestimate their number; Domesday Book names fifteen such in less than half of Kent.[2]

When Maitland, however, accuses Cnut and Edward the Confessor to "reckless liberality" in abandoning their rights and duties to subjects, he is not concerned so much with the ancient traditional formula as with Cnut's list of royal dues, which he appears to equate with the "highest criminal jurisdiction".[3] Miss Hurnard[4] has made out a good case for the limited scope of these "rights," but she also uses the term "criminal" without defining its meaning as applied to eleventh-century justice. The system of *bot* and *wite* is hardly compatible with the distinction between crime and tort, and when any man was entitled to execute a red handed thief without trial and the blood-feud was sanctioned by law,[5] terms drawn from modern classifications of justice seem anachronistic.

Emergence from a state of society where self-help did the work done today by policemen, gaolers and hangmen was bound to be gradual. Both church and monarchy were endeavouring to curb the vendettas and to organize the protection of property by various devices. From Alfred onwards, the kings accepted the responsibilities later formulated in the coronation oath, of upholding peace, forbidding robbery and seeing that justice was

[1] "Cnut's attempt to save for himself certain pleas of the crown looks to us like the effort of a strong king to recover what his predecessors have been losing." *Domesday Book and Beyond*, p. 282.

[2] Stenton, *Anglo-Saxon England*, p. 491; *Domesday Book and Beyond*, p. 90.

[3] *Domesday Book and Beyond*, pp. 282-283.

[4] "The Anglo-Norman Franchises," *E.H.R.*, 1949, pp. 290-310.

[5] D. Whitelock, *The Beginnings of English Society* (1952), pp. 40-44.

done to all men, and did their utmost to enforce order and punish theft. But this could not be effected solely by their own agents, and they called upon their magnates to help them in the task. Edward exhorted his councillors to apply themselves to the keeping of the peace and to be in that fellowship that he was;[1] Athelstan gave his official approval to the London association for thief catching.[2] In Goebel's words, "The *hlafords* were deliberately worked into the main structure of law enforcement, as this was reconstituted in the course of the tenth century, as a part of the policy of strong kings,"[3] whether, as he believes, only by being given a share in the profits of thief catching and so forth, or by being encouraged to use courts that they were already holding for the enforcement of the new laws.

The eleventh-century king of England inherited not only laws resulting from an enlarged conception of the royal office but also the new administrative organization made necessary by the addition of Mercian, Northumbrian, and East Anglian lands to the old West Saxon kingdom. His position was very different from that of the earliest royal benefactors of churches. He had more to give and more to withhold. A grant of all the royal dues arising in the hundred hides centring in a king's *tun* in the seventh or eighth century would certainly not have conveyed the same assets or the same responsibilities as the grant of a hundred in the days of Edgar.[4] Nor could freedom from suit to shire and hundred have been granted before the days of Edward the Elder. In some at least of the hundreds it seems certain that the reeves of the grantees not merely collected the profits of the hundred court but presided over its judgements. The evidence of Domesday as to the hundred of Oswaldslaw is unequivocal,[5] and the authentic writ of Edward the Confessor to Abbot Baldwin of Bury St. Edmunds grants not only the judicial profits of the eight and a half hundreds but also all the dues and services owed to the king by

---

[1] II Edward.

[2] VI Athelstan. Note Stenton's comment, *Anglo-Saxon England*, p. 351.

[3] J. Goebel, *Felony and Misdemeanour* (1937), p. 359.

[4] See below, pp. 59-67.

[5] Domesday, I, 172b: "Ecclesia S. Mariae de Wirecestre habet unum hundret quod vocatur Oswaldeslau . . . ita ut nullus vicecomes ibi habere plossit querelam, nec in aliquo placito, nec in alia qualibet causa."

the suitors of the courts,[1] whilst the abbots of Ely were almost certainly holding courts and not merely drawing profits in their Cambridgeshire and Suffolk hundreds under the Confessor.[2] The probability is that many other hundred courts were being held by subjects' reeves before 1066, but all the records are far more concerned to register "fiscal" than "justiciary" rights. And this holds good of the statements in II Cnut 12-14. Miss Harmer has emphasized the concrete character of the word *gerihta*.[3] The "king's rights" were royal dues; the law that states that he may honour a man highly by granting *mundbryce* and *hamsocne*, *forsteal* and *fyrdwite* gives no indication either in what court these profits of justice had normally accrued to the king,[4] or in what court the grantee would in future claim them. Edward the Confessor's writ to Bury St. Edmunds strongly suggests that these special royal dues would be levied in the courts of the eight and a half hundreds along with the ancient customary dues "that lawfully pertain thereto."[5] We seem justified, then, in assuming that those honoured by a grant of the new royal dues named by Cnut would collect them in the same place and in the same manner as they had exercised their prescriptive rights of sake and soke and toll and team and infangthief before these were defined in writing.

To sum up: the charters and writs of the eleventh-century kings testify neither to the abandonment of a struggle to recover lost ground nor to the irresponsible surrender of a ruler's duties. They reflect the need to define the scope of the rights which had come, in the course of centuries, to be bound up with the receipt of royal revenues. If the kings had taken on the responsibility for

---

[1] Harmer, *Anglo-Saxon Writs*, pp. 441-442; R. H. C. Davis, *The Kalendar of Abbot Samson*, p. xl.

[2] E. Miller, *The Abbey and Bishopric of Ely* (1951), pp. 27-28, 31.

[3] *Anglo-Saxon Writs*, pp. 441-442. In like manner Goebel stresses the financial aspect of the term *placitum*, which in the *Leges Henrici* is as often to be rendered "mulct" as "plea". He questions the prerogative interpretation of *placita coronae* for any date earlier than Henry II (*Felony and Misdemeanour*, p. 402).

[4] Miss Hurnard's doubts (*E.H.R.*, 1949, pp. 444 ff.) as to the competence of the hundred court to deal with the breaches of the peace covered by these terms seem hardly warranted by the evidence. See Morris, *Mediaeval English Sheriff*, p. 20; Goebel, *Felony and Misdemeanour*, p. 367, where payment "to the hundred" is equated with payment to the Crown; and Harmer, *Anglo-Saxon Writs*, p. 125.

[5] Harmer, *op. cit.*, pp. 164 f.

putting down fighting, peacebreaking, robbery by violence and harbouring of outlaws, it was only sound policy to give the great landholders a money interest in punishing these offences. And whilst there is reason to believe that these rights were often exercised in courts held by the grantees, of a competence equivalent to that of the ordinary hundred court, there is only the scantiest pre-conquest evidence of the right to exclude the ordinary officials of the shire.[1] The "well-endowed immunist" of St. Edward's day, who "has jurisdiction as high as that which any palatine earl of after ages enjoyed,"[2] is fiction, not fact. The immunity, in the Continental sense, did not exist.

II

The Norman Conquest introduced a new element into the history of private jurisdiction in England. The feudal relation of lord and man involved the right of a lord to summon his tenants to a court and the duty of a lord to see that justice was done in that court (as before, by its suitors). No special grant was required to authorize this practice. But William's policy of "conserving the laws of Edward the Confessor" meant that the churches' rights had to be maintained, and many laymen also succeeded to the rights as well as the lands of Anglo-Saxon predecessors. Legal historians of a later date distinguish between feudal and franchisal justice,[3] but the evidence of Anglo-Norman charters suggests strongly that the first generations after the Conquest did not think that way. The right of sake and soke, toll and team and infangthief went with the land and could be transferred with the land.[4] In particular, the right to a hundred was frequently regarded as appurtenant to the tenure of a particular manor, and two hundred years later men were still basing their claim to hold a hundred court on enfeoffment of their ancestors by a lord, rather than by royal grant.[5] And, as late as 1280, the justices in

[1] Miss Harmer quotes two instances (*Anglo-Saxon Writs*, p. 128).

[2] *Domesday Book and Beyond*, p. 283.

[3] e.g., W. S. Holdsworth, *History of English Law* (1922), I. 28; G. B. Adams, *The Origin of the English Constitution*, p. 78; W. O. Ault, *Private Jurisdiction in England* (1923), p. 1.

[4] Stenton, *English Feudalism* (1920), pp. 99-102.

[5] See H. M. Cam, *Liberties and Communities*, pp. 64 ff.

eyre in Somerset doubted whether special mention of a hundred was necessary in any charter older than John's reign to convey it along with the manor to which it pertained.[1] But the new conditions of tenure, notably the imposition of knight service on churches which had hitherto held lands and privileges unconditionally, made it the more desirable for the holders of ancient liberties to assure their continuance by royal charter. The demand for more exact definition stimulated the art of forgery, not unknown before 1066. Post-Conquest terms were inserted into genuine pre-Conquest charters, and these, or complete fabrications, were successfully submitted for royal endorsement. Miss Lancaster has told the story of the growth of the privileges of Coventry abbey, formerly associated with its founders, Earl Leofric and the Lady Godiva. She shows how Robert of Limesey, bishop of Lichfield 1086-17, obtained a judgement for the abbey from the court of Henry I about 1107-11 on the strength of forged Anglo-Saxon and Norman deeds, and how his forgeries were supplemented some twenty years later by those of the monks, and how these doubly improved charters were confirmed by Stephen and Henry II and ultimately enrolled on the Charter Roll of Henry III.[2] The smoke-screen cast over Anglo-Saxon written evidence by this school of highly experienced forgers is only gradually and laboriously being thinned,[3] though Maitland's hopes for a new edition of the landbooks[4] are still, after fifty years, unrealized.

On the other hand, in the genuine charters of the Anglo-Norman kings between 1066 and 1100 a new clause appears; that which forbids royal officials to interfere in the privileged land.[5]

[1] *Placita Quo Warranto*, p. 694. I owe this reference to Mr. D. Sutherland.

[2] J. C. Lancaster, "The Coventry Forged Charters: a Reconsideration." *Bulletin of the Historical Institute*, XXVIII. 76 (November 1954), 113-135. The hand of the forger of the Coventry writs has recently been recognized among Westminster and Gloucester documents. (Information from Miss Harmer.)

[3] Note, for instance, the discrediting of the writs granting Hormer and Godley hundreds (Harmer, *op. cit.*, pp. 18, 205) and Professor Stenton's warning against all the charters attributed to Edward the Elder (*Latin Charters of the Anglo-Saxon Period* [1955], p. 51).

[4] "The Laws of the Anglo-Saxons," *Coll. Pap.*, III. 472.

[5] Of the authentic charters containing this clause in H. W. C. Davis, *Regesta Regum Anglo-Normannorum*, I. three belong to the reign of William I (Nos. 162, 235, 252) and seven to that of William II (Nos. 294, 306, 311, 344, 408, 421, 453). The grantees are all clerics; for possible lay holders of the privilege in this period see S. Painter, *The English Feudal Barony* (1943), pp. 110 f.

It is evidence of the growing efficiency and aggressiveness of that invaluable agent of the crown, the Anglo-Norman sheriff.[1] This might serve in the eleventh century; in the twelfth the holders of ancient rights had to face mightier rivals than sheriffs. Under Henry I royal justices visited the shire courts, ousting the suitors from their function of judging, and holders of infangthief from their right of hanging thieves. They asserted the royal right "alone and above all men in the land, for the establishment of security"[2] to penalize men for some twenty-four offences, including, besides those enumerated by Cnut, the building of unlicensed castles, breach of the forest laws and, most significantly, *injustum judicium, defectus justiciae*. Only the crown had the right to supplement or correct the judgements given in subjects' courts, and in vindication of this right, an increasing variety of royal writs announced the king's intention of doing justice if courtholders failed to do so. And in the exchequer every claim of fiscal privilege was scrutinized. Confronted by this growing activity at the centre, the lords of liberties had either to acquiesce in the automatic devaluation of their rights or acquire new privileges. These might be silently assumed, if the central authority was incurious, or, as under Stephen, ineffective. The enforcement of royal regulations by supervising frankpledge and by fining those who infringed the assize of bread and ale brought its profit, and many twelfth-century landlords must have taken these functions upon themselves without express grant. But we have also to reckon with the conscious and deliberate acts of strong rulers. Whilst the majority of Henry I's charters confirm ancient customary rights in traditional language, and a fair number reserve to the crown pleas of murder and theft, a few specifically exclude not only sheriffs but royal justices from the privileged area.[3] Henry may have been induced to endorse the forged charters of Robert of Limesey for Coventry, but there is nothing questionable in his

---

[1] W. A. Morris, *The Mediaval English Sheriff*, pp. 71-73.

[2] *Leges Henrici*, x. 1.

[3] See *Regesta Regum Anglo-Normannorum*, II. (Oxford, 1956), Nos. 644 (St. Edmund's), 767 (Durham), 774 (Chertsey), 859, 1651 (Battle). For other exceptional privileges see the grants to St. Pancras, Lewes (510), St. Albans (596), Christchurch, Canterbury (840), Bath (988), and St. John's, Colchester (1204).

writ for Gerard of York. The archbishop is to have all the privileges that his predecessors had had under the two Williams, and, in addition, is to enforce the king's new statutes for the judgement of thieves and coiners, in his own court and by his own justice, so that he loses nothing on account of the new statutes.[1]

This writ foreshadows the development of the palatinates and great ecclesiastical franchises of the thirteenth and fourteenth centuries. They were to reflect or duplicate the royal machinery of government, and many of the great churchmen who secured royal sanction for their powers knew that machinery from the inside. Gerard of York, Robert of Lichfield and Coventry, Hugh Pudsey of Durham, and William Longchamp of Ely had all served the king in chancery or exchequer. "The liberty had to move with changing times if it was to remain an immunity,"[2] and their knowledge and influence forwarded the process.

Of recent years evidence has been accumulating which discredits the traditional antiquity of the greatest franchises. We used to find the origins of the liberties of the Isle of Ely in Etheldreda's dower lands; Mr. Miller has shown that they had their first beginning in Edgar's grants, three hundred years after Etheldreda, and that it is doubtful whether even ordinary hundredal jurisdiction resulted from those grants. Ely's extraordinary privileges only began in the later twelfth century, with Richard I's charter.[3] Mr. Barraclough has demonstrated that the characteristics which distinguish the "palatine" earldom of Chester from other earldoms did not appear before the middle of the twelfth century. The development of the "regalities"—the private exchequer and chancery, the register of writs, the explicitly named "pleas of the sword"—belongs to the days of Ranulf Blundeville (1187-1234).[4] A writer of 1195 says that these special Chester privileges were

[1] "Nova statuta mea de iudiciis sive de placitis latronum et falsorum monetariorum exequatur et faciat per suam propriam iustitiam in curia sua nec aliquid perdet uel ecclesia sua pro novis statutis set ea ut dixi in curia sua faciat per propriam iustitiam secundum statuta mea" (W. Farrer, *Early Yorkshire Charters*, I. 31). The writ is dated Easter, 1101, by the editors (*Regesta Regum Anglo-Normannorum*, II. 8).

[2] E. Miller, *The Abbey and Bishopric of Ely* (1951), pp. 25, 240 ff.

[3] *Ibid.*, p. 30.

[4] G. Barraclough, *The Earldom and County Palatine of Chester* (Oxford, 1958), pp. 27-28.

acquired *per indulgentias regum atque excellentias comitum*,[1] and an express grant of *jura regalia* by the crown is lacking in Chester, as in Durham.[2] The origin of the Durham palatinate has been found in the Northumbrian earls' independence of West Saxon rulers,[3] though in fact their title rested on royal acquiescence in steadily advancing prescription. Mr. Lapsley has traced the growth of the bishop's liberties from the lordship of a private shire in the eleventh century to the "little judicial system organized on the royal model"[4] described in the Northumberland eyre of 1293, with chancellor, register of writs, justices for all pleas, coroner and moneyer.[5] "As to his temporal holdings," said the king's counsel in parliament that year, "he has the status of a count of the palace."[6] He was a second king "wearing his mitre in place of a crown as the sign of his regality," his steward asserted in 1302.[7] This duplication of royal machinery had not been solely due to the enterprise of bishops trained in the royal court. Hugh of Pudsey had secured from Henry II confirmation of his exclusive jurisdiction over the men of the county, including presumably the pleas of the crown, but it was the knights and freeholders of the liberty who bought from John the charter of 1208. In spite of the opposition of Bishop Philip they obtained, during the vacancy that followed his death in 1208, the right to have the same assizes and legal customs in freehold pleas as were used in the rest of the kingdom.[8] To borrow Powicke's phrase, the liberties "fed upon the new processes of government."[9] What happened conspicuously in Durham happened in a lesser degree in the liberties of Ely, Bury, Glastonbury, St. Albans and many more, with their special sessions of the eyre, their right to receive the amercements

---

[1] *Liber Luciani de laude Cestria*, p. 65. Cited by Barraclough, *op. cit.*, p. 29, n. 4.

[2] Barraclough, *op. cit.*, p. 29, n. 4.

[3] W. Page, "The Northumbrian Palatinates and Regalities," *Archaeologia*, 1888, pp. 143-145. Though Lapsley does not accept this view, it is supported by Barraclough and by Bayley, who finds the origins of the bishop's "palatine" rights in the charter of 1094, when the earl, with royal approval, transferred his rights between Tyne and Tees to the bishop. *V. C. H. Durham*, II. 137-138; H. W. C. Davis, *Regesta*, No. 349.

[4] G. T. Lapsley, *The County Palatine of Durham* (1900), p. 171.

[5] *Placita Quo Warranto* (Record Commission), p. 604.

[6] *Rot. Parl.* I. 103.

[7] Justice Itinerant Roll 1/226 m.1d (cited by C. M. Fraser, *Speculum*, XXXI. 329).

[8] Lapsley, *op. cit.*, pp. 167-168.   [9] *Henry III and the Lord Edward* (1947), p. 50.

levied in the eyre on their dependents, their private justices and coroners, and their writs "in the form of" the petty assizes.[1]

To the acquisition of palatine or near palatine rights by the greater franchises corresponded the acquisition of new privileges by the lesser liberties. Mr. Painter has noted the first appearance of the liberty of return of writs on the Curia Regis Rolls of John's reign,[2] and the right to hear pleas of replevin or *vee de naam* belongs to the same period, though in both cases the practice was certainly older than the official label.[3] Both of these liberties arose from the procedural innovations of Henry II, and in the thirteenth century, along with view of frankpledge and the assize of bread and ale, they were far more valuable to landlords than the rights of ordeal or infangthief that survived from earlier days. They were widely extended in the thirteenth century, as was the right to hold a hundred court. A recent study of the liberties of Wiltshire shows that in 1066 four or possibly six hundreds were in private hands; by 1194 the number had risen to twelve or thirteen and by 1275 to twenty-seven, leaving only eleven under royal bailiffs.[4] And so with the other judicial liberties just mentioned. "It may seem surprising," says Mr. Hodgett, "that this period, which was marked by a significant growth in the activity of the king's courts, should witness what appears to be an extension of private jurisdiction.[5] But if the history of the franchises has been rightly interpreted above, it is just what might be expected.

Are we then, as Miss Hurnard suggests,[6] to abandon Maitland's picture of an attack on franchisal justice by Henry II, or to say that it failed? We have gone some way with her in questioning the existence of the exalted jurisdiction that Maitland ascribed to the early "immunists". They could not have equalled the later palatine earls;[7] Edward the Confessor himself exercised no such

---

[1] Painter, *English Feudal Barony*, pp. 114-116; E. Miller, *op. cit.*, p. 216; M. D. Lobel, "The Ecclesiastical Banleuca in England," *Oxford Essays presented to H. E. Salter* (1934), pp. 126-140; A. E. Levett, *Studies in Manorial History* (1938), pp. 152-153.

[2] Painter, *op. cit.*, p. 116.

[3] *Ibid.*, pp. 107-108. It should be observed that "withernam" (reprisal) is not a correct rendering of *de vetito namio*, and is not used by Maitland. See Holdsworth, *History of English Law*, III. 283-284 and F. A. Enever, *The Law of Distress* (1931), pp. 106 f.

[4] *V. C. H. Wilts*, v. 44-51. [5] *Ibid.*, p. 56.

[6] *E.H.R.*, 1949, pp. 310 ff. [7] See above, p. 30.

jurisdiction. The wording of Henry I's charters, we may agree with her, leaves us in some uncertainty as to the scope of the liberties effectively exercised by lay and ecclesiastical franchise-holders between 1066 and 1135. But we have to bear in mind the nineteen years that preceded the accession of Henry II. As Stenton has shown, the failure of the monarchy to discharge what were coming to be considered its functions had stimulated the barons to take new responsibilities on themselves. From both good and bad motives, many of them must have enlarged their franchises. Henry II's declared aim to return to the days of his grandfather was bound to involve some restriction of usurped liberties. But his attack, as Maitland's description indicates,[1] was indirect rather than direct. His power to innovate in legal procedure enabled him to compete successfully with the feudal courts in civil litigation—indeed the barons played into his hands by preferring his courts to their own. His grandfather's rule that a man need not answer for his freehold in his lord's court without a royal writ was the thin end of the wedge, and in criminal justice also Henry I had pointed the way. Though Henry II's attack was on crime rather than on franchisal jurisdiction, it was bound to reduce the franchises. The developing doctrine of felony and the royal monopoly of the inquest process, enforced by the agency of the itinerant justices, did in fact oust the jurisdiction of all but the greatest lords, and they, as we have seen, were able to secure recognition, tacit or express, of new powers. The lesser franchises were weakened, the greater franchises strengthened, as a result of the Henrician reforms. As under Cnut, the crown had more to give and more to withhold.

But this is not the whole picture. In the sixty years since Maitland wrote our views of the feudal baron have been transformed by the work of many scholars, above all Stenton and Powicke. We do not today assume that the Angevin kings saw the barons as their natural enemies, or a franchise as a *malum in se*. The long term result of Henry's reforms was to integrate the franchise, whether great or small, into the general pattern of royal govern-

---

[1] *D. B. and B.*, p. 283; *History of English Law* (2nd ed.), I. 576.

ment. The beginning of "deliberate archive-making"[1] under Henry's sons makes it possible to see what was happening. The earliest pipe rolls had recorded payments for the grant of liberties, which abound under Richard and John.[2] It followed that royal liberties bought and registered by charter were protected by royal process. Many of Henry I's charters had imposed a "royal forfeiture" of £10 on any official or other person who should infringe the liberty granted,[3] but we lack evidence of its exaction. The Curia Regis rolls of John's reign, however, show the holders of liberties claiming and being allowed their jurisdiction.[4] Both these and the earliest eyre rolls record pleas between subjects that indicate the king's readiness to uphold the legal possession of a liberty as of any other form of property.[5] A writ of course, *ne vexes abbatem contra libertatem*, appears on the Register before 1236.[6]

On the other hand, along with the protection of seisin in liberties went the extension to them of the feudal principle of conditional tenure. Liberties should involve obligations. Henry II's Inquest of Sheriffs inquired into the conduct of the baron's bailiffs as well as the king's.[7] His Assize of Clarendon authorized the sheriff to pursue fugitive criminals "even into the Honour of Wallingford," and laid down that lords could only claim the chattels of thieves and felons if they had arrested them themselves, thus, in effect, making the liberty of infangthief or gallows dependent on its effective exercise.[8] The principle of the writ of right was being extended from feudal civil justice to franchisal criminal justice: "Enforce the law; if you will not, my sheriff or my justice shall, and you lose your 'court'." Thus the privilege was insensibly being turned into an obligation, the exemption into a burden. Even more is this true of the liberty of

---

[1] V. H. Galbraith, *Studies in the Public Records* (1948), p. 70.

[2] Madox, *History of the Exchequer*, Ch. xi.

[3] Some twenty instances, ranging from 1106 to 1134, occur in the *Regesta Regum Anglo-Normannorum*, II. e.g., Nos. 754, 1145, 1167, etc.

[4] For instances of claims of liberties in eyre and exchequer see Hurnard in *E.H.R.*, 1949, p. 320, n. 3.

[5] *Curia Regis Rolls*, VII. 13, 82, 144 (1214); *Pleas before the King or his Justices 1198-1202* (Selden Society, LXVIII), cases 851, 885, 971, 1005, 1012, 1055, 1061, 1073.

[6] Holdsworth, *History of English Law* (1923), II. 608.

[7] cc. III, X, XV (Stubbs, *Charters*, pp. 176, 177, 178).

[8] c. 5, 11 (Stubbs, *Charters*, p. 171).

return of writs. Almost as soon as it is traceable on the Curia Regis rolls the writ *non omittas propter libertatem* comes into use.[1] If the bailiff of a liberty sailed to execute the writ delivered to him by the sheriff, the sheriff was commanded to disregard the royal exemption and enter the liberty to carry out the royal mandate himself.

Between 1066 and 1216, then, a whole crop of new franchisal privileges had developed, corresponding to the new powers and functions of the monarchy. The purchase of them from kings willing to supplement their revenues, and the registration of them in the royal archives, secured for their holders the protection of their rights both judicially and administratively. "The king's government stood behind the liberty not only as mentor, but as its support."[2] More and more the franchise holder was becoming involved in the royal system of government. The Magna Carta of 1217, when it regulates the holding of the tourn and the view of frank-pledge, expressly reserves the rights of those lords who have private views and leets. "Every man is to have his liberties as he had in the time of Henry our grandfather."[3] But whether the view is held by the sheriff or by a franchise-holder, "the king's peace is to be enforced and the tithings duly made up". The right to a private view might rest on a written grant or on prescription; in either case he who held it was in effect exercising a delegated jurisdiction, and was a royal agent, to be held to account just as much as the man who failed to exercise his right to hang a redhanded thief. Thus in 1237 Henry III writes to the abbot of Peterborough: "Since we ordered all the bailiffs in our realm to see that watches were kept by night against the disturbers of our peace and commanded that the holders of liberties should see that this was observed in their liberties, we marvel greatly that you in your liberty of Peterborough have allowed homicide and theft to be committed, and have taken no steps to keep our peace. . . . We enjoin you therefore that, as you wish to retain

---

[1] The earliest instance I have noted is in the Michaelmas Term of 1204 (*Curia Regis Rolls*, III. 241). A year earlier, for a similar case in the same franchise (Ely), another form of words had been used (*ibid.*, p. 46).

[2] E. Miller, *op. cit.*, p. 244, where instances of such support to the Ely liberty are given.

[3] c. 42 (Stubbs, *Charters*, p. 243).

your liberty, you take care to deal with malefactors and peace breakers, so that it may appear that you are a lover of our peace, and that we may not have to lay our hands upon your liberty because you have failed."[1]

As the integration of the franchise-holder into the national system proceeded, the question of title was bound to arise. Claims to liberties had been scrutinized in Exchequer as early as 1200,[2] but it was the overall confirmation of liberties in Magna Carta, it would seem,[3] that led the government of Henry III's minority to demand more precise statements of what liberties were claimed and of the title by which men claimed them. *Quo Warranto* queries occur sporadically on the Eyre rolls from 1218 onwards.[4] More general inquiries were initiated in 1223.[5] The writ of 1225, following on the re-issue of Magna Carta, links the liberties of king and subject as correlative.[6] In 1238, in the eyre of Devon, every lord of a private hundred was asked by what warrant he held it, and for eighteen of the thirty-two their answers, though no judgements, are on record.[7] The writ of 1244 commanded the sheriffs to see that no one of their bailiwicks exercised a liberty unless it was warranted by royal grant or by ancient tenure or by use up to the time of Runnymede.[8] And in the nation-wide inquest of 1255 the jurors had to answer such questions as "Do the men who have return of writs have that liberty by royal grant or by permission of the sheriff? What men are holding views of frankpledge or pleas of replevin without royal warrant? What men claim to have liberties without the king's charter, and of what kind?" and the inquiry was headed

[1] *Close Rolls, 1234–1237*, p. 556. A similar threat to the bishop of Ely in 1225 is quoted by Mr. Miller, *op. cit.*, p. 244, n. 1.

[2] E. Miller, *op. cit.* For instances of claims of liberties in eyre and exchequer, 1202–1232, see Miller, p. 216; Hurnard in *E.H.R.* 1949, p. 320, n. 3.

[3] Powicke, *Henry III and the Lord Edward*, pp. 110, 323 ff.

[4] Return of writs: Eyre of York, 1218 (Selden Society, LVI. 422); Wapentake (*ibid.*, p. 147); Gallows: Eyre of Gloucester, 1221 (Selden Society, LIX. 123 ff.)

[5] R. S. Hoyt, *The Royal Demesne in English Constitutional History* (Ithaca, New York, 1950), p. 155, n. 65.

[6] Powicke, *Henry III and the Lord Edward*, p. 323.

[7] Justice Itinerant Roll 1/174. Enough rolls survive for the twenty-one eyres known to have been held 1234–38 to make it probable that the inquiry was confined to the S.W. circuit. (Information from Mr. C. A. F. Meekings.)

[8] Powicke, *Henry III and the Lord Edward*, p. 111.

"Concerning the rights and liberties of the crown, and what archbishops, bishops, earls, barons, knights and other freeholders have usurped to themselves rights and liberties pertaining to the crown; and what those liberties are."[1]

The time was ripe for a clear-cut theory of franchise, and Bracton was there to formulate it.

Certain matters are, as it were, sacred. They pertain to the royal person and cannot be transferred to any save to the king's own justices. Such are views of frankpledge, pleas of replevin, the amendment of breaches of the assizes, judgement over thieves, and everything of this kind that belongs to the peace and consequently to the crown. . . . Matters of jurisdiction and of peace and what is bound up with justice and peace belong to no man save only to the crown and the royal dignity. They cannot be separated from the crown since they make the crown what it is. For the crown exists to do justice and give judgement and maintain peace. Such rights and jurisdictions cannot be transferred to persons or lands; they cannot be possessed by a private person either as the enjoyment or as the exercise of a right, unless this has been granted as a delegated jurisdiction. And it can only be delegated in such a way that the ordinary jurisdiction remains with the king.[2]

Nor can such a delegated jurisdiction be delegated to another.[3] Further, in the dictum "Time does not run against the king" Bracton rules out prescription as a title to a liberty; only a written grant, it would seem, is good warrant in his eyes.[4] And as to the terms of a charter, not even the king's justices are entitled to interpret them; it is for the king alone to interpret its meaning.[5]

After Bracton there should no longer be any question of confusing "feudal" and "franchisal" justice. This consciousness of a distinction between public and private functions may be due in part to the legal renaissance of the twelfth century, but also, surely, to the transformation of royal power and to the growth of a governmental system of which Bracton himself was part.

Maitland doubted whether Bractonian theory corresponded to existing practice,[6] and Holdsworth characterized it as "prophetic rather than true."[7] There seems to be no evidence as to the rules

---

[1] *Annales Monastici* (R.S.), I. 337.   [2] Bracton, ff. 14, 55d.
[3] So Glanvill had already said, *De Legibus et Consuetudinibus Angliae*, lib., XII. c. 19.
[4] Bracton, ff. 14, 56.   [5] Bracton, f. 34.
[6] Pollock and Maitland, *History of English Law* (2nd ed.), p. 572.
[7] Holdsworth, *History of English Law*, I. 87.

applied in the earlier years of Henry III's reign in Quo Warranto cases, but the inquest of 1255 evoked a protest from the holders of ancient ecclesiastical liberties which suggests that Bracton's precepts were being applied in practice in the years between 1255 and 1258 at least.

Although the king in the great charter confirmed to the churches all the liberties which they had exercised before that date, nevertheless he compels prelates to answer by what warrant they exercise such liberties. And if the prelate so compelled produces the charter of the donor, even though it declares that the donor gave all the rights that he possessed in the land, nevertheless that general statement will not help the prelate unless the charter expressly mentions the liberty that he claims, and the intention of the donor is made of none effect. Moreover, even if there is express mention, it is of no avail unless usage is proved, whilst if long usage is proved *without* mention, it is said that long possession is of no avail against the king.[1]

The *subtilitas modernorum* of which the bishops and abbots complained in 1257 was in a sense inevitable. A charter of Offa's granting "all royal liberties," even if it were genuine, could hardly cover return of writs.[2] History was on the king's side.

But when the investigations interrupted in 1258 were renewed on a more comprehensive scale in 1278, it is by no means clear that the Bractonian theories were fully accepted by Edward I's judges. Their initial statement of the law in 1279[3] admitted immemorial tenure as good warrant, and examination of the pleadings in the eyres of 1278-94 reveals widespread inconsistency, not only in the judgements but in the arguments of the king's counsel, from case to case, and from eyre to eyre.[4] Immemorial tenure was repeatedly accepted as good warrant, especially in the earlier eyres, well before the statute of 1290. The alienability of a liberty and the appurtenance of a liberty to an estate are admitted as lawful. As late as 1321 the notion that a liberty was heritable and alienable property appendant to a tenement was not questioned

[1] Matthew Paris, *Chronica Majora* (R.S.), VI. 363-365.

[2] In 1275 the abbot of Glastonbury claimed return of writs, by charter, from the days of King Ine. *The Great Chartulary of Glastonbury*, Somerset Record Society, LIX (1947), 220.

[3] Cam, *Liberties and Communities*, p. 182.

[4] For a full exposition of this see D. Sutherland's account of the Quo Warranto proceedings of Edward I, due to appear shortly. (1962).

by the king's counsel in the eyre of London, the redoubtable Geoffrey le Scrope.[1]

If we turn from the law courts to the law books, it is noticeable that Bracton's successors are far less clear on regalian rights than he is. Fleta, chiefly concerned with what the king may grant, and on what terms, classes escheats and ancient demesne manors as liberties. When making the point that it is convenient to the people that some barons should have *minutae libertates* he includes with such franchises as market, gallows, and warren the right to hold a court baron.[2] Similarly, Britton groups the power of holding plea in a writ of right along with infangthief as a franchise.[3] The dictinction between feudal and franchisal justice has again become blurred. The high regalian theory is scarcely traceable. The liberty seems to be rather a form of property than something "sacred", uniquely bound up with the royal office.[4] Gilbert of Thornton, who, as royal counsel in the eyres, had used or abandoned Bractonian theory as suited him, abridged Bracton more intelligently in his *Summa*, but noted that the maxim "nullum tempus occurrit regi" was no longer valid in relation to franchises. "Today if a man and his ancestors have used a royal liberty since time immemorial he may enjoy the possession of it by King Edward's statute."[5]

Bracton's theory was not and never could be applied with the logical consistency of the jurist who framed it. The statute of 1290 was not so much a surrender as a recognition of historical fact and political realities, notably the common interest of king and magnates. But the basis of the theory was valid. It was indeed for the king to do justice and maintain the peace. The ideal had been expressed in Edgar's coronation oath; by the thirteenth

[1] e.g. *Rex* v. *Fitzwalter* (Brit. Mus. MS. Harl 1062, f. 8; Brit. Mus. MS. Egerton 4811, f. 28d).

[2] Fleta, *lib.*, III. c. 6.   [3] Britton, ed. E. M. Nichols, I. 222.

[4] Fleta uses the term *res sacra*, but without comment or explanation.

[5] Sed hodie si quis usus fuerit aliqua libertate regali ipse et antecessores sui a tempore quo non exstat memoria gaudeat possessione, sua et hoc per statuta regis Edwardi" (Harvard Law Library, MS. 77, f. 25). The relation of the statute of 1290 to the custom of the Welsh March cannot be discussed here, but it may be noted that the position of the lord of Gower, whose palatinate claims could be checked by a royal charter, was weaker than that of his fellow Marchers who could allege immemorial tenure. See A. J. Otway-Ruthven in *Trans. R. Hist. Soc.*, 1957.

century the implications of the task had grown out of all knowledge. Edward I, like Edward the Elder and Cnut, was prepared to share the work with his more powerful subjects; it was neither practicable nor desirable to replace them by a ubiquitous bureaucracy. But the transformation in the functions of government meant that "What the king had to give" now included obligations as well as revenues. The lords of franchises found themselves loaded with "a great and continual labour"[1] undreamt of by the Anglo-Saxon beneficiaries of unconditional grants. Moreover, the monarch now had resources which enabled Edward I to implement Bracton's doctrine of delegated regalian rights. Such powers, he had said, could only be transferred to the king's justices.[2] Whilst Edward was prepared to describe himself as "the minister and maintainer of St. Cuthbert's franchise,"[3] he could say to the irresponsible holder of that franchise, three years later, "*Because* you have these powers, you are my minister, and if you fail to execute my writs or enforce my assizes or maintain my peace, you must answer for it to me. For the king's power extends within liberties as well as without."[4]

Liberties, whether great or small, still had their financial, as well as their prestige value in the later Middle Ages, but their place in the national scheme of things had been completely transformed in the course of centuries which had seen the evolution of the English monarchy. As the itinerant court of a tribal leader had grown up into the centre of that nation-wide organization for law, justice, trade, finance, defence and diplomacy of which Edward I was master, so the lords of liberties had learned to exercise governmental functions un-imagined by their forerunners, under a control equally inconceivable to them.

---

[1] See Cam, *Liberties and Communities*, p. 186, for this description of the lordship of the liberty of St. Edmunds. It should be noted that it is a fifteenth-century writer who puts these words into Edward the Confessor's mouth.

[2] Bracton, f. 14. [3] *Speculum*, XXXI, 338, n. 51.

[4] "Episcopus, cum libertatem predictam a corona exeuntem et dependentem habet per factum Regis, in hoc minister ipsius Regis est ad ea que ad regale pertinent infra eandem libertatem loco ipsius Regis modo debito conservanda et exequenda" (*Kings Bench, Placita*, Michaelmas 33-34 Edward I [KB 27/182] m. 103d). For a detailed account of the events leading up to this judgement, see C. M. Fraser, "Edward I of England and the Regalian Franchise of Durham," *Speculum*, XXXI. 329-342.

II

The Quality of English Feudalism[1]

"WHAT DO we mean by feudalism?" Maitland asked in 1887, and offered as an answer "A state of society in which the main social bond is the relation between lord and man— a relation implying on the lord's part protection, on the man's part service and deference. This personal relation is inseparably involved in the tenure of land, and the national organization is a system of these relationships with the king at the head as lord of all."

Maitland was speaking to law students, and the indelible feudal stamp set on the law of real property in England is one of the reasons why for English historians land tenure is an essential element in feudalism. But when Maitland goes on to say that in Anglo-Saxon England "the facts of feudalism seem to be there: what is wanting is the theory to express the facts, and that came to us from Normandy" he differs from such twentieth-century scholars as Sir Frank Stenton, for whom the theory—the doctrine of tenure—is the *sine qua non* of feudalism. Lacking "the great feudal principle of dependent tenure in return for definite service," Stenton says, we cannot, without abuse of language, call Anglo-Saxon England feudal.[2]

Between 1887 and 1929, when Stenton gave his Ford Lectures on "English Feudalism 1066-1166," Round's articles on the introduction of Knight Service into England[3] had initiated a fresh approach to the study of English feudalism. Stubbs' theory of a gradual evolution from Anglo-Saxon to Anglo-Norman military tenure had been replaced by the conception of the Norman Conquest as "a break away from Old English tradition".[4] But as

[1] Paper read to the Anglo-Soviet Conference of Historians in London, September 1958 (revised 1962).

[2] *The First Century of English Feudalism 1066-1166* (1932), p. 122.

[3] E.H.R., 1891-2, reprinted with additions in *Feudal England* (1895).

[4] *English Feudalism 1066-1166*, p. 121.

Stenton pointed out, the brilliance of Round's technique could blind his readers to the limited scope of his demonstration. He had established that "the whole elaborate system of knight service in England could be traced to the conditions which the Conqueror had imposed on his leading followers", but this had not all the implications that some assumed. Now, after another thirty years, we are witnessing in some quarters what might almost be called a return to Stubbs which even goes so far as to revive his suggestion that the Norman knight's fee derives from the Anglo-Saxon five hide unit.[1] In general, the tendency is to emphasize the very considerable continuity between Old English and Anglo-Norman institutions. Along with the writ, the Treasury, and the Danegeld, we are being reminded the Norman kings not only inherited from their predecessors the Old English fyrd, and used it as an effective military arm, but also followed them in employing mercenaries and exacting payment for exemption from military service.[2] Moreover, as Vinogradoff insisted,[3] service of various kinds was widely associated with the possession of land, and if knight service was new, the same cannot be said of serjeanty. The riding service recorded in *Bracton's Notebook* seems identical with that of Oswaldslaw and the *Rectitudines*.[4]

In considering whether these are "facts of feudalism" we need to bear in mind that the term *feudalism* is of modern coinage. It is an umbrella word, used to cover a wide stretch of facts and relationships—military, administrative, judicial, economic, social, political. In the following pages the social and economic factors which gave the *feudum* or fief its practical value are not discussed. Manorialism, the material basis on which the legal and political

[1] M. Hollings, "The Survival of the Five-Hide Unit in the Western Midlands", *E.H.R.*, 1948, pp. 453-487; E. John, *Land Tenure in Early England* (1960), pp. 140-151.

[2] C. W. Hollister, "The Norman Conquest and the genesis of English Feudalism", *Amer. Hist. Rev.*, LXVI 1961, 654-663; "The Five-Hide Unit and Military Obligation", *Speculum*, 1961, 61-74. Mr. Hollister's views are criticized in "Feudalism Revisited", *Economic History Review*, 1961, pp. 333-340 by Mr. J. C. Holt, who has also pointed out to me that according to C. Cahen, *Le Régime Féodal de l'Italie Normande* (1940), p. 63, the Italo-Norman evidence indicates the existence of the forty-day period for normal military service in Normandy before 1051.

[3] *English Society in the Eleventh Century* (1908), pp. 60-7.

[4] *Bracton's Notebook*, 758, cited Vinogradoff, *op. cit.*, pp. 66-7; Maitland, *Domesday Book and Beyond*, pp. 305, 307, 327.

structure of "feudalism" rested, is taken for granted, though it is recognized that the unfree villein, like his lord, owed service in respect of tenure.

What then, in general terms, were Maitland's Anglo-Saxon "facts"? Stenton's "Old English tradition"?

First, the relationship of lord and man, entered into by commendation—"common to the whole Teutonic world", consecrated by traditions of loyalty reflected in Anglo-Saxon literature from Beowulf to the battle of Maldon.

Secondly, the acceptance and utilization of this relationship in the laws, which gave the lord responsibilities for the behaviour of his man and recognized both his right and his duty to do justice on him and for him in courts whose existence seems certain, but at whose constitution we can only guess—the courts indicated by the formula *sake and soke*.

Thirdly, the possession by many land owners of rights— "superiorities" is Maitland's term—granted to them by the king, to take to themselves certain financial dues—toll, tribute, and the profits of justice which would otherwise have gone to the king himself and which, from the modern point of view, involve the performance of governmental functions.

All these facts or traditions are ingredients in English feudalism, and their existence made possible that continuity in evolution, that "uninterruptedness" of which Powicke has spoken,[1] which was maintained in spite of the catastrophic event of the Norman Conquest. William the Conqueror was able to keep his word to the English. He preserved the laws and customs of Edward the Confessor "in land and other matters. with those additions which he had made for the welfare of the English people".

It was the fact of conquest which made possible the "additions" which in effect created the English feudal system. In no other European country was the overlordship of the king ubiquitous as in England. Because all the land was the king's by conquest, the allod disappeared. Every man, to the smallest holder of half a virgate, held mediately or immediately of the king. Further, the introduction from Normandy of knight service standardized the

[1] *Medieval England* (1931), p. 15.

relation of the king to his magnates. A definite military obligation was imposed on all the king's tenants in chief, and for the first time the possession of lands and financial privileges by the great ecclesiastical foundations and bishoprics became conditional and not absolute.

To make sure that they could supply the knights whose service they had undertaken to provide, the tenants in chief had themselves to make their own contracts. At first the knights might be members of their household; *milites domestici*; or they might be retained by an annual money payment—the *fief-rente* of which Sczaniecki and Bryce Lyon have written[1]—but the typical *feudum* or knight's fee came to be a holding of land. The ladder of infeudation and sub-infeudation came into existence, whereby the same piece of land became liable to a series of contracts, linking each tenant with the lord above him and the dependent below him—and the land law—(outside the boroughs at least) became completely feudalized.

Political results also followed from this standardization and definition of the king's relation with his magnates. Tenants in chief, laymen and ecclesiastics, whilst succeeding to the traditions of the Anglo-Saxon Witan, were now bound by the feudal obligation to give counsel and aid to their lord: he in return, by the same convention, as well as by common sense, found it advisable to seek their counsel and consent in his military undertakings, in law making and in taxation. The new centralization of tenure combined with the older institution of king's sheriffs and king's treasury to strengthen the monarchy. On the other hand, the feudal baron in his attendance at the king's courts and councils was, as Powicke has pointed out,[2] becoming involved in the processes of government, and receiving a political education.

The same was true at the lower levels. The lord, as in Anglo-Saxon times, was bound to see that his men had justice. Now, by the feudal contract, he could exact the attendance of his men at his court, where they exercised the function of judging their

---

[1] Bryce Lyon "The Money Fief under the English Kings", *E.H.R.*, 1951, pp. 161-193; M. Sczaniecki, *Essai sur les fiefs-rentes* (1946).

[2] *Stephen Langton* (1928), p. 123.

47

peers. Stenton's researches into the records of these early baronial courts have taught us what valuable work was done in them in adjusting Anglo-Saxon and Norman custom and building up a working system of customary law on which the great lawyers of the twelfth and thirteenth centuries could base their innovations.

By the twelfth century the pattern of English feudalism seemed firmly set. The common law of the king's court, framed to protect the subject's rights of property, was based on a completely feudalized land law; its adjustments to changing economic conditions in later centuries were to be seriously complicated by its origin in a period when land was the main form of wealth.

Politically speaking, the magnates, the royal tenants in chief, were using feudal principles to establish their position as royal counsellors. The theory that vassals can repudiate their contract if the lord fails to keep his part of the bargain was applied both in 1215 and in 1264, when the barons of John and Henry III, by the ceremony of *diffidatio*, declared themselves entitled to take up arms against their lord. In 1215 they asserted their right to refuse financial aid demanded without their consent. In 1258, by the exercise of this right, they compelled the king to promise to seek their counsel, in parliaments or discussions to be held three times a year. In 1297, by refusing to supply the military aid the king requested, they extorted from him a promise not to levy taxes without consent that covered the whole nation, not merely tenants in chief, and covered non-feudal sources of revenue. The use of feudal conventions to legalize resistance to the crown was in effect laying the foundations of the English political tradition of "Her Majesty's Opposition"—the recognition of a right to criticize and oppose governmental policy, and, along with it, the responsibility for providing an alternative solution of national problems. The lawyers who helped the barons to draft Magna Carta—the manifesto of revolt which became the first statute on the statute book—were preparing the way for those members of fourteenth-century parliaments whose petitions were transformed into the statutes of the later Plantagenets.

Edward I himself was prepared to exploit feudal theory for the benefit of the monarchy. Whilst his lawyers, following Bracton's line, argued that governmental functions belonged to the king alone and could never, as had been assumed in Anglo-Norman times, be attached to the tenure of land, Edward maintained and enforced the doctrine that such privileges, granted by the Crown to magnates, were held conditionally, like fiefs. The right to hang thieves or to serve royal writs involved the duty of hanging thieves and serving royal writs; if the magnate who had such a right failed to do his duty he forfeited the privilege. Thus the holders of franchises—some of great antiquity, others of recent origin— were in effect transformed into royal agents, liable, like any civil servant to lose their office for dereliction of duty.[1]

But well before the reign of Edward I there are clear signs that feudalism is changing its character; that the facts and the theory are at war with each other. The causes for this transformation are economic, social, legal and political.

Even in the Norman period the kings had been supplementing the feudal army by employing mercenaries.[2] The advance of trade and commerce stimulated the growth of a money economy. Services could more readily be paid for in money than in land, and with the increasing complexity of agricultural organization on the one hand and of military organization on the other it was often more convenient to receive money instead of service. Scutage was in full use in the twelfth century, and reduced quotas and fines began under Richard I. The providing of a knight was far more costly in 1250 than it had been a hundred years before: with the advance in military techniques his equipment had become more and more elaborate. So the old contracts of knight service were in effect impossible of fulfilment, and the Crown had to find other means of recruiting an effective army for the wars in France and later in Wales and Scotland. New types of contract for supplying troops are found under John.[3] The military indenture, deriving in part, as Bryce Lyon has shown,[4] from the *fief-rente* of the twelfth

[1] See above, pp. 37-39.

[2] J. O. Prestwich, "War and finance in the Anglo-Norman State," *Trans. R. Hist. Soc.*, 1954, pp. 19-43.

[3] Powicke, *The Loss of Normandy*, 2nd ed. p. 213, n. 26. I owe this reference to Mr. J. C. Holt, who has also pointed out to me John's *prestita*, or additional payments, to the armies, largely feudal, of 1210 in Ireland and of 1213 at Dover.

[4] Bryce Lyon, *From Fief to Indenture*, Harvard University Press, 1957.

century, is coming into use under Edward I. It is a contract between king and subject for so many men at such and such wages,
for such and such a period, with such and such equipment, and
similar contracts between subject and subject are securing the
supply of the soldiers bargained for. But such contracts do not
involve land tenure, nor always personal fealty.

There were further reasons making the old knight service
contracts obsolete. Constant sales, gifts and exchanges of land
had led to so much subdivision of holdings that one tenant might
be bound, as on the St. Albans estates, to supply $\frac{4}{17}$th or the
22nd part of a knight.[1] The complications resulting from
subinfeudation are frequently illustrated in the Hundred Rolls of
1279. In the village of Little Paxton, Hants, Roger of St. Germains
holds a message of Robert of Bedford, by the service of 3d. paid
to the said Robert and 6d. on Robert's behalf to Robert's lord
Richard of Ilchester, and Richard holds of Alan of Chartres, and
Alan holds of William le Butler and William holds of Sir Gilbert
de Neville and Sir Gilbert holds of the lady Devorguilla of
Balliol and the lady Devorguilla holds of the King of Scotland and
the King of Scotland holds of the King of England. And the
relationships created whenever lands changed hands are further
illustrated by the fact that in this one village this same Robert of
Bedford holds various small parcels of land from five other lords
besides Richard of Ilchester, and two of the five also hold land
from him. Tenures like these were obviously incompatible with
the personal loyalty formerly associated with feudalism. Moreover such a fragmentation of holdings, some as small as half an
acre, made impracticable the exaction of the traditional obligations of service, suit and aid.

At higher levels, as G. A. Holmes has shown,[2] the holders of
great estates were finding new legal devices for evading the feudal
incidents which had been such valuable sources of revenue to the
Crown in the twelfth and thirteenth century. By the end of the
fourteenth century magnates were using the trust "to by-pass the

---

[1] H. M. Chew, *English Ecclesiastical Tenants in Chief and Knight service* (1932), p. 125.

[2] G. A. Holmes, *The Estates of the Higher Nobility in England in the Fourteenth Century*
(1957), pp. 41-57.

operation of feudal law" and deprive the Crown of its feudal rights of wardship and relief, and limiting its power to control the transfer of the great blocks of property which were being accumulated in the hands of a smaller number of wealthier tenants in chief. This exploitation of the common law is one aspect of the legal and political consequences of the development of a nation-wide system of royal administration and justice. Whereas in the eleventh and twelfth century men sought and found justice in their lord's courts, these were no longer needed. Great and small men alike preferred to use the king's courts. The king's sheriffs were the financial and administrative agents of the royal Exchequer, and the lords of franchises copied royal procedures and themselves functioned as agents of the national administrative system.

Edward I recognized and accelerated these tendencies. His Welsh wars, as J. E. Morris showed long ago, were the occasion of the first large scale use of the military indenture system. His statute of *Quia Emptores*, by putting an end to further sub-infeudation, prevented the creation of new feudal ties of the old type, and made inevitable, as G. A. Holmes has recently pointed out, the dissociation of personal dependence from the tenure of the land.[1] On the other hand, two of his new articles of the eyre indicate his recognition of the dangers arising from this dissociation and from the exploitation of royal processes of justice.

The lord's obligation to back up his tenant seeking justice in the king's court was expressed in the institution of warranty, des-cribed by Maitland as "one of the most powerful forces which had given society its feudal form."[2] Men could, he says, give up their land and take it back as rent paying tenants in order to gain the right to vouch a high and mighty lord to warranty in their law suits. In 1280 the eyre juries were asked to report "on those who had taken money payment to become the warrantors of men who were not their tenants".[3] The good lordship of the fifteenth century, the lordship whereon hang the law and the prophets, as

[1] G. A. Holmes, *op. cit.*, p. 83.
[2] Pollock and Maitland, *History of English Law* (1898), II. 663.
[3] Cam, *Studies in the Hundred Rolls* (*Oxford Studies in Legal History*, XI), p. 60.

John Paston described it, is already on the way, and the royal justices are expected to check it. Very similar instructions had been given to the justices of the special eyres of 1259.[1] The other new article, based on a royal writ of 1279, is aimed at the exploitation of the jury system by those who conspire by mutual oaths to make false accusations and defeat justice.[2]

Professor Dunham has distinguished between lawful and unlawful maintenance. It is proper for a lord to uphold his man in a court of law, in lawful and reasonable causes, as by warranty: but to uphold those who are not your men, or to uphold any man in conduct against law and order is unlawful maintenance, and the various devices by which in the fourteenth and fifteenth century great men maintained the cause of any one who had bought their support are the theme of a series of statutes from 1305 onwards.[3] These devices were well summarized in 1487 in the so-called Act of Star Chamber: "By unlawful maintenances, giving of liveries, signs and tokens, retainers by indenture, promises, oaths (in) writing or otherwise, by embraceries of his subjects, untrue demeanings of sheriffs in making of panels (as we should say today, by packing juries) and by taking of money by juries, the laws of the land in execution may take little effect."

Maintenance, the bringing to bear of influence by an external party upon proceedings in a law court, is still a legal offence and newspapers have been charged with it in this century. But the means by which it was exercised in the fourteenth and fifteenth centuries are characteristic of that later stage of feudalism which was first labelled "bastard" by Plummer in 1885.[4] It is described as illegitimate because it is divorced from the tenure of land, because the relationship is not hereditary and because it derives its vigour from a non-feudal source. It is parasitic on a system of royal justice. There is nothing feudal about juries, justices of the peace, or justices of oyer and terminer, but it is through them that the lord is maintaining the cause of his dependents. A statute of 1429 states specifically that the statutes against liveries are not being

---

[1] Powicke, *Henry III and the Lord Edward*, p. 406.
[2] Cam, *op. cit.*, pp. 58-9.
[3] W. H. Dunham, *Lord Hastings' Indentured Retainers 1461-83* (1955), pp. 8-13, 67-88.
[4] Sir John Fortescue, *The Governance of England*, ed. Charles Plummer (1885), p. 15.

enforced because maintenance prevents juries from indicting.[1]

"Giving of liveries", the second abuse mentioned in 1487, was again a perfectly legitimate practice in its proper place. Wages to members of a lord's household were normally supplemented by "robes". But when liveries were worn by men not of the household and supplemented by badges, easily recognizable by the illiterates as indicating a man's affinities, and thus serving, like modern blackshirts, or brownshirts, as rallying points for gangs of men, they would become menaces to public order. Lady Stenton has noted a north country robber who clothed his fifteen followers in one livery "as if he had been a great lord" as early as 1218.[2] The statute of 1305 against conspirators defines them as men who receive men in the country in their liveries or fees to maintain their malicious enterprises. In 1322 when Edward II was pursuing his savage vengeance on the supporters of Thomas of Lancaster, a number of petitioners to parliament tried to prove that though they wore the livery of rebel lords they had not supported them actively.[3] The so-called Malmesbury chronicler tells the story of the sheriff of Hereford, Roger of Elmbridge, who had held the shire court clothed in the suit which the barons had given to their knights to know them by, and for this insult to the king he was found guilty of treason and hanged in that very suit, in February 1322, so that the punishment might fit the crime for all men to see.[4] Dunham has summarized the series of statutes from 1305 to 1468 by which the wearing of liveries was ultimately restricted to the bona fide household of great magnates.

"Retainers by indenture" belong to a society accustomed to contracts recorded in writing. The retinue itself is the direct descendant of Tacitus' *comitatus*. As Powicke has said, the *bacheleria* who demonstrated at the parliament of 1259 were the retainers of the great barons there present.[5] We are told similarly in 1327 that the knights of the retinues of four great earls swore

---

[1] St. *8 Hen. VI*, ch. 4.
[2] *Rolls of Justices in Eyre for Yorkshire, 3 Henry III*, ed. D. M. Stenton. (Selden Society, 1937), p. 424.
[3] *Rot. Parl.* i. 388, 389, 391, 394, 395.
[4] *Vita Edwardi Secundi* ed. N. Denholm-Young (1957), pp. 119-20.
[5] Powicke, *Henry III and the Lord Edward*, p. 407, n. 1.

with them to uphold the cause of Isabella.[1] As the estates held by the greater earls were increased by marriage to heiresses and other means, their organization became more elaborate, and the number of dependents increased. Dr. Holmes has described the host of officials, councillors, soldiers, servants and followers of all kinds who were fed and paid by a great lord, and has analysed the retinue of various fourteenth-century magnates, resident in their various castles and manor houses of their estates.[2] Of these dependents more and more, as the century went on, were retained by written contracts, the terms of which, to judge by the fraction that survives, varied considerably. Professor Otway Ruthven has recently discovered in the Red Book of Kildare and kindly communicated to me transcripts of a series of contracts between John fitz Thomas, Baron of Offaly and later the first earl of Kildare and persons who are becoming his *familiares*. The dates are of 1289-91; the form varies from contract to contract. One provides for the wearing of squire's livery until the *familiaris*— practically his lord's social equal—shall be able to wear knight's livery. The sanction of the contract is generally a sum of money, ranging from 40 silver marks to 1,000 pounds sterling, payable at the exchequer of Dublin, but one contract simply says "on pain of perjury". None refers specifically to military service: faith, aid, counsel and service are pledged against all men saving the king and, in one case, as many as six other lords. These Irish contracts do not use the indenture form, the cyrograph, of which each party retained a duplicate, as the contemporary English contracts do. The English contracts also vary considerably. Some are for military service, for a specified period, with specified wages and agreements as to compensation for loss of horses and so on. Some add to the specific military contract a retaining fee for peacetime. Some contracts are for life, but none provide for a renewal on the death of either party, though in fact the relationship certainly was carried on to the next generation in some instances. Mr. Dunham has printed a collection of indentures

---

[1] *Calendar of Plea and Memoranda Rolls of the City of London 1323-1364*, ed. A. H. Thomas (1929), p. 12.

[2] Holmes, *op. cit.*, pp. 58-74.

entered into between Hastings, the friend and follower of Edward IV, beheaded by Richard III, and a number of Hastings' retainers. They were mostly drawn up after the Statute of 1468, which, whilst appearing to prohibit retaining by indenture, permits retaining "for lawful service done or to be done". The clause included in most of Hastings' indentures that the retainer promises to take Hastings' part against all men *saving the allegiance that he owes the king*, and the clause by which Hastings promises to be good and favourable lord to the retainer and help him in all matters *according to the law*, or *as law and conscience requireth* presumably kept these indentures within the statutory limits. But the retainer's undertaking "to be ready to come at all times with as many men as he may bring, defensibly arranged at the costs and expenses of his lord" indicates very clearly the possibilities of civil war contemplated in these indentures. Tenure by knight service in Norman times meant the duty of furnishing knights to fight for the king: in these contracts the military service is owed to a subject. Mr. Dunham insists that though the terms of the contract have changed, the old feudal tradition of loyalty and devotion to your lord are still very much alive. But, as Mr. McFarlane has shown, the same man might be bound to a number of different lords in succession, or even simultaneously.[1] The links of loyalty were shifting and transitory. And reservation of faith to the lord king might be a very empty form—not only in the fifteenth century, when two different dynasties were competing for the crown, but also in the fourteenth. Another significant incident from the reign of Edward II, the period in which so many of the features of bastard feudalism became evident, illustrates the conflict of loyalties between lord and king. At the time when baronial opposition to Edward II was developing into armed revolt in Wales and in northern England, the rector of Wigan, Lancashire, *ex officio* lord of the borough of Wigan, preached a sermon to his parishioners telling them that it was their duty as liege men of the earl of Lancaster to follow him against the king, as the earl's cause was just and the king's cause unjust. He caused prayers to be said in his church for the earls that they

[1] "Bastard Feudalism," *Bulletin Inst. Hist. Research,* 1945, pp. 170-177.

might be given grace as pillars of the land to maintain the crown and the peace of the land, and he declared that he would absolve from all their sins those who went to fight in this just cause. He himself sent his son with another mounted soldier and four foot soldiers to serve in Lancaster's forces. The fact that he had himself been a chancery clerk for many years counted for nothing against his loyalty to Lancaster, the leader of the baronial rebels—and it was presumably because he was a cleric that he escaped the fate of the sheriff of Hereford and got off with a fine of 300 marks.[1]

Does loyalty to a lord, as Mr. Dunham suggests, make feudalism? The "lordship" of the fifteenth century has been described as a throw-back to Anglo-Saxon lordship when a man was free to go to whatever lord he pleased; but fifteenth-century ties were not as permanent, and fifteenth-century loyalties seldom reached Anglo-Saxon standards of faithfulness to death. And when land tenure and heredity have dropped out of the relationship, can it be called genuinely feudal?[2] I know no better epithet than that which Plummer coined seventy years ago. It is a bastard feudalism, the illegitimate descendant of a once mighty stock; illegitimate because deriving its vitality illicitly from the non-feudal stock of monarchic institutions.

If we regard European feudalism as the response of Western civilization to the challenge of the barbarian invasions, it becomes clear that that challenge took a different form in our island. Our invaders came by sea; the feudal castle and the feudal horsemen, regarded by Stenton and Stephenson as essential features of feudalism, were not here before the Normans came.[3] Lordship was here, and lordship was used by the Anglo-Saxon kings to help them in their task of maintaining peace and justice, but it was the Normans who brought in the feudal army, the feudal tenures, the feudal revenues, the feudal courts which for two

[1] *Rot. Parl.* i, 406; *Vict. Co. Hist. Lancashire*, II. 201; G. H. Tupling, *South Lancashire in the reign of Edward II* (Chetham Society, 1949), pp. 71-3.

[2] It might be said that this applies equally to the *fief rente* and the baronial mercenaries of the twelfth century.

[3] Stenton, *op. cit.*, p. 215; C. Stephenson, *Mediaeval Institutions* (1954), pp. 252-4. As against Hollister and Stephenson, however, it has been argued that the Anglo-Saxons did fight on horse back. See J. H. Clapham in *E.H.R.*, 1910, pp. 287-293, and R. Glover in *E.H.R.*, 1952, pp. 1-18.

centuries best met the needs of government. By the thirteenth century that need had dwindled. The military, judicial and financial institutions of feudalism were being supplemented and partly supplanted by non-feudal practices and institutions. The law of real property was set in a feudal pattern; the feudal doctrines of counsel and consent had become part of the national political tradition. But social and economic changes were modifying the structure of politics. The towns had always been outside feudalism and apart from the City of London they played no large part in English *politics*. But a growing number of substantial smaller landholders, who had become useful if not essential to the monarchy for the running of local government, were beginning to count as a political force. Magnates and rulers are competing for their support from the Barons' Wars of Henry III's reign onwards. The king will use them to recruit soldiers for his wars by the muster and the indenture systems; he will summon them to his parliaments, where the feudal doctrine of consent is being extended to cover the newer, non-feudal taxes, or to solicit their support against the demands of the magnates. The magnates, for their part, will seek to attach these middling men not only for political reasons, but because of their need of lawyers and business men to manage their ever-growing groups of estates. Mr. Denholm-Young,[1] Mr. Somerville,[2] and Mr. Holmes,[3] have given us some idea of the vast numbers of dependents who served the great lord or lady in their private exchequers and chanceries, in their councils and in their manors. Mr. Roskell and Mr. McFarlane have indicated their importance in the fourteenth- and fifteenth-century House of Commons.[4] The stewards of the great lords who figure in the parliaments of Edward III were able and independent men; we must not assume that they were merely the tools of their masters. But the system of retainder by indenture extended far beyond the bona fide members of a noble household or the active officials of a great estate. When the Commons in

---

[1] *Seignorial Administration in England* (1937).

[2] R. Somerville, *History of the Duchy of Lancaster* (1953).

[3] *Op. cit.*

[4] J. S. Roskell, *The Commons in the Parliament of 1422* (1954); K. B. McFarlane, "Parliament and Bastard Feudalism," *Trans. R. Hist. Soc.*, 1944, pp. 53-99.

parliament after parliament petitioned against the abuses of retainder, of livery and of maintenance, they were complaining of a pest that riddled the countryside, of practices that were making law and justice a dead letter there, whatever might be the case at Westminster. From the reign of Edward II onwards this complex of private loyalties threatened revolt and civil war; a danger only averted if overseas military adventure offered an outlet, or if a strong ruler like Henry V or Edward IV was on the throne. Bastard feudalism was indeed a disease of the body politic, which, like the anarchy of Stephen's reign, gave genuine feudalism a bad name; a disease which had to be mitigated, if not eradicated, by the Tudors.[1]

Looked at as a whole, the most characteristic quality of English feudalism seems to be its intimate association with royal government. Knight service, baronial courts and feudal revenues in the Anglo-Norman period; feudal land law the basis of the national common law as it developed from Henry II to Edward I; the traditions of counsel and consent handed down from the great councils of the Normans and Angevins to the parliaments of the later Middle Ages; the integration of the franchise holder into the national system of government by the rule of responsibility; even the invasion of the governmental machine by bastard feudalism—all these are evidence of what might be called the marriage of feudalism with the non-feudal monarchic system thatWilliam the Conqueror inherited from Edward the Confessor. Even when Henry Tudor set out to destroy bastard feudalism he made use, alongside his invaluable Star Chamber, of the ancient feudal prerogatives of the Crown to fill his coffers—setting up the Supervisor of the Royal Prerogative to revive and exact ruthlessly the moribund feudal incidents of escheat, wardship and marriage.

[1] For the survival of lordship, maintenance and livery under the Tudors see McFarlane, *Bulletin Inst. Hist. Research*, 1945, pp. 179-80; J. E. Neale, *The Elizabethan House of Commons* (1949), pp. 24-7, 152-3; Dunham, *op. cit.*, pp. 44-6, 78, n. 91-110.

III

The "Private" Hundred in England before the Norman Conquest[1]

IN THE year 1316, when an inquest was held throughout England into the lordship of every township and hundred, it was possible to give precise answers to precise questions. Of the 628 hundreds named at that date 240 were royal and the remaining 388 were held by subjects.[2] In many instances various forms of written evidence enable us to assign the grant of such a hundred to a post-conquest date, but where immemorial tenure rather than charter is the holders' warrant, a search for the origin of their rights may take us back beyond Domesday Book, even, it would seem, beyond the days of the hundredal organization, introduced, as most authorities now agree,[3] by the West Saxon Conquerors of the Danelaw in the tenth century.

Over how many hundreds were subjects holding rights before 1066? What follows is an attempt to assemble the scattered evidence, none of it new, which may enable us to make a reasonable guess at an answer. Much of this evidence is to be found in writings of post-conquest date, some as late as the thirteenth or fourteenth century, and even when searching diplomatic criticism has been applied to it, only an approximation can be hoped for. We need not for that reason, however, refuse to use the great mass of charters transcribed in royal records and monastic

---

[1] Reprinted from *Studies presented to Sir Hilary Jenkinson*, ed. J. Conway Davies, Oxford University Press, 1957. Their permission to reprint is hereby acknowledged.

[2] The returns, printed in the five volumes of *Feudal Aids*, cover twenty-seven counties; the facts for the remaining six can be deduced from the *Rotuli Hundredorum* or the Sheriff's Accounts at the P.R.O.

[3] e.g. Liebermann, *Gesetze der Angel-Sachsen* (1912), II. ii. 516; Corbett in *Camb. Med. Hist.* (1922), III. 366; Stenton, *Anglo-Saxon England* (1943), p. 289 f.; Whitelock, *English Historical Documents* (1955), p. 393.

cartularies,[1] and the returns to inquests which record old traditions.

It is necessary to begin by defining one's terms. What do we mean by "lordship of a hundred" in the tenth or early eleventh century? The existence of a judicial or administrative unit such as we see in the thirteenth century is only possible under a centralized monarchy with effective control over the agencies of local government. The existence of clearly delimited geographical areas involves settlement by a population whose utilization of the soil has gone so far that there are few gaps left between community and community. We must not visualize a royal map-maker parcelling out shires into neat districts, much as the French Constituent Assembly planned the departments in 1790. Sir Richard Hoare speaks most aptly of the causes for

almost infinite irregularity in the bounds of hundreds . . . the felling of part of a primeval forest . . . the draining of a marsh, the cultivating of a waste by any one individual could extend the limits of the hundred in that direction. . . . To have drawn a map at this period assigning boundaries to the hundreds would have been like writing on the sand or like attempting to give a permanent representation of a surface of water when agitated by the wind.[2]

Above all, rights of property might modify the pattern. The lord of a private hundred granted by the king, he pointed out, "will wish to connect other lands he holds to the hundred and compel attendance at his court, and may attract tenants from another hundred".[3]

Hoare is here using feudal terminology, but it is equally true before 1066 that the lord of a hundred is the person who has the hundredal soke; the right, that is, to exact attendance at the hundred court and the right to take some if not all of the profits of justice arising there. So Maitland described it;[4] Corbett later defined the grant of hundredal soke as the transfer to the grantees of the king's rights in the area in question, and the subjection to them, for police and judicial purposes, of men who were not their tenants. Such men would henceforth have to appear before

[1] See G. J. Turner in introduction to *Black Book of St. Augustine* (1915), p. xvii; F. E. Harmer in *Anglo-Saxon Writs* (Cambridge, 1952) and F. M. Stenton, *The Latin Charters of the Anglo-Saxon period* (Oxford, 1955).

[2] *Modern Hist. of Wiltshire* (1822), I. 172 f.   [3] *Ibid.*, p. 74.

[4] *Domesday Book and Beyond*, pp. 92-97.

officials appointed by the grantees, if charged with any crime, and if convicted be liable to pay them fines.[1] It has long been recognized that the king's rights in the area, frequently if not invariably, included the receipt of various ancient customary dues deriving most probably from the primitive right to *feorm* or entertainment,[2] and Mr. Davis, in his recent edition of Abbot Samson's Kalendar,[3] points out that "soke, as used in Domesday Book, meant far more than jurisdiction"[4] and argues that, in East Anglia certainly and probably elsewhere, the grant of hundredal soke carried with it not only the profits of justice in the hundred court and the right to exact the attendance there of certain suitors or sokemen, but also the right to receive from the sokemen or holders of socage lands in the hundred such customary dues as wardpenny, averpenny, foddercorn and hidage.[5] Edward the Confessor's grant of the eight and a half hundreds of Bury St. Edmunds to the abbot had transferred these revenues to him, *quia sunt regalia*.[6] The evidence he adduces, remarkably full and clear, is post-conquest, but there is no reason to doubt its validity for Suffolk in the days of Edward the Confessor. How far are we justified in arguing backwards from the eleventh to earlier centuries, and from East Anglia to other regions?

Mr. Davis may go too far in suggesting that "the primary purpose of hundreds was fiscal"[7], but it is arguable that interest in their judicial and police aspects has tended to throw their fiscal aspect into the shade. Whatever the primary purpose of hundredal organization, the primary purpose of royal grants of hundreds to subjects was clearly financial. Anglo-Saxon kings had only a limited amount of land or money at their disposal; if they wished to make a gift an obvious means of enriching a monastery or

---

[1] *Camb. Med. Hist.*, III. 376-377.

[2] Note especially the articles of E. B. Demarest, *E.H.R.*, 1918, pp. 62 ff.; 1920, pp. 78 ff.; 1923, pp. 161 ff.; and of C. Stephenson, *E.H.R.*, 1924, pp. 161-174, and see F. M. Stenton, *The Latin Charters of the Anglo-Saxon period*, p. 56.

[3] *The Kalendar of Abbot Samson of Bury St. Edmunds and Related Documents*, edited for the R. Hist. Soc. by R. H. C. Davis (C.S. 3rd ser., LXXXIV), 1954.

[4] *Ibid.*, p. xl.   [5] *Ibid.*, pp. xxxii-xliv.

[6] *Ibid.*, p. xiv, n. 4. For other post-conquest examples of such ancient dues in addition to that cited by Mr. Davis see N. Neilson in *Oxford Studies in Social and Legal History*, vol. II. *Customary Rents*, ch. vi, vii; and L.T.R. Miscellaneous Rolls, Bundles 5, 6. (P.R.O.).

[7] *Op. cit.*, p. xxx.

rewarding the loyalty of a great man was to exempt the beneficiaries from fiscal obligations, and so, frequently, transfer to them
the right to receive royal revenues. Such grants go back far
beyond the tenth century. The triple hundred of Oswaldslaw
would seem to be co-eval with the other hundreds of Worcestershire, but when we seek for the origins of such private hundreds as
those of Crediton (Devon)[1] or Glastonbury Twelve Hides (Som.)
we are driven to conclude that the holders' claim to regalian
rights is older than the hundredal system itself, and that the
introduction of that system by Alfred's descendants not only
remodelled the pattern of royal administration and justice, but
also regularized or standardized long-established rights enjoyed by
subjects over their lands and men under the grants of Alfred or his
predecessors. If such a view be accepted the eleventh- and twelfth-
century "forgeries" of charters and the thirteenth-century claims
made at Quo Warranto inquests take on a fresh complexion.
Neither the absence of authentic charters granting a hundred, nor
the silence of Domesday Book, will compel us to reject an ancient
tradition when no contradictory evidence exists.

The subjoined list of hundreds presumably in private hands
before 1066 is thus based only to a slight extent on reliable pre-
conquest charter evidence. A few documents of the reign of the
Confessor, when, as Mr. Galbraith says, it would seem that "a
necessity for showing title deeds for rights that were being actually
exercised arose",[2] explicitly record a grant of hundredal soke.
Such are the grants of Hormer hundred (Berks.) to Abingdon
Abbey, of Godley (Surrey) to Chertsey Abbey, of Clackclose
(Norfolk) to Ramsey Abbey, and of the eight and a half hundreds
of Bedricsworth to Bury St. Edmunds.[3] The charters registering
Edgar's grants to Ely, Peterborough and Worcester, if not
authentic, may fairly be regarded as corresponding with the facts.
No earlier grant in terms of hundredal soke can be relied on. And
this is hardly surprising, since neither the positive right to receive

---

[1] W. H. Stevenson, *Crawford Charters*, p. 1.   [2] *E.H.R.*, 1920, p. 382.

[3] Harmer, *Anglo-Saxon Writs*, pp. 126, 127. For the grant of the soke of Stow or Well
Wapentake to St. Mary of Stow by Godeva and its later absorption by the Bishop of
Lincoln, see Davis, *Regesta Regum Anglo-Normannorum*. i, no. 333; Dd. i. 376; and J. W.
F. Hill, *Medieval Lincoln*, pp. 74-76.

the profits of a hundred court nor the negative right of exemption from suit to the hundred could be granted before the establishment of the hundredal organization.

Our second main source, Domesday Book, is erratic in the information it gives. It is our sole source for the existence of lay lords of hundreds before the Norman Conquest, (with the exception of Edward's charter to Bury, which states that the eight and a half hundreds had been granted to his mother by her first husband Cnut): but the evidence is fullest and least equivocal for the three eastern counties of the second volume. The compilers of the final version for the rest of the country may not have been so much interested in hundredal soke.

Domesday evidence is, however, significant in establishing the relation of the hundred to the hundredal manor—a subject that has been fully discussed elsewhere[1]—and with this clue we can carry back our investigations beyond the tenth century. As Sir Frank Stenton pointed out long ago[2] there are early instances of grants of a hundred hides "belonging to" manors which correspond closely with later hundreds. Such are the hundred hides of Micheldever and of Chilcomb (Hants), of Chalk and of Downton (Wilts.), of Abingdon (Berks.) and of Taunton (Somerset).

Maitland and others have discussed the grant to Winchester of the hundred hides belonging to Chilcomb,[3] which correspond to the later hundred of Fawley and possibly included Buddlesgate hundred[4] which seems later to have centred in Crawley. These were only two of the nine hundreds held by Winchester in Hampshire in 1316,[5] and for none of these are specific charters extant. The Chilcomb grant was of special importance as evidence for the beneficial hidation claimed by the bishop. These Hampshire hundreds consisted almost exclusively of lands held by St. Swithun's, the Old Minster of the bishopric. The same is true of its Somerset hundred of Taunton; of the Glastonbury hundred of the

[1] H. M. Cam, *Liberties and Communities*, pp. 64-90.

[2] *The Early History of the Abbey of Abingdon* (1913), p. 46.

[3] *Domesday Book and Beyond*, pp. 449 f., 496 ff.; N. S. B. Gras, *Economic and Social History of an English village* (Crawley), pp. 170 f.

[4] *V. C. H. Hants*, I. 463, n. 5, III. 315.

[5] Buddlesgate, Crondall, Evingar, Fareham, Fawley, Meon, Overton, Sutton, Waltham. (Sutton was a post-conquest acquisition.)

Twelve Hides and of the St. Albans' hundred of Cashio in Herts. The only Domesday evidence of St. Albans' rights in the last is its name: Albanstou Hundred. In 1275 the monks alleged they held it by grant from Offa, who obviously could no more have granted a hundred than return of writs, but who might very well have granted some or all of the lands that were to make up the hundred when it was later constituted with St. Albans as its administrative centre, and who may also have made over to the abbey some or all of his regalian fiscal rights in its lands.

Maitland speaks of the generous endowments bestowed upon the Church by the West Saxon kings;[1] grants of large tracts of land reinforced by fiscal privileges that included profits of justice. As royal justice, finance and administration developed under the kings of the tenth and eleventh centuries the privileges would come to assume more definite form to correspond to the system from which they claimed exemption.[2] The scattered lands belonging to the church of Worcester would be constituted the triple hundred of Oswaldslaw, as the detached Glastonbury lands in North and South Wiltshire were constituted the hundred of North and South Damerham, and the eight outlying portions of Deerhurst in Gloucestershire were constituted Deerhurst hundred.[3] Such hundreds are in marked contrast with the eight and a half hundreds of West Suffolk, a solid block of land inhabited by many other landowners besides the abbot's tenants. Here the grant meant the transfer of royal rights over administrative districts whose bounds had not been determined by the previous possessions of the grantees. In such cases a charter or a writ to the shire court announcing the gift was desirable. Again, where possessions and privileges accumulated through the centuries had been invaded by predatory ealdormen or other layfolk, restoration and confirmation in writing might be solicited, but where they were peacefully enjoyed such title-deeds might not be needed. There is a significant statement in the Quo Warranto pleas for Suffolk in 1286. That Hoxon hundred, called Bishop's Hundred in Domesday Book, had been an episcopal possession from early times may be inferred

---

[1] *Domesday Book and Beyond*, p. 498.   [2] See above, pp. 25-29.
[3] C. S. Taylor, *Domesday Survey of Gloucestershire*, p. 96.

from the fact that the church of Hoxon had been since 951 at least a *sedes episcopi*.[1] In 1286 the bishop was called upon to state the warrant by which he held various liberties. Three entries refer to the hundred. The first records that the bishop was summoned to answer by what warrant he held the hundred of Hoxon, which belonged to the Crown and dignity of the king, without his will and license. In the second the king's counsel admitted himself unable to frame a writ of Quo Warranto in the proper form because "It cannot be certified what king was seized of the hundred"; and in the last entry a third party successfully claimed that he need not answer to the king concerning suit to the hundred court of Hoxon because the hundred was the bishop's.[2] Of many other ecclesiastical hundreds beside Hoxon for which no charter of grant exists, it would have been difficult if not impossible to say what king had been seized of it. As some parliamentary boroughs were born rotten, so some hundreds were born private.

In especial, it seems highly probable that from very early times endowments of bishoprics carried with them rights that would in course of time crystallize into titles to hundreds. Winchester and Norwich are by no means alone in holding hundreds for which no attempt was made to produce pre-conquest charters. Of the bishop of Worcester's hundred of Henbury in Gloucestershire, the jurors of 1275 could only say, "Nihil, quia de tam longo tempore."[3] The bishop of Lincoln's title to Dorchester hundred, Oxfordshire, or the bishop of Salisbury's title to Sherborne, Dorset, and Ramsbury, Wiltshire, obviously went back to the centuries when their dioceses had centred in other sees. The practice of a comprehensive grant confirming all existing liberties only begins, it would seem, under Cnut, but no such grants specify hundreds. Edward the Confessor continues the practice. The writs which announce the grant of the bishoprics of Winchester to Aelfwine (1042-7),[4] of Wells to Giso (1060-61),[5] of Hereford to Walter (1061)[6] and of Worcester to Wulfstan (1062)[7]

---

[1] *E.H.R.*, 1925, p. 223. Dd. ii. 379. The bishop also held a quarter of Wangford or, the "ferting" of Elmham, the name of the East Anglian see down to 1070.

[2] *Placita Quo Warranto*, pp. 732 ff.   [3] *Rot. Hund.*, i. 168.

[4] Harmer, *Anglo-Saxon Writs*, pp. 381, 398.

[5] *Ibid.*, pp. 272, 277.   [6] *Ibid.*, pp. 229, 231.   [7] *Ibid.*, pp. 407, 410.

include the grant of everything pertaining thereto, with sake and with soke, as fully and completely as ever they were held by any bishop before them. The Winchester writ refers to Cnut's charter.[1] Miss Harmer regards these writs as fully authentic; indeed she accepts that to Worcester in its existing form as "an original writ, written and sealed by the clerks of King Edward's secretariat".[2] There can be little doubt that such grants would cover all the hundreds belonging to a bishopric before the Norman Conquest, and it seems hardly too much to assume that such rights would be regarded as the natural appurtenances of a bishopric—to use Domesday terminology, *semper de episcopatu.*

Other passages in Domesday suggest that hundreds may also have been attached to the office of earl. The existence of "comital hundreds" after 1066 has been assumed or accepted by various writers, but the evidence for them before the conquest is inevitably more dubious. The office of earl lacked the continuity of that of abbot or bishop; muniments are correspondingly lacking. Domesday Book indicates that hundreds or hundredal manors were held by Harold,[3] Gurth,[4] Waltheof,[5] earl Ralph[6] and possibly Robert fitz Wymark,[7] but we cannot tell in what capacity, though we may feel sure that Stigand's hundreds in Norfolk[8] were not attached to the archiepiscopate. Even more doubtful is the category to which one should assign the wapentake of Newark held by Countess Godeva[9] or the hundreds held by Githa[10] or Queen Edith[11]: such lordships underline the preponderantly financial aspect of hundredal soke.

The rights and revenues accruing to the lords of private hundreds before 1066 may well have varied from shire to shire and from hundred to hundred. The detailed statements set down by Abbot Samson for the hundreds of St. Edmund are exceptional,

[1] *Ibid.,* p. 382.

[2] *Ibid.,* p. 407. Henry I's writs granting the sees of York, Hereford and Chichester are very similar. *Regesta Anglo-Normannorum,* II. Nos. 885, 1101, 1243, 1424.

[3] Witham and Harlow (Essex); Hitchin (Herts.); Stratford, Cutethorn, Radelau, Thornlau and Plegeliet (Hereford), North Curry (Som.), and possibly Melksham (Wilts.).

[4] Lothingland (Essex).   [5] Hamfordshoe and Wimersley (Northants.).

[6] Shropham (Norfolk).   [7] Clavering and Rochford (Essex).

[8] Hersham, Smithdon, Launditch, Forehow.   [9] Dd. I. 280d. (Notts.).

[10] Higham (Northants.); Cocker (Som.); the six hundreds belonging to Wallop (Hants).

[11] Bath, Chewton, Keynsham, Martock, Milverton (Som.); Martinsley (Rutland).

and we cannot be certain that they are valid for the period before 1066. The hundred-pennies of Taunton have been variously interpreted.[1] The most specific clause in Edward the Confessor's grant of Godley hundred is regarded by Miss Harmer as a later interpolation.[2] All that we can be sure of is that certain rights to revenue that normally went to the kings had been ceded by them to the holders of the hundreds, and that such concessions, whether sanctioned by written record or by long custom, were accepted by post-conquest kings as good titles to administrative and judicial functions unknown to the original donors and confirmed later either in general terms or by the uncritical endorsement of charters condemned by modern scholars.

LIST OF "PRIVATE" HUNDREDS BEFORE THE NORMAN CONQUEST

The names of the hundreds correspond to those of Domesday Book, generally in their modern form. In some cases the bounds have been greatly altered since 1086.

The nature of the evidence is indicated by numerals as follows:

1. Statement of grant of 100 hides.
2. Statement of grant of a hundred.
3. Statement in Domesday Book as to profits or soke of a hundred.
4. Lordship of manor to which hundred was later appurtenant.
5. Ownership of the whole area of the hundred.
6. Name of the hundred.

County	Hundred	Holder	Evidence
Berkshire	Blewbury	Bp. of Sherborne or Ramsbury	1. B.C.S. 596; Stenton, *The Early History of the Abbey of Abingdon*, p. 46.
	Hormer	Abbot of Abingdon	1, 2. *Hist. mon. de Abingdon*, II. 258; Harmer, *A.-S. Writs*, pp. 126, 132.
	Sonning	Bp. of Sherborne or Ramsbury	4, 6. Dd. i. 58; *Sarum Charters*, 12.
Cambridge	2 hundreds of Ely	Abbot of Ely	2, 3. Dd. i. 191d, 192; B.C.S. 1266.
Cornwall	Pautone (Pider)	Bp. of Crediton or Exeter	4, 5. Dd. i. 120d; *Exon Domesday*, 66.
Devon	Crediton	Bp. of Crediton or Exeter	4, 6. *Crawford Charters*, 1; Dd. i. 101d.

[1] See above, p. 61, n. 2., and *V. C. H. Somerset*, I. 403 ff.
[2] *Anglo-Saxon Writs*, p. 205 f.

County	Hundred	Holder	Evidence
Dorset	Beaminster	Bp. of Sherborne or Ramsbury	4. Dd. i. 77.
	Sherborne	Bp. of Sherborne or Ramsbury (before and after Queen Edith)	4, 6. Dd. i. 77.
	Yetminster	Bp. of Sherborne or Ramsbury	4. Dd. i. 75d.
	Henley	Abbess of Shaftesbury	4. Dd. i. 78d.
	Buckland Newton	Abbot of Glastonbury	4. Dd. i. 77d.
Essex	Claverin3 } Rochford }	Robert fitz Wymark (?), (father of Suen of Essex)	3, 4. Dd. ii. 46b. 3. Dd. ii. 45b.
	Harlow	Harold	4. Dd. ii. 2. (Hatfield manor).
	Witham	,,	3, 4. Dd. ii. 1b, 2.
	Winstree	St. Ouen	3, 4. Dd. ii. 22. (West Mersea manor.)
Gloucester	Deerhurst	Abbot of Westminster and Abbot of St. Denys	4, 5. Harmer, A.-S. Writs, pp. 330 ff., 363 ff.; Dd. i. 166.
	Bernintreu (later Henbury)	Bp. of Worcester	4, 5. Dd. i. 164d.
	Pucklechurch	Abbot of Glastonbury	4, 5. Dd. i. 165; B.C.S. 887
	Tidenham	Abbot of Bath	4, 5. Dd. i. 164; B.C.S. 927.
Hampshire	Buddlesgate	Bp. of Winchester (Old Minster)	(Crawley manor?) B.C.S. 629; Dd. i. 40.
	Crondall	,,	4, 5. Dd. i. 41; B.C.S. 1307; Whitelock, A.-S. Wills, p. 16.
	Evingar	,,	5. Dd. i. 41.
	Fareham	,,	4, 5. Dd. i. 40d.
	Fawley	,,	1. (100 hides belonging to Chilcomb.) 4. Dd. i. 41; B.C.S. 620, 1147.
	Meon	,,	4. Dd. i. 40d; B.M. Add. MS. 15350 fo. 4.
	Overton	,,	4, 5. B.C.S. 625; Dd. i. 40.
	Waltham	,,	4. B.C.S. 613; Dd. i. 40.
	Micheldever	Abbot of Hyde (New Minster)	1, 4, 5. Liber de Hyda, p. 85; Dd. i. 42d.
	6 hundreds	Githa	3, 4. Dd. 1. 35d. (Wallop manor.)
	Welford (Wherwell)	Abbess of Wherwell	5. Dd. 1. 44.
Hereford	Stratford and Cutethorn	Harold	Dd. i. 186. (Burghill manor.)
	3 hundreds	,,	Dd. i. 186. (Cowarne manor.)
Hertford	Albanestou (later Cashio)	Abbot of St. Albans	4, 5, 6. Dd. i. 135d, 136.
	Hitchin	Harold	4. Dd. i. 132d.
Kent[1]	Achestan (later Codsheath)	Abp. of Canterbury	5. Dd. i. 3. (Otford manor?)

[1] See footnote on next page.

The "Private" Hundred in England before the Norman Conquest

County	Hundred	Holder	Evidence
Kent[1]	Bircholt	Abp. of Canterbury	5. Dd. i. 4. (Aldinton manor?)
	Boughton	,,	4, 5. Dd. i. 3d.
	Calehill	,,	5. Dd. i. 3d.
	Esturset	,,	Dd. i. 4. (St. Martin manor?)
	Maidstone	,,	4. Dd. i. 3d.
	Pecham	,,	4, 5. Dd. i. 3d.
	Roculf	,,	4. Dd. i. 3d.
	Sandwich	,,	4. Dd. i. 3.
	Toltentrow	,,	5. Dd. i. 4d.
	Wingham	,,	4, 5. Dd. i. 3d.
	Wrotham	,,	4, 5. Dd. i. 3.
Lincoln	Well (or Stow) (1) Godeva (2) St. Mary of Stow		3. Dd. i. 376; Davis, *Regesta*, i. no. 333.
Norfolk	Clackclose	Abbot of Ramsey	2. Harmer, *A.-S. Writs*, p. 250; Dd. ii. 215b.
	Forehow	Stigand	4. Dd. ii. 137b. (Windham manor.)
	Smithdon	,,	Dd. ii. 142. (Snetisham manor.)
	Hersham	,,	4. Dd. ii. 139b.
	Launditch	,,	4. Dd. ii. 136b. (Mileham manor.)
	Mitford	Abbot of Ely	3. Dd. ii. 214.
	Shropham	Earl Ralph	3. Dd. ii. 126b. (Buckenham manor.)
	Tunstead	Abbot of St. Benet of Hulme	2, 4. *Monasticon*, iii. 83; Dd. ii. 218d, 220.
Northants	Higham	Githa	4. Dd. i. 225b.
	Hamfordshoe	Waltheof	{ 4. Dd. i. 228, 228d. (Yardley
	Wimersley	,,	{ manor.)
	The 8 hundreds of Oundle	Abbot of Peterborough	2, 3. B.C.S. 1281; Dd. 221d.
Notts.	Newark	Godeva	3. Dd. i. 280d; Davis, *Regesta*, i. no. 333.
Oxford	Banbury	Bp. of Dorchester	4. Dd. i. 155.
	Dorchester	,,	4, 6. Dd. i. 155.
	Thame	,,	4. Dd. i. 155.
Rutland	Martinsley	Queen Edith	2. Harmer, *A.-S. Writs*, pp. 323, 359.
Somerset	Bath	Edith	4. Dd. i. 87.
	Chewton	,,	4. Dd. i. 87.
	Keynsham	,,	4. Dd. i. 87.
	Martock	,,	4. Dd. i. 87.
	Milverton	,,	4. Dd. i. 87.
	Cocker	Githa	4. Dd. i. 87.

[1] Two factors complicate the evidence in Kent. The hundredal system is alien and artificial; and the privileges granted to the archbishop, presumably covered by Cnut's writ to Archbishop Aethelnoth (Harmer, p. 183) gave him a share in the profits of something like three-quarters of the Kentish hundreds; (see Cam, *The Hundred and the Hundred Rolls*, pp. 270-2.) The hundreds listed here are those in which he appears to have been the sole lord in 1065.

County	Hundred	Holder	Evidence
Somerset	Chew	Bp. of Wells	4. Dd. i. 89d.
	Kingsbury	,,	4. Dd. i. 89.
	Wells	,,	4. Dd. i. 89.
	North Curry	Harold	4. Dd. i. 89.
	Taunton	Bp. of Winchester	1, 2, 3. Whitelock, A.-S. Wills, p. 16; Dd. i. 87d.
	12 Hides	Glastonbury	3. Dd. i. 90.
Suffolk	Bishops Hundred (Hoxon)	Bp. of Elmham or "Suffolk"	4, 6. Dd.ii . 379.
	The ferting of Elmham ($\frac{1}{4}$ of Wangford Hundred)	,,	2. Dd. ii. 379.
	The $8\frac{1}{2}$ hundreds of Bedricsworth or Thingoe	Abbot of Bury St. Edmunds	2. Harmer, A.-S. Writs, pp. 146, 154-5.
	The $5\frac{1}{2}$ hundreds of Wichlau	Abbot of Ely	2, 3. B.C.S. 1266; Dd. ii. 385b.
	Lothingland	Gurth	4. Dd. ii. 283. (Gorleston manor.)
Surrey	Farnham	Bp. of Winchester	4, 5. B.C.S. 627, 1156; Dd. i. 31.
	Godley	Abbot of Chertsey	2, 5. Harmer, A.-S. Writs, pp. 205-8.
Sussex	Bury	Goda	4. Dd. i. 17.
	Bexhill	Bp. of Selsey	4, 5. Dd. i. 18.
	Bocse	,,	4, 5. Dd. i. 16d.
	Hamfelde (Tipnoak)	,,	4, 5. Dd. i. 16d.
	Somerleg (Manhood)	,,	5. Dd. i. 17.
Warwick	Patelau	Bp. of Worcester	Dd. i. 238d. (P.Q.W. p. 783)
Wilts.	Bradford	Abbess of Shaftesbury	4. Dd. i. 67d.
	Chalk	Abbess of Wilton	1, 4, 5. B.C.S. 917; Dd. i. 68.
	Damerham	Abbot of Glastonbury	5. Dd. i. 66d.
	Downton	Bp. of Winchester	1, 4. B.C.S. 690; Dd. i. 65d.
	Ramsbury	Bp. of Sherborne or Ramsbury	4, 5, 6. Dd. i. 66. (Rot. Hund. ii. 231.)
	Potterne and Cannings	,,	4. Dd. i. 66.
	Underditch	,,	5. Dd. i. 66.
	Weresdone	Abbess of Romsey	4, 5. Dd. i. 68. (Rot. Hund. ii. 235.)
	?Melksham	Harold	4. Dd. i. 65.
Worcester	Fishborough	Abbot of Evesham	2, 5. Dd. i. 175d.; Davis, Regesta, i. no. 106.
	Oswaldslaw	Bp. of Worcester	2, 5. B.C.S. 1135; Dd. i. 172d.
	Pershore	Abbots of Pershore and Westminster	4. Dd. i. 174d, 175; Harmer, A.-S. Writs, pp. 330, 363 ff., 519.

IV

The Community of the Vill[1]

IT IS A commonplace to say that the vill and the manor are not synonymous in England of the high Middle Ages. The township was an entity both older and longer lived than the lordship, and even in the heyday of feudalism, the township, the *villata*, the community of the vill imposes itself on our attention—not only as an indispensable unit in the governmental system but also, in many parts of the country, as a community conscious and active in its own right.

As with the more conspicuous community of the shire, the Anglo-Norman and Angevin kings preserved and invigorated the township by making use of it. When facts were needed, as in the Domesday inquest and in numerous other inquests down to those of 1255 and 1274-5 recorded in the so-called Hundred Rolls, the township was called upon to supply them by four or six men, with or without priest and reeve. Similar deputations had to attend the shire and hundred courts periodically, and, if Miss Hurnard is right,[2] they were being expected to report the names of suspicious characters long before the Assizes of Clarendon and Northampton required every township of a hundred to present on oath the names of suspected criminals to the sheriffs and justices; a task fulfilled, as the records prove, at the tourn, the county court, and the general eyre. In particular, from 1194 at least, the coroner, inquiring into sudden deaths, treasure-trove, and the like, always summoned the four vills nearest to the scene of the event, by four men from each vill, to report upon oath what they knew about the matter.[3] The decrees of 1233, 1242, and 1285 laid on the

[1] Reprinted, by permission of the editors, from *Medieval Studies presented to Rose Graham*, 1950.

[2] *E.H.R.*, 1941, pp. 174 ff. See also Van Caenegem, *Royal Writs in England from the Conquest to Glanvill* (Selden Society 1959), p. 58.

[3] *Select Charters*, p. 414. After 1300 each vill was represented by twelve to sixteen men. Hunnisett, *The Medieval Coroner* (1961), p. 14.

vill the duty of keeping watches by four or six of its number, and the following of the hue and cry by the whole township; it was responsible for seeing that every one of its members was in frank-pledge or tithing, and for the custody of any criminal committed to its keeping by the sheriff. Hardly separable from its police duties were its military obligations. Though Henry II's Assize of Arms had expressly excluded the villein from its scope, all men were liable for the defence of the realm,[1] and this responsibility was riveted on the township in a series of regulations. John's measures against threatened invasion in 1204 had provided for the registering and leading of the village forces, whilst the regulations of 1242 set up constables in every township; the regulations of 1253 made the township responsible for providing the arms required; and both men and weapons were to be ready for inspection by the shire authorities when demanded; an inspection held twice a year, according to the Statute of Winchester in 1285. An entry on the court rolls of Halesowen shows a village picking its own men for the call-up to the Welsh wars in 1295,[2] whilst for the same campaign a Lincolnshire vill contributed 4s. to the expenses of its soldiers[3] and "all the men" of a Durham vill were penalized for not compensating their fellows for their war service.[4] The invaluable *Nomina Villarum* of 1316 is the fruit of an inquiry arising from the provision in the Parliament of 1315 that one man should go from every whole vill of the kingdom for the Scottish war, as are the returns, preserved for three counties, of the weapons in the keeping of the constables of each vill for the use of the militia men.[5] The vill is also under the ancient obligations of keeping up roads, causeways, and bridges, referred to in Clause 23 of the Charter of 1215; the sheriff in his tourn will inquire into their discharge of such duties. Analogous, but of more recent origin, is the duty of keeping the walls of a royal park in repair, shared by ancient custom between a number of Northamptonshire townships whose names, according to an ancient deponent in 1548,

---

[1] Cf. Petit-Dutaillis, *Les Communes françaises*, pp. 117-18.
[2] G. C. Homans, *English Villagers in the Thirteenth Century*, p. 330.
[3] W. S. Thompson, *Lincs. Assize Roll*, pp. xxiv. 59.
[4] *Durham Halmotes* (Surtees Society, 1889), p. 1.
[5] *Feudal Aids*, I. xii; P.R.O. Ex. Ac. 15/10.

are "engraven upon the stones upon the walles of the said parke".[1]

Again, new forms of taxation made new work for the townships. The sheriffs had been accustomed to collect the ancient customary dues which went to make up the farm of the shire by hundred and vill;[2] when the regulations for levying the taxes on property began they fell into the same pattern.[3] In 1225 the payment was made by four lawful men and the reeve of each vill to the county knights;[4] and the fortieth of 1232 and the thirtieth of 1237 were assessed in the same way. Willard has shown that under Edward I the responsibility for assessment rested directly on the vill, with no intervention from the hundred; and the final assessment of 1334 was drawn up on the basis of agreement between the chief assessors and the communities of the cities, boroughs, and men of the vills.[5] Whilst Mr. Thompson has shown that the actual subtaxor in the vill was sometimes a villein,[6] Mr. Homans has found an instance in 1306 of the distribution by the vill itself among its own members of the war-time requisitions levied by the sheriff: an admirable instance of the common sense of the township. A substantial villager is assessed by the whole vill at half a quarter of oats for the use of the king "because he has more than he needs for his own sustentation".[7]

"The township", says Maitland, "is a community which, even if it has not rights, certainly has duties";[8] and he, like Madox before him,[9] gives illustrations from the reign of Henry II onwards of the money penalties inflicted on the vill for failure to discharge these duties and for other delinquencies—for taking no action when a man is found slain, for receiving a man who is not in frank-pledge, for exceeding its powers by putting men to the ordeal of water or hanging a thief, for infringing the Crown's monopoly of the great fish, for not raising the hue and pursuing the criminal, for ploughing up the king's highway, for failing to resist a Flemish raid, even

---

[1] R. Glover, *Kingsthorpiana*, p. 110.   [2] See *Liber Memorandorum de Bernewelle*, pp. 238 ff.
[3] *Select Charters*, p. 278.   [4] *Ibid.*, p. 352.
[5] J. F. Willard, *Parliamentary Taxes on Personal Property, 1290–1334*, pp. 55 ff.
[6] W. S. Thompson, *Lincs. Assize Roll*, pp. xliii, xlvi.
[7] Homans, *op. cit.*, p. 332 (454).   [8] Pollock and Maitland, I. 564, 567.
[9] Madox, *Exchequer*, cxiv, "Of Amercements"—Sections vi, vii, xiv. See also Maitland, *Pleas of the Crown for the County of Gloucester, 1221*, for numerous examples of the criminal liabilities of the township.

for remaking a ditch before authorized to do so by the royal justices. In every case it is the *villata* that is amerced; in these matters the lord of the manor, if such there be, is ignored; the penalty, like the obligation, is on the community. But other records show the lord of the manor himself treating his tenants as a community. Study of the Durham halmotes, to which Maitland directed our attention, shows that commands to the vills are most frequently couched in the form *injunctum est omnibus tenentibus*, whilst money penalties are inflicted on the *communitatem ville*. Financial obligation has a communalizing effect; and it is difficult, in view of the evidence noted above, to accept Maitland's sugges-tion[1] that the distribution of the financial burden was stereotyped by annexation to holdings so that no discussion was needed when the community had to find a sum of money for any purpose. Stenton has propounded the contribution of the primitive levies of Anglo-Saxon tributary rulers towards the growth of the earliest folkmoots;[2] there can be little doubt that collective financial responsibility was one of the causes of the preservation of an active communal organization.

Another force, as is generally accepted, was the need for co-operation in agriculture, for though much may be stereotyped by custom the English climate is not, and emergencies of all sorts may demand initiative or innovation. The plainest evidence of communal agriculture action are the by-laws drawn up by com-mon agreement. Mentioned from early in the thirteenth century by such names as Le Belawe (Wilburton 1222), *statutum autumpni* (Herts. 1228), *statutum villate*, Le Byelawe (Ely 1303-9), even the *plebicetum*[3] (Yorkshire 1297), found recorded in writing from 1329,[4] they are described as being agreed upon *inter communam ville* (Durham 1296) and as being enforced, in Yorkshire, by the *custodes statuti autumpni*.[5] A judge refers in 1370 to "the usage

[1] Pollock and Maitland, I. 611. [2] *Anglo-Saxon England*, p. 294.
[3] *Wakefield Court Rolls*, i. 298 (Yorks. Arch. Soc. 1901) cited by Homans, p. 427.
[4] W. D. Ault, *E.H.R.*, 1930, p. 212.
[5] For a bibliography on by-laws see G. C. Homans, *English Villagers in the Thirteenth Century*, p. 427. Note also the Durham halmotes, and the manuscripts of the dean and chapter of Ely, Sutton Court Rolls, 31 Edward I onward, for which reference I have to thank Mr. Edward Miller. (It should be noted, however, that Mr. Lennard, reviewing Homans, adduced considerable evidence to show that the initiative in the framing of by-laws often came from the lord of the manor. *Econ. Journal*, 1943, pp. 850-6. Dr. Patzelt of Vienna argued to the same effect with regard to the *Weistümer* of German villages).

throughout the land called Bie-laws" by which neighbours can levy a sum by common assent, assess each man and distrain for non-payment.[1] Penalties for disobedience are frequently mentioned; sometimes they go entirely to the township or *communitatem plebiceti*, sometimes they are shared between the lord and the township.[2] In sixteenth-century Kingsthorpe, a long-lived community, they may be shared between the town officers and the town.[3]

Another well-known illustration of the township acting as a body in agrarian concerns is the practice of inter-commoning in fen or marsh country, mentioned by Maitland,[4] and very fully discussed by Nellie Neilson in her edition of the *Terrier of Fleet* in Lincolnshire.[5] Seven townships have rights of common in Gruntifen, and three in Thetfordheyfen along with the Templars of Denny Abbey.[6] As Miss Neilson observed, though most of the documentary material belongs to the period when the lord of the manor has assumed control, "the villata still has its part to play", and it seems clear that the origins of such agreements go back far beyond the manorial origins.[7]

The township is indeed tough. Beatrice Lees in her edition of the Templars' inquest of 1185 comments on the fact that, apart from the *villa integra* whose entity is preserved by the enforcement of public obligations,[8] "the vitality of the ancient local group" asserts itself against both "the administrative organization of the preceptory and the feudal organization of the manor".[9] She cites the spirited protest of the small community of Lockridge, Wilts., against the innovations of the Order "when Osbert of Dover held the bailiwick";[10] the sworn statement of the men of Kerby, Yorkshire, who owe rent but no service, as to the customs of their court and as to the forfeitures which they retain intact and those which they divide with the brothers;[11] and the statement of the township of Willoughton, Lincolnshire, as to the Templars' lands

---

[1] Y.B. 44 Edward III, Trinity Term.
[2] Homans, *op. cit.*, pp. 104, 427. Cf. *Records of Templars*, edited B. A. Lees, p. 130.
[3] *Kingsthorpiana*, pp. 84-9; cf. pp. 39 f.   [4] Pollock and Maitland, I. 619.
[5] *Terrier of Fleet*, pp. xli ff.   [6] *Ibid.*, p. xli, see also p. 168.
[7] *Ibid.*, pp. viii, xlix.   [8] See *E.H.R.*, 1926, pp. 98-103.
[9] *Records of Templars*, pp. cxciii f.   [10] *Ibid.*, pp. cxxxi, 53, 57.
[11] *Ibid.*, pp. ccxiii, 130.

in their village: "all this land is of the gift of Simon de Canci and Roger de Bussei. But the *villata* knows not how to separate the fee of Simon from the fee of Roger except for five tofts".[1] This incapacity to apply the complexities of feudal tenurial theory to the actual fields on which they lived is paralleled by a statement in the Hundred Rolls of 1255. The villagers of Oving, Buckinghamshire, asked to say who holds the vill of Oving, start off bravely with the statement that Robert of Oving is lord of the vill and holds one knight's fee of the honour of Doddeley and answers for three hides. They then proceed to enumerate four other tenants, three of them each holding one-seventh of the vill of a different lord, and the fourth holding one-fourteenth of the vill of yet another lord, and then break down. "Of this vill we know nothing else, nor can we discover anything, save that William de Bello has view of frank-pledge."[2] In such villages, as in the many Cambridgeshire villages of three, four, or five lords of manors described in the Hundred Rolls of 1279, "the villar unity persists".[3] It may be, as Joan Wake suggests, apropos of a Northamptonshire village with six lords, that "the sense of unity at Harlestone, its corporateness, has come from the very fact of its divisions which have forced on the village the necessity of centralization in what must have been a series of village meetings for the organization and administration of its corporate affairs".[4] The *villata* of Harlestone that sets up a joint committee to represent itself and the lords of the vill in 1410,[5] probably to tackle the changeover from a two-field to a three-field system of cultivation, has taken joint action before, notably in 1294 when it delivered an acre of land to the rector for providing adequate bell-ropes for the church.[6] Similar charitable actions by various Danelaw villages are noted by Stenton: the endowment of a chapel by the men of Hutthorpe, Northamptonshire, about 1155;[7] the endowment of a church at

---

[1] *Ibid.*, pp. xxxi, cxciii, 101.
[2] *R.H.* i. 23. For the more exact description that the villagers failed to give see *V. C. H. Bucks.* IV. 86-7.
[3] *Records of Templars*, p. cxciv.　　　　[4] *E.H.R.*, 1922, pp. 407-8.
[5] *Ibid.*, pp. 409-13. Cf. the regulations for Wymeswold, Leicestershire, made by common assent of the township and of three lords of manors, *Danelaw Charters*, p. lxii, note 1.
[6] *Estate Book of Henry de Bray* (Camden Society, 1916), p. 43.
[7] *Danelaw Charters*, p. lxx, No. 465.

Keddington by the joint donation of the lord and the men of Keddington of an acre for every bovate of the vill;[1] the witnessing of gifts to Greenfield Priory by the townships of Driby and Holton in Lincolnshire, an action which he thinks was probably taken on behalf of the two townships by their representatives in the shire courts.[2] It is in connexion with one such transaction that we hear of a common seal of the township, when the whole community of the vill of Wellow in Nottinghamshire in 1250 bind themselves and their heirs and successors by a common oath to provide a chaplain for the chapel of Wellow, and provide for his support and the proper upkeep of the chapel, affixing to the two charters that record their pledge the seal of their community.[3] The whole community of the vill of Towcester, Northampton-shire, by a unanimous agreement of the vill, appoints proctors to collect alms for the repair of the bridge at the north end of the town.[4] Again, the levying of a sum to repair the roof of their church by the parishioners of an unnamed village in 1370 is the occasion of the judicial pronouncement as to the validity of by-laws cited above.[5]

The township can act in a less eleemosynary manner. The estate book of Henry de Bray registers a convention of *la commune de la vile* of Harlestone with Henry as to bull and boar in 1309.[6] The men of Toddington, Bedfordshire, by unanimous consent in an assembly grant some land to the prior of Dunstable at an annual rent of 6*d*., and their grant is upheld by the justices of Novel Disseisin in 1293.[7] The community of the vill of Kings-thorpe repeatedly farms out the town mills,[8] and grants a vacant place for enclosure to two members of the community.[9] The

---

[1] *Ibid.*, p. lxi, note 1.
[2] *Ibid.*, p. lxiii, Nos. 142, 143.
[3] *Antiquissimum Registrum of the Cathedral Church of Lincoln*, Linc. Rec. Soc. iii. 311-13. The only other references to the common seal of a township of which I am aware are that noted by Mr. Homans at Bromham, Wiltshire, in 1295, where the villeins are penalized for having taken upon themselves to have a common seal (Homans, p. 332), and those at Kingsthorpe, the common seal of which, attributed to the reign of Richard II, is repro-duced on the title-page of Glover's *Kingsthorpiana*.
[4] *E.H.R.*, 1922, p. 413.
[5] Y.B. 44 Edward III, Trinity Term.
[6] *Estate Book*, p. 13.
[7] *Annales Monastici*, iii. 378.
[8] *Kingsthorpiana*, pp. 3, 36, 54-7.
[9] *Ibid.*, p. 26.

whole community of the vill of Brightwaltham effects an exchange of common land with the abbot of Battle in 1294.[1]

We have seen the community of the vill acting with the lord and without the lord; we have next to consider it acting *vis-a-vis* the lord. Economic historians have found numerous instances of lords of manors letting the manors to the men of the township at farm. Sowerby is held of the Templars by the men of the vill for £10 as early as 1185;[2] the priory of Worcester has farmed out Hallow and Tibberton to the *villani* of those two townships by 1250;[3] Richard of Cornwall has farmed out Bensington to twenty-seven men of the vill by 1257.[4] Ramsey Abbey has farmed out Hemingford by 1280, and Elton by 1312 in like manner; and so on in Essex, Yorkshire, Somerset, Wiltshire, Herefordshire, and Berkshire.[5] And the king himself is the first to farm out the manors of his ancient demesne. Madox has noted many instances when a vill, most often a royal vill, farmed itself to the Exchequer; a process so near to that by which a borough paid its farm as to illustrate aptly the observation that the dividing line between a vill and borough was not easy to draw. In Chapters II-V of his *Firma Burgi* he gives numerous instances of unincorporated vills holding the vill at farm. His instances can be supplemented from the printed pipe rolls. In Northamptonshire alone there are seven royal manors whose men are farming them in 1242,[6] including Kingsthorpe, to which the farm of the hundred of Spelhoe was appendant.[7] As with the chartered borough, the right of a vill to pay its own farm at the Exchequer involves the right to appoint an agent who will be recognized by the Exchequer as its accredited representative. An interesting instance of the temporary commitment of vills to the administration of their own community has been pointed out by Mr. Homans; it would seem that when

---

[1] *Select Pleas in Manorial Courts*, p. 172; also see Maitland's comment on p. 163.
[2] *Records of Templars*, p. 128.
[3] *Cartulary of Worcester Priory* (Camden Society), pp. 47a, 54b.
[4] M. T. Pearman, *History of the Manor of Bensington*, p. 30.
[5] Homans, p. 453.
[6] *Pipe Roll 26 Henry III*, p. 319. I owe this reference to Mr. H. G. Richardson.
[7] Other examples of hundreds held by the men of a vill are Basingstoke, Hampshire, held by the men of Basingstoke; Elmbridge and Kingston, Surrey, by the men of Kingston; whilst Ainsty, Yorkshire, was held by the mayor and burgesses of York.

Kirtlington, Oxfordshire, escheated to the Crown as a Norman fief in 1203 it was handed over to the reeve and four men for the time being until the manor was granted out to a new tenant. He notes a parallel instance in Oxnead, Norfolk, in 1290.[1] The vills further resemble the boroughs in purchasing privileges from the king; to take one of several instances which have been pointed out to me by Mr. H. G. Richardson, the men of Lothingland, Suffolk, in 1230 request a charter from the king granting them the farm of the manor of Lothingland, and also other special privileges, very likely the hundred of Lothingland as appendant to the manor, for which they are prepared to pay £160. There have been protracted negotiations; the representatives of Lothingland have had to return to their fellows at home for fresh instructions.[2] Unincorporated vills may hold charters from the king, and the men of a vill may hold a charter of privileges from their lord.[3]

The community of the vill, then, besides being compelled to accept "public" responsibilities in matters of taxation, militia, police, criminal liability, road and bridge service, and the like, is in a position voluntarily to accept fresh responsibility, to bind itself to the fulfilment of obligations, and to incur financial liabilities. In an age when the legal principles of incoporation had not yet been worked out, its legal status is not easy to define. Both Madox and Maitland, however, have noted instances where vills sue or are sued.[4] But it would seem that medieval legal writers have not pronounced on the matter, and this lends some interest to an entry on the Close Roll of 39 Henry III which, so far as I know, has not hitherto been discussed in print by any legal historian:

Pro hominibus Imberti Pugeys.—Rex ballivis B(onifacii) Cantuariensis archiepescopi de Cantuaria salutem. Quia secundum legem et consuetudinem regni nostri hucusque optentum est quod villate et communitates villarum ejusdem regni nostri querelas et querimonia suas per tres vel per quatuor ipsorum in curiis nostris et aliorum possint prosequi, vobis mandamus quod, si

[1] Homans, p. 336.　　　　　　　　[2] *Royal Letters*, (R.S.) i. 381-2.

[3] *Terrier of Fleet*, pp. 77, 114. Charter of Thomas fitz Lambert of Multon to his free tenants in Fleet and to all the men of the vill, free and villein. Date before 8 Edward I. See also the Bensington Charter mentioned above, p. 78, n. 4.

[4] See below, pp. 80, 81.

homines dilecti et fidelis nostri Imberti Pugeys, qui nobiscum stat in servicio nostro, de villata de Sybeton, aliquas querelas habent prosequendas vel defendendas pro communitate sua in curia domini vestri de Cantuaria, ipsos per tres vel quatuor ex eis, prout superius dictum est, prosequi permittatis, tantum facientes quod dictum fidelem nostrum iterato non oporteat super hoc fatigari. Teste rege apud Westmonasterium vij die Marcii (1255).[1]

Imbert Pugeys was one of Henry III's "foreign favourites", being probably a native of Le Puy en Velay, Haute-Loire, and had come over to England with Queen Eleanor about 1235. He served Henry for twenty-five years as yeoman of the Chamber, keeper of the Tower of London, and steward of the Household, holding the last office down to his death in 1263. He was rewarded for his services by lands in various counties where his descendants succeeded him, and his name survives in Stoke Poges, Buckinghamshire, the scene of Gray's *Elegy written in a Country Churchyard*. His rights in Sibton,[2] a knight's fee held of the Archbishop of Canterbury, were derived from his wife, Joan, *née* Aguillon, who held it as part of the dower of her first marriage to Ralph fitz Bernard.[3] He was thus in a strong position to ask for favours, but it is, in fact, the men of the village whose interests seem to be chiefly affected, and it is their rights that are declared by this, apparently unique, statement as to the law and custom of the realm.

Uncorroborated, this incidental statement might carry little weight, but the examples of townships figuring in legal proceedings are numerous enough to lend it credibility. The community of the township of Helpringham appears before the justices in eyre at Lincoln in 1272 by four men to plead against the communities of two other Lincolnshire townships, each represented by four men.[4] The township of Graveley by its attorney brings a plaint against a stonemason for breach of contract in the Court of the Fair of St. Ives in 1275;[5] the communities of the vills of Holbeach and Quappelode enter into a final concord with Thomas de

---

[1] *Close Rolls of Henry III, 1254–1256*, p. 173.

[2] Sibton in Lyminge; not, as the index to the Close Rolls identifies the name, Siberston near Houghton in Bewsborough Hundred.

[3] *Book of Fees*, iii. 490; *Close Rolls, 1237–42*, pp. 72, 79; *1261–4*, pp. 174, 209; *Patent Roll Calendar, 1249–58*, pp. 195, 547, 578, 614, 638; *1259–63*, pp. 198, 203, 233, 266.

[4] Assize Roll 481.   [5] *Select Pleas in Manorial Courts*, p. 150.

Holbeach before the royal justices in 1287;[1] the bailiff of Headington sues for the king, and for himself, the reeve and the men of
Headington against the prior of St. Frideswide's in 1294.[2] The
men of Little Hormead, Herefordshire, sue the men of the hamlet
of Bordesden, and get 100s. damages in 1387.[3] And only two years
before the date of this writ the whole community of the vill of
Faversham, Kent, pleading by their alderman, had been involved
in a lawsuit.[4]

Mr. H. G. Richardson has kindly pointed out to me some even
more relevant cases from the rolls of the King's Court. The suit
between the villagers of Culham, Oxfordshire, and Sutton, Berkshire, recorded on the Rolls of the Curia Regis for 1212, though
it ends in a number of individual appeals, is initiated by a plaint
from "the men of Culham", speaking apparently by the mouth
of one man; not their lord, the abbot of Abingdon, who remains
aloof throughout the controversy.[5] In 1258 one man, acting
apparently as the spokesman of the other men of Witley, Surrey,
complains that Peter of Savoy has raised the rent of the manor,
which it would seem they formerly farmed of the king and now
farm of him.[6] The men of Norbiton, Surrey, who have a plaint
against a neighbouring township, are advised by the court to
proceed by writ,[7] which appears to indicate that the justices not
only accept the statement that vills may sue by *querele* and *querimonia*, but also recognize their right to proceed by writ. By far the
best instance, however, for bringing out both procedure and legal
personality is the case recently discussed by Powicke,[8] recorded on
the rolls of the Court *Coram Rege* for the year 1266.[9]

Four days after Evesham, some royalist soldiers came through
the village of Peatling, Leicestershire, and were greeted by the
villagers with abuse "eo quod fuerunt contra utilitatem communitatis regni et contra barones". Words were followed by violence,

---

[1] *Terrier of Fleet*, pp. 110 f.   [2] Madox, *Firma Burgi*, p. 65.
[3] *Ibid.*, p. 110. See also instances cited by Maitland from *Durham Halmotes*, pp. 22 (1358)
and 33-4 (1364).
[4] *Abbreviatio Placitorum*, 140.   [5] *Curia Regis Rolls*, vi. 390-1.
[6] *Select Cases of Procedure without Writ* (Selden Society), ed. H. G. Richardson and G. O.
Sayles, pp. 91-2.
[7] *Ibid.*, p. 92.   [8] *Henry III and the Lord Edward*, pp. 509-10.
[9] *Select Cases of Procedure without Writ*, pp. 42-5.

and the beaten and wounded men carried back the report of their handling to their lord, Peter de Neville, who sent a larger body of men to demand amends. The men of the village took refuge in the church. As the royalists threatened to burn it down, one of the village wives took it upon herself to arrange that a fine of twenty marks should be paid, and when the men came out of the church, the village reeve confirmed the bargain on behalf of the township, and handed over five villagers as hostages for the payment of the sum in four days' time. The men of the village sent the hostages money for food, but failed to pay the fine, and the hostages remained in prison until the following January, when the case came before the king. Thomas the reeve, Philip the clerk, and four other villagers including the husband of the woman who had taken the first steps to make the fine, appeared "pro se et communitate ville predicte". They complained that Peter de Neville had seized the hostages by force to extort money from them, and claimed damages. Peter declared that the bargain had been freely made and properly authorized by the reeve on behalf of the community that had attacked his men. The hostages also claimed damages because they had been made hostages without their own consent and had then been left to lie in prison in wretchedness—*miserrime*—for four months and more. The jury which gave the final verdict found that the township was responsible both for the bargain made with Peter de Neville and for the sufferings of the hostages. The reeve had acted *pro communitate*, in proper form, and the township had sanctioned the bargain by sending money for the hostages' food. So judgement was given against the township, which had to pay the twenty marks to Peter and one mark as damages to each of the five hostages.

The community of the vill of Peatling Magna is seen in this case acting through its traditional representatives, the priest, the reeve, and the four men, suing as a litigant in the king's court, bringing its *querimonium* against Peter de Neville, impleaded by Peter de Neville for breach of contract, sued for damages by the five hostages, and liable as a community for payment of the penalties imposed by the king's court, "to be levied from the lands and chattels of the whole township".

If we turn back to the statement of 1255 we are inclined less to question the validity of this *obiter dictum* than to ask why it was called for. The *Leges Henrici* had said that the lord of a vill, or his steward, or the priest, the reeve, and the four men, might discharge the obligations of the vill in the shire and hundred courts. Imbert Pugeys was unable to attend the court of the archbishop of Canterbury; it seems that the archbishop's bailiffs were unwilling to recognize the status of his tenants in pleading or defending their cases. It may be that the significant words are *in curiis aliorum*, since a large proportion of the cases noted above were heard in royal courts.

However that may be, the statement seems to clinch observable facts. Maitland, without citing any authority, says: "The men of C., a mere rural township, or a hundred, can sue and be sued; their bailiff or their reeve with four men will represent them ... But ... as a group, they have no rights to assert or to defend ... What is lacking is not a common seal but common property."[1] Maitland's treatment of the township in *The History of English Law*, even in view of the facts that he himself cites, seems over-legalistic to the student of social and constitutional history. Was he perhaps, in 1899, still fighting the ghost of the Mark? The cases cited above suggest that even from the legal point of view the community of the vill had rights against its own members, as against outsiders. If the statement of 1255 is to be taken as true, the law of the realm gave it procedural rights, and an accepted status in the courts.

By and large, however, the passage is most interesting in the field of constitutional history. It adds one more scrap of evidence to support the contention that representation in England was not a device introduced in the thirteenth century by canon lawyers, but a practice long familiar at the lowest levels, and taken so much for granted as to need no special description. It was a common-sense device, bound to come into existence in a country which combined a strong respect for legal process with a deeply rooted tradition of community. The community of the realm was becoming

[1] Pollock and Maitland, I. 632-3. In the *Pleas of the Crown for the County of Gloucester*, however, he had spoken of "the half-corporate character" of the *villata*, illustrated by the fact that the word governed now a singular and now a plural verb (p. xxv); and in *Township and Borough* he was to say much of its "communalism".

aware of itself in the thirteenth century; at Great Peatling in 1266, as Powicke points out, it had impinged on the consciousness of a far older community—a community older than that of the borough or the shire—the community of the vill.[1]

[1] I should like to acknowledge here my debt to the many friends with whom I have discussed the significance of this passage—particularly to Sir Maurice Powicke, Professor J. G. Edwards, Professor Postan, Miss K. E. Major, Mr. Edward Miller, and, above all, Mr. H. G. Richardson.

Page 85.
[1] Reprinted, by permission, from *In Memoriam Werner Näf: Schweizer Beiträge zur Allgemeinen Geschichte*, 1960/1961.

The Law-Courts of Medieval London

LONDON WAS unique among English towns, and this uniqueness was reflected in its courts and its officials. As far back as we can trace its history, it seems to have been the jurisdictional centre of a region which came to be defined, probably in the tenth century, as the shire of Middlesex. In the days of Edward the Confessor the town reeve (*port-gerefa*) of London was also the Sheriff of Middlesex, and soon after the Conquest charters are addressed to the Sheriff of London. Henry I granted to the citizens of London the right to elect their sheriff, who should render account at his Exchequer of the farm at which they held the shire of Middlesex. But under his grandson Henry II, twenty years later, there were two sheriffs of London, and London was a shire of itself, no other English town having that status until Bristol was created a shire in 1373.

The two sheriffs were not, as might be supposed, the sheriffs of London and Middlesex. It is possible that the second sheriff was the successor of the *Justiciar* of London, the local justice with power to hear the pleas of the Crown, elected in London by the citizens under Henry I's charter, but later appointed by the king. He disappeared under Henry II, being replaced by the justices itinerant.

Henry I's charter mentions what was undoubtedly the oldest London court, namely the Folkmoot, probably the successor of the court that had served Middlesex and London in the tenth century, and the equivalent of the shiremoot in ordinary shires. After the Norman Conquest it had three special sessions in the open air outside St. Paul's Cathedral, where St. Paul's Cross still stood in the seventeenth century, and at one of these three sessions the sheriffs were elected. It was called together by the ringing of St. Paul's great bell, and in times of crisis it became the focus of popular feeling, and was appealed to by city demagogues and royal agents alike. But as a court of justice it was becoming obsolete by the twelfth century, if not earlier, and we have no record of its meeting after the thirteenth century.

Before we turn to the main city courts, mention should be made of the smallest London courts—the wardmoots and the sokemoots. London was divided into wards, at first twenty, later twenty-four, and these are compared in the fourteenth century to the hundreds of a normal shire. No evidence exists, however, that the ward-moots exercised the civil jurisdiction of a hundred court in the twelfth or later centuries. They were summoned by their alderman for police and military purposes, and they supplied juries to report crimes and nuisances and to meet other royal demands. Elections were held in the wardmoots in the fourteenth century, for a short period of the alderman of the ward, but more frequently of representatives to attend the great assemblies at the Guildhall.

The sokemoots were a different matter. Henry I's charter of 1132 provides that the barons and citizens of London shall have their *sokes* or private jurisdictions, and in the twelfth century there were at least twenty of these seignorial complexes,[1] whose lords, from great men like the King of Scotland, the Bishop of London, or the Earl of Gloucester to many lesser folk, had their own soke courts, attended by their London tenants. As the jurisdiction of the city courts developed, the soke courts became superfluous, and gradually ceased to meet. As late as the reign of Edward II, however, a few, like those of St. Paul's and St. Martin's, were still functioning, and, according to the reports made to the royal justices in eyre in 1321, were still hanging thieves, a right only granted to the city in 1327.

"We have three sokes in the city," say the Dean and Chapter of St. Paul's, "one at Cornhill, and one at Holborn, and the third at Bishopsgate, and we hold our court for those sokes by our servants at Cornhill, and in that court thieves taken redhanded within our sokes are judged, and on such malefactors convicted in this court judgement is executed at our gallows at Stepney or Finsbury outside the city."[2]

[1] W. Page, *London, its origin and early development* (1923), ch. iv.
[2] *Placita Quo Warranto* (Record Commission) (1818), p. 456.

There was no rivalry between the officials and courts of the sokes and those of the city; the sheriffs were prepared to back up the authorities of the sokes if they were in difficulties, and, as we shall see, if a soke man failed to get justice in his lord's court he could carry the case to the sheriff's court.

The court at which the main judicial business of the city was done in the twelfth century is first mentioned towards the end of the tenth. Its name, the Husting, shows strong Scandinavian influence, and may derive from the short period in the ninth century when London was in Danish hands. However that may be, Henry I's charter, in declaring that no citizen shall plead outside London for any plea, recognizes the Husting as the court where their pleas are held and their customs maintained, saying it may meet every Monday. At this date the sheriff presided, and, according to customary procedure, the suitors were the judges, namely the aldermen of the city wards. It was presumably in the Husting that the Justiciar held the pleas of the Crown until Henry II withdrew that privilege. In the Husting, held in the Guildhall, the Londoners transacted all their civil litigation, real and personal, according to the laws and customs of London, recognized by all the kings from the Conqueror onwards. As the wealth and population of the city increased, so did the activity of the court. By 1193, when the city acquired a mayor, who henceforth took premier place at the Husting, it was sitting two days a week, on Mondays and Tuesdays, and as its business continued to expand, it ramified, like the king's own court, into different branches and developed different jurisdictions. Thus early in the thirteenth century we hear of separate sessions, held in alternate weeks, for common pleas and pleas of land, these last being initiated by a royal writ. Further, a distinction was being established between the courts held by the sheriffs and those where the mayor presided, assisted by sheriffs and aldermen.[1]

The Sheriffs' Courts, held at first in their own houses, dealt with the offences coming to be known as trespasses, and also with pleas of contract and debt. And just as the ordinary shire-courts

[1] For an account of this evolution, see A. H. Thomas, *Calendar of Early Mayor's Court Rolls* (1924), Introduction, pp. xiv-xxv.

could hear the case of a man whose lord had refused to listen to him in his court, so the sheriffs of London could hear complaints of default of justice in a soke court. Lastly, there was from 1221 a "Pie Powder" court, held by the sheriffs with or without the mayor and aldermen on days other than Mondays or Tuesdays, for foreign merchants passing through the city, in which the Law Merchant was followed.

At the same time the mayors with the aldermen were holding, besides the regular Hustings at the Guildhall, courts on other than the set Husting days at which not only the pleas of foreign merchants, but all kinds of pleas initiated by plaint or bill were heard. Pleas initiated by writ were heard in the Husting of Common Pleas or the Husting of Pleas of Land. The development of these jurisdictions can be followed in the rolls of the courts, preserved at the Guildhall, and in the various city custumals.[1] It was in the Mayor's Court that public order was enforced, and brawlers and others who disobeyed city ordinances were punished. There was some overlapping of jurisdictions, but it was the Mayor's Court whose functions grew steadily. It heard citizens' complaints against the sheriffs, dealt with the violation of royal statutes and punished fraudulent traders. But until 1327 it could not inflict capital punishment, and criminals were taken to the king's gaol of Newgate. It was distinguished by the fact that most actions in it were by plaint or bill rather than by writ.

One feature of this London judicial system has a special interest in a wider field. It has been suggested that it was in connexion with the London courts that the common law writ of error was first evolved.[2] The history of jurisdiction in error in the City of London has two facets: the revision by the mayor, in the thirteenth and fourteenth centuries, of judgements given in the Sheriffs' Courts, and the correction of judgements given in the court of Husting by special commissions of royal justices, sitting at St. Martin's le Grand, from the thirteenth to the sixteenth century.

[1] See the *Calendar of Early Mayor's Court Rolls* and the series of *Calendars of Plea and Memoranda Rolls of the City of London*, 1926, and *Munimenta Gildhallae Londoniensis* (Rolls Series), I/II. 1859 1860.

[2] By S. F. C. Milsom, in his unpublished Cambridge thesis, "Origin and early history of judicial review" (1948).

The Statute of Marlborough, in 1267, had laid it down that none save the king might exercise jurisdiction in error, that is to say, might revise the judgement of a lower court. But there is clear evidence that the Mayor's Court was hearing complaints, not of failure of judgement, but of wrong judgement in the Sheriffs' Court, by well established practice, by 1280, for in that year it was declared to be the law and custom of the city that if it seem to the pleaders in the Husting or the Sheriff's Court that an erroneous judgement has been given they shall make a complaint to the mayor, who will redress the error, if error there be.[1]

The Mayor's Court, as we have seen, heard complaints of the sheriffs' misconduct—very generally of trespasses committed by them. On the Mayor's Court Rolls, which begin in 1298, there are twenty instances of plaints of error of judgement brought against the sheriffs between that date and 1307, the actions concerned being of debt, detinue, covenant and assault. The procedure is for the mayor to order the sheriff to bring the record and process of the case in his court to answer before the mayor to the plea of error. The judgement of the Mayor's Court is recorded on seven occasions: in five instances the judgement of the Sheriff's Court is confirmed; in two it is annulled. On two occasions the plaint is withdrawn; on one, where Law Merchant is involved, the plaintiff is advised to seek his remedy at Common Law. In the other cases the outcome is not recorded. The record of the Sheriff's Court is enrolled in eleven instances, showing in what detail the actions were entered, and what careful and experienced lawyers the clerks of the Sheriff's Court were. One case had begun in a soke court, whose record is also enrolled.[2]

In all these entries on the Mayor's Court Rolls there is no indication that the party complaining of error of judgement has brought a writ; he appears to have proceeded by plaint. But in 1315 a petition to the king from the citizens of London states that when a defendant alleges that a wrong judgement has been given against him in the Sheriffs' Court he purchases a writ to have the record brought *before the mayor* or before Justices

---

[1] *Mun. Gild. Lond.*, II. p. 281.
[2] *Cal. of Early Mayor's Court Rolls*, pp. 89-91.

assigned,[1] and the royal reply to the petition clearly recognizes this procedure.[2]

Nevertheless, when in the London Eyre of 1321 a Quo Warranto was brought against the mayor and community, the king's counsel, Geoffrey le Scrope, attacked the mayor for having violated the statute of Marlborough, which laid down that writ of error of judgement ought to be heard nowhere save in the king's own court, "and to this statute you yourself and all the community assented,[3] to which the mayor replied that they had done this from time immemorial whenever the king's writ came to them to redress errors done before the sheriff. "They correct in the court of Husting the errors of judgements given in the Sheriff's Court, if errors there be, by authority of the writs of the lord king and not by their own authority".[4]

No judgement was given in the Eyre on the matter; the Quo Warranto proceedings against the city were adjourned for the Council to hear, and when Edward III succeeded his father the case was still undetermined.[5] In the charter granted by the new king to the city, largely in gratitude for their help in overthrowing his father, the liberties of the city were confirmed in general terms, and though there is no specific reference to the mayor's jurisdiction in error the confirmation of their liberties as used before the Eyre is expressly granted, "non obstantibus aliquibus statutis seu judiciis in contrarium editis vel promulgatis",[6] which in effect exempts them from the operation of the Statute of Marlborough.

If the practice had been discontinued from 1321 to 1327 we have evidence that it was resumed. In 1338 the mayor and bailiffs of Oxford wrote to the mayor and sheriffs of London asking for particulars of their procedure in holding the assize of Fresh Force.

---

[1] *Mun. Gild. Lond.*, I. p. 408. A number of such writs are entered on the rolls of the Husting of Common Pleas for the years before 1321, and there is a complete record of the hearing of such a case in the Husting, up to the judgement which confirms the judgement in the Sheriff's Court, on the roll for 1318-19 (Hustings of Common Pleas, Roll 43; Monday after St. Luke's day, 12 E 2. Guildhall Record Office).

[2] *Ibid.*, p. 409-410, from Close Roll of 8 Ed. 2, m. 4.

[3] Brit. Mus., MS. Harl. 453 (Report of Eyre), fo. 30 v.

[4] *Mun. Gild. Lond.*, II. 324 (The City's transcript of the Eyre roll, that at the P.R.O. being defective).

[5] *Bulletin Inst. Hist. Research*, No. 19 (June 1929), p. 37.

[6] *Chronicles of Edward I and Edward II* (Rolls Series), 1882, I. p. 330.

The reply, enrolled on the Plea and Memoranda Rolls of the city, after describing the assize, adds that by writ of error the record and process could be revised in the Husting.[1] Again, in 1355, when a litigant obtained a writ summoning a case from the city into Chancery, the return to the writ stated plainly that in an action terminated outside the Husting an aggrieved party might obtain a writ *de venire faciendo* to have the record and process brought before the mayor and aldermen in the Husting for review.[2] Lastly, in a collection of legal formulae which appears to be especially concerned with the City of London there occurs a writ *De errore corrigendo in Londoniis*, addressed to the mayor and sheriffs of London on behalf of a certain William of St. Albans, who asserts that in the record and process of a plea heard without a writ before the sheriffs of London, according to London custom a manifest error had occurred in the judgement given. The king, willing that this error, if it did occur, should be corrected and justice be done, orders the mayor and sheriffs to have the record and process recited and examined before them in the presence of the parties in full Husting, that justice may be done according to the custom of the city.[3] The writ is undated, but it is among documents belonging to the reign of Edward II, and a William of St. Albans occurs on the record of a city court held on 18 July 1355.[4] There is no evidence as to when the practice was discontinued. A parallel practice, by which the mayor could intervene in the Sheriffs' Court before a case was submitted to a jury and call in into his own court, is described in a custumal of about 1327,[5] and was continued to a late date under the title *querelae levatae*, namely, complaints taken away from the sheriffs by the mayor.

We now have to turn to the history of the royal commissioners appointed to revise judgements given by the mayor. In the reply cited above given to the citizens of Oxford in 1338,[6] as to the

---

[1] *Cal. of Plea and Memoranda Rolls, 1323-1364*, p. 169.   [2] *Ibid.*, p. 247.

[3] MS. Dunn 52, Law School Library, Harvard University. My attention was called to this MS. by Mr. Milsom's thesis, mentioned in note 5. The wording closely resembles that of the fourth writ under the heading "De errore" in *Registrum Brevium*, fo. 130-130 v.

[4] *Cal. of Plea and Memoranda Rolls, 1323-1364*, p. 256.

[5] *Mun. Gild. Lond.*, I, 219.

[6] See note 1 above, and see a very similar account of the practice in a custumal that should be dated 1321-1327, not 1419; Bateson, *Borough Customs* (Selden Society, 1906), II, 18.

mayor's jurisdiction in error, it is added that if the aggrieved party is not satisfied with the judgement given by the mayor and sheriffs in the Husting he can obtain another writ of error to have the record brought before a session of royal justices, appointed *ad hoc* to sit at St. Martin's le Grand.

St. Martin's le Grand was geographically within the city, but legally outside it; it was a very specially privileged royal liberty. There is frequent mention of royal justices sitting there with various commissions. The first recorded instance of their hearing a complaint of wrong judgement in the Husting is in 1248, when Henry of Bath heard the complaint of one Margery Vyel who had obtained a writ from the king ordering the record of the case to be brought before him. The mayor and citizens appeared before the Justice, who found the judgement false and the city was taken into the king's hands.[1]

From this time on the Patent Rolls contain a growing number of commissions to justices to sit at St. Martin's in order to hear the record, brought by the mayor and sheriffs, of specific cases in the Husting of London, and to correct the judgements, if necessary, according to the custom of London. There are seven such entries under Henry III, and twenty-four under Edward I down to 1285, the year when the city was again taken into the king's hands.[2] By 1304 it was regarded as an immemorial privilege that appeals from the Husting should be heard only at St. Martin's. In that year the mayor, summoned to bring the record of a plea of trespass before the Treasurer in the Exchequer, protested, saying "we ought to make no record save at St. Martin's le Grand, as you well know".[3] In 1319 the citizens obtained from Edward II a charter confirming their liberties, which consists for the most part of a recitation of earlier grants, but has a new clause granting "that the king will appoint no justices to hear cases arising in the city or the suburbs save only justices to hold an Eyre at the Tower, justices to deliver the gaol at Newgate and justices to correct errors at St. Martin's le Grand, as has been done by old custom".[4] The Charter

---

[1] *Liber de Antiquis Legibus*, ed. T. Stapleton (Camden Society, 1846), pp. 13-14; *Close Rolls, 1247-1251*, p. 79.

[2] London remained without a mayor until 1298.

[3] H. T. Riley, *Memorials of London* (1868), p. 51. [4] *Mun. Gild. Lond.*, II. 267.

of 1327 makes a more general promise—"all inquisitions to be taken by our justices shall be taken at St. Martin's, except for eyres at the Tower and the Gaol Delivery at Newgate".[1]

And the justices continued to hold sessions at St. Martin's under special commissions down to 1517, the city having the special privilege of bringing the record and process of cases heard in the Husting before them orally (*ore tenus*) by their Recorder.[2]

The majority of writs of error make no reference to a previous hearing, but there are instances when it is clear that the case had been heard both in the Sheriff's Court and in the Mayor's Court before it was called to St. Martin's.[3] In 1314 when the mayor had failed to take action on an appeal from the Sheriff's Court, the record and process was summoned to St. Martin's in his default.[4]

The statements of 1338 and 1355 make it clear that the mayor was still exercising jurisdiction in error in the middle of the fourteenth century, and this undoubtedly contributed to exalt the status of his court above the sheriffs'. Moreover, as by various emergency commissions the mayor was coming in the early fourteenth century to exercise the functions of a justice of the peace,[5] and as by the Charter of 1327 he was *ex officio* a justice of Gaol Delivery, he had acquired a measure of criminal jurisdiction.

It will be seen that the jurisdiction of the city courts was varied and comprehensive. Their oldest charters had guaranteed to the citizens their own legal customs, and the grant that they should not have to plead outside the city enabled them to develop procedures for securing their rights which, though differing in detail, were the effective equivalent of those available in the king's own courts. The Hustings of Common Pleas, the Hustings of Pleas of Land, the Sheriffs' Courts and the Mayors' Courts made it unnecessary for the Londoner to apply to the common law courts. From the middle of the thirteenth century a large body of city lawyers were available to plead his cause in the city courts, and if he did, in fact,

---

[1] W. de Gray Birch, *Historical Charters of the City of London*, 1887, p. 58.

[2] *Cal. of Plea and Memoranda Rolls, 1323-1364*, p. 169 (1338); *Mun. Gild. Lond.*, I. 42 (*ca.* 1419). The charter of 1518 transferred the sessions to Guildhall, but the court was not abolished until 1857. See W. E. Jones, *The Corporation of London* (1953), p. 87.

[3] e.g. *Beauflour* v. *Totenham*, 1305, *Cal. of Patent Rolls, 1304-1317*, p. 403.

[4] *Cal. of Patent Rolls, 1314-1317*, pp. 147-148.

[5] Thomas, *Cal. of Plea and Memoranda Rolls, 1323-1364*, Introduction, pp. xi-xxxiii.

apply to a royal court, the representative of the Mayor and Community followed him there and claimed and recovered cognizance of the plea for the city in accordance with the liberties of London. Only in criminal matters or in matters that came within the growing equitable jurisdiction of the Crown would a citizen find himself in a royal court.

The tradition of the city was that their Assize of Fresh Force had anticipated Henry II's Assize of Novel Disseisein.[1] It is not too difficult, in the light of the facts given above, to believe that the earliest precedents for writs of error are to be found in London, and that the earliest stages in the evolution of the commission of the peace are to be found in London.[2]

[1] Bateson, *Borough Customs*, I. 232 (*c.* 1215).
[2] See footnote 5, p. 93.

VI

Cases of Novel Disseisin
in the Eyre of London 1321[1]

O<small>N</small> 14 J<small>ANUARY</small> 1321, the royal justice Hervey of Stanton, with three colleagues, opened an *iter ad omnia placita*, or general eyre, at the Tower of London. We are not concerned here with the possible reasons that led Edward II to revive a moribund institution.[2] The interest to a historian of law in the proceedings of January to July 1321 is twofold. There survive two parallel accounts of the proceedings in court; the official record in Latin,[3] and the reports of discussions of some of the cases by counsel and judges, as taken down by reporters who were either students of the law or caterers for their needs.[4] In character they belong to the class of documents known as Year Books, though they stand outside the regular series so-called of the reports of the cases heard in the Common Bench at Westminster, year by year, and term by term. As only six eyres have been thus fully reported, and the reports of only one of these have been printed,[5] those for 1321 have a scarcity value. But they stand alone in reporting the judicial visitation of a city, and in the evidence they afford as to the relation of the common law to the custom of London and as to the legal remedies most in request among its citizens in the first quartier of the fourteenth century.

This brief study concerns only one type of case reported by these vigorous and lively note-takers, the cases of Novel Disseisin.

---

[1] Reprinted from *Études d'histoire du droit privé offertes à Pierre Petot*, Paris, 1959.

[2] In the reign of Edward I some sixty eyres had been held, but since his death only one General Eyre, that of Kent, had been held, in 1313; after 1321 only the eyres of Bedford, Northampton, Nottingham and Derby (1330-1) were carried through before the practice was finally abandoned.

[3] Assize Rolls 546, 547. (Public Record Office.)

[4] Eight MSS. are extant, no two of them alike in selection or order of cases.

[5] *The Eyre of Kent* (Selden Society, 1909-1913).

It will be recalled that this action had been introduced by Henry II about 1166,[1] and had proved immensely popular, as providing a rapid means of enabling a man to recover by jury trial land which had been taken from him *"injuste et sine judicio"*. In the century and a half since the writ of Novel Disseisin had been devised, the doctrine of seisin had been extended and applied not only to land but to a series of rights arising out of land, notably, well before Bracton wrote, to rents.[2] The Statute of Westminster II, in 1285, had further enlarged the scope of the Assize.[3] A remedy devised primarily for an agrarian society could now be used to protect "incorporeal things" in an urban society.

As regards the use of the writ of Novel Disseisin in the London eyre of 1321 three points should be noted. First, in a general eyre, from at least 1204,[4] the writs were issued not from the Chancery, but by the justices of the eyre themselves. Those of 1321 had fixed a date, 2nd February, by which all such writs were to be procured.[5] In technical terms, they were judicial, not original, writs, and the report of the first case of Novel Disseisin brought in the eyre begins by quoting the judicial writ in full to make this clear. It is tested not by the Chancellor, but by Hervey of Stanton, the presiding justice. In the second place, the formula as to the date of the disseisin is not that used for cases brought in the Common Bench. There the disseisin was supposed to be novel —recent—but by 1321 this was pretty much of a legal fiction, for the date was 1242.[6] When the assize was brought in a general eyre, however, the date named was always "within the summons of the eyre", in this case, 30 November, 1320.[7] And lastly, the citizens of London were in a different position from the men of other counties; they could bring the assize of Fresh Force (*frisca forcia*), identical in scope with the assize of Novel Disseisin and probably

---

[1] Pollock and Maitland, *History of English Law*, I. 145-6; Joüon des Longrais, *La conception anglaise de la saisine*, pp. 48-9, 54-5; Plucknett, *Concise History of the Common Law* (5th ed.), pp. 358-9.

[2] Pollock and Maitland, *op. cit.*, II. 126 ff.; Holdsworth, *History of English Law*, III. 96-101.

[3] Stat. Westm., II, c. 25 (*Statutes of the Realm*, I. 84).

[4] *Select Cases of Procedure without Writ*, (Selden Society 1941), pp. xl-xli.

[5] Brit. Mus. MS. Harl. 453, fo. 12d.

[6] Pollock and Maitland, *op. cit.*, II. 51.

[7] Brit. Mus., Add. MS. 38131, fo. 91.

of equal antiquity,[1] in the court held every Saturday before the sheriffs and coroners of London. Thus the eyre brought them no added facilities in this field, whilst it actually debarred them from the use of the writ of right which they could normally plead in the Hustings of Common Pleas, which met fortnightly. The effect of an eyre was always to suspend the sessions of all local courts, but it was the special privilege of London that no pleas of land except those of Novel Disseisin could be held in a general eyre, and consequently from January to July 1321 no citizen could use a writ of right to establish his right to a tenement. One result was the use of the assize of Novel Disseisin to seek a remedy in cases where the plaintiff would normally have used, or actually was already using a writ of right in the court of Husting.

To come now to the cases themselves.

On the rolls of the London eyre there are eighty-one cases of Novel Disseisin. About half of these concern houses or shops, *cum pertinenciis*; an equal number are about rents. Of the thirty-two cases *reported*, twelve are concerned with houses and eighteen with rents; the law students found rents a more interesting topic, it would seem.

I. House cases

In few of the cases do the litigants come directly to the point of the question, has the defendant disseised the plaintiff? Almost always a special issue is raised, intended to show that the plaintiff has no right to bring the assize, that "he was never seised so that he could be disseised". In one instance[2] the landlord who has a life interest in the house and lives in the country has entered it to distrain because the house rent is eighteen months in arrears;[3] the tenants complain that they have been disseised. The jury find that the tenants had offered to pay the arrears and the landlord has

---

[1] *Mun. Gild. Lond.,* I. 114, 195-7. This assize lay in most towns; *Borough Customs,* (Selden Society), Publ. 18, pp. 231-242.

[2] *Alegate* v. *Bamme,* Assize Roll 546, m. 27d.

[3] The right to distrain did not in London expire after twelve months, as it did in Paris. Olivier-Martin, *Coutume de Paris* (1922), I. 467.

refused to accept them; the arrears are paid in court, the tenants are re-seised of the house, and the landlord has to pay 40s. damages as well as an amercement. In the second case[1] where house rent is in arrears, the house in question had been devised to two parties, and as it was impossible to divide it into equal halves, the devisee who had the larger half undertook to pay rent to the other devisee in respect of the difference. The rent (10s. 1d.) was in arrears, so the other devisee, having distrained for the rent more than once, finally took possession of the other part of the house. Was this disseisin? The jury say it was not disseisin, but a reasonable distress, and the plaintiff is amerced for a false claim.

In these two instances there was no dispute as to ownership, but in other cases the assize is clearly being brought to establish the seisin—the possession—of one party. Two of the houses involved had notable owners. A number of relatives of John Kirkby, a former bishop of Ely, brought the assize against John Hotham, the present bishop of Ely, complaining that he had disseised them of a certain house "in the suburb of London" most probably in Holborn.[2] The bishop brought evidence to show that the house had been in the possession of the bishops of Ely ever since the days of Kirkby, and further produced deeds whereby the plaintiffs had quitclaimed all right in the house in question, together with the king's licence to hold the house in mortmain. But for that licence, the justice said, he would have dismissed the case as a collusive action; as it was, it went to the jury,[3] who found that there was no disseisin. It certainly looks like a collusive action to establish the title of the bishops of Ely to the house, which they held down to the Reformation.

Another case[4] concerned a house held by the famous Lombard merchants, the Bardi, later sold by them to Edward III, and occupied jointly or alternately by the Great Wardrobe (a government office) and by the De la Pole family.[5] The house had belonged to Robert Turk, and the Bardi had acquired it, with the sanction

---

[1] *Langton* v. *Vilers*, Assize Roll 546, m. 7.
[2] *Prilly and others* v. *the Bishop of Ely*, Assize Roll 546, m. 14.
[3] As provided by Stat. Westm., II. ch. 32.
[4] *Turk* v. *Ardinguelli and others*, Assize Roll 546, m. 9.
[5] Tout, *Chapters in Administrative History*, IV. 401-5.

of Edward II, in 1318: now, in 1321, his son Walter Turk asserts that his mother alienated the tenement while he was a minor and overseas, and that he has thus been disseised by the Lombards. The sale had been acknowledged in the court of Husting, and by the custom of the City, forty weeks' occupation precluded use of the assize of Fresh Force. The nature of the widow's title and the question whether the disseisin had taken place, legally speaking, since the summons of the eyre were issues raised in court. The production by the defendants in court of a quitclaim from the plaintiff would make one again suspect collusion, did not the reports show clearly that the quitclaim represents a settlement arrived at midway in the proceedings.[1] Presumably this quitclaim was one of the sixty-two title-deeds which the Bardi handed over to Edward III in 1328 when he bought the house from them for £700:[2] an indication of the complexities of title that might be involved by the tenure of a London house.

Beverley v. *Beverley*[3] is a family affair. John, the grandson of William of Beverley, brings the assize against Salerna, William's widow, for disseising him of a house and five shops. Salerna alleges that she holds one-third of the property as her dower and that the other two-thirds were devised to her by her husand on his deathbed. John's counsel says that she was assigned a rent charge of 40s. a year on the property, but admits that William's son had left her in peaceful possession for ten years. Salerna's counsel says the assize ought not to be held because the case is pending in the court of Husting by writ of right—"bref de plus haut nature",[4] but as John is a minor the judges decide that the assize shall be held, and the jury find for him against Salerna.

In two other instances, where the parties are of full age, the fact that a case is pending in the Guildhall under a writ of right cuts the pleading short. In *Winchester* v. *Acre*[5] the judge refuses to let the issue go to the jury; in *Pyper* v. *Pilk*[6] the plantiffs' counsel advises them to withdraw, and they do so.

---

[1] The record gives the date—25 February, 1321, Assize Roll 546, m. 9.

[2] *Calendar of Close Rolls, 1327-30*, pp. 362, 378-9. For 21 of these deeds see Chanc. Misc. 47/9/6 (P.R.O).

[3] Assize Roll 546, m. 28d. [4] Brit. Mus. MS. Harl. 1062, fo. 5d.

[5] Assize Roll 546, m. 13. [6] Assize Roll 546, m. 25d.

Finally, one attempt is made to use the assize to protect a right that has not yet materialized. The house in question had been alienated to the defendants for their lives, with remainder to the plaintiff, who was still a minor when he brought the case. The defendants were granting the house in fee to a third party, thus depriving the plaintiff of his remainder rights. The plaintiff, it seemed, could gain little by the assize. The judge observed that no action was provided for such a case, but he awarded the assize. After a series of adjournments, however, the minor failed to appear to prosecute his claim, and the case went against him by default.[1]

II. RENT CASES

Bracton, as Maitland tells us,[2] distinguishes three types of *redditus*, or rent. There is the rent due from a tenant to his lord, in France called *cens*; this came to be termed "Rent Service" by the lawyers. The non-tenurial rents, corresponding to the *rente constituée* of the *coutumes*,[3] were of two kinds; first the *redditus que detur alicui ex tenemento cum districtione*, known as "Rent Charge" by the time of Edward I, which could, like Rent Service, be exacted by distress; and secondly, the *redditus sine districtione*, which could not be exacted by distress, and which came to be known as *redditus siccus*, or Rent Seck. If the rent could not be regarded as issuing out of a certain place it could not be recovered by the assize; a writ of *annuity* must be used,[4] But if the annual rent was payable in a certain place (a corrody) it ranked as freehold after 1285, and the assize could be used to recover it.[5]

Rent Service, whether called by that name or not, was as old as feudalism. The rent charge, in England as in France, came into use in the twelfth century, and was very generally applied, at first to the purposes of charitable endowment,[6] but later as a form of

---

[1] *Reyner v. Reyner*, Assize Roll 546, m. 4d.

[2] Pollock and Maitland, *op. cit.*, II. 129.

[3] Olivier-Martin, *Coutume de Paris*, I. 441-457; Petot, *La constitution de rente dans les pays coutumiers* (Publications de l'Universite de Dijon, fasc. I. 1928).

[4] Pollock and Maitland, *op. cit.*, II. 133.

[5] Pollock and Maitland, *op. cit.*, II. 135.

[6] Olivier-Martin, *op. cit.*, I. 454; Petot, *op. cit.*, pp. 4-6. The cartularies of St. Paul's and of St. Mary's, Clerkenwell, one of the London nunneries (edited in the Camden Series 1939, 1949) supply numerous examples of rents bestowed on London religious houses by all manner of English donors.

investment, acquired by purchase as well as by gift.[1] Already by Bracton's time rents had come to be regarded as freeholds—*libera tenementa*—and as such the assize of Novel Disseisin was appropriate for them.[2] The statute of 1285, which extended the use of the assize to estovers, corrodies, tolls, bailiwicks and common rights in turfland, made no reference to rents, already fully accepted as freehold property.

The eighteen rent cases reported in the London eyre concern Rent Service, Rent Charge and, it would, Rent Seck, and there is one case of a corrody. In one instance the action of debt is employed to demand rent for a house let for a term of years. When counsel queries the use of the writ of debt, seeing that the plaintiff was able to distrain, the justice says that he knows nothing more natural than writ of debt for the recovery of arrears of rent in a case of this kind—"en chescun lieu a la comune ley la ou terre est lesse a terme des ans plus naturellement git action de dette qe destresce".[3]

Two of the cases concern Rent Service. In the case of *the Prioress of Clerkenwell* v. *Gilbert of Taunton*,[4] where she alleges that she has been disseised of 26s. of rent due from him as her tenant, the defendant says that he is no longer her tenant, as the land had been granted to another since the Statute of *Quia Emptores* had been passed,[5] so that the rent is due to the overlord of the Prioress and not to her; but he fails to prove this and she is awarded the assize.

The second is a suit between two graduates.[6] Master William of Melford, archdeacon of Colchester, complains that Master Ralph of London, a surgeon, has disseised him of 30s. rent (the arrears for a year). Master Ralph and his wife had gone elsewhere during the Christmas holidays and, unable to find a tenant, had left the house empty. When the landlord came to distrain for the rent he found the house locked up, and when the key was demanded by a city

[1] Pollock and Maitland, *op. cit.*, II. 130. In 1238 a case between two laymen concerning a rent of 67s. 6d. was being heard before the mayor and sheriffs of London. *Close Rolls, 1237–1242*, p. 148.   [2] Pollock and Maitland, *op. cit.*, II. 130-1.

[3] Brit. Mus. MS. Harl. 453, fo. 27; MS. Harl. 1062, fo. 9; MS. Egerton 2811, fo. 31d.

[4] Assize Roll 546, m. 4d.

[5] This statute, passed in 1290, forbade further subinfeudation; alienation was henceforth to be by substitution, with an equitable apportionment of the services.

[6] Assize Roll 546, m. 28.

official Master Ralph refused to hand it over. Unable to distrain,[1] Master William brings the assize. The pleadings reveal that the house had been leased to Master Ralph and his wife for the term of their lives by a previous landlord who had later granted both the rent and the reversion of the property to Master William, who thus became the landlord to whom rent service was due. Ralph and his wife had "attorned to William as his true tenants"; that is, they had legally acknowledged the transfer and their new obligations, and now Ralph declares himself "willing to pay the rent, but unwilling to let William enter his house". The jury find that William has been disseised, and he is awarded 36s. 8d. damages as well as the arrears of rent.

The part played by Rent Charges in the London economy is very well illustrated by the cases reported in the eyre. The Prior of Blackmore,[2] a house of Austin Canons in Essex, produces the will of the pious donor proved in the court of Husting by which, according to the custom of London, he had devised the rent to him in 1294, along with Edward I's licence to hold the rent in mortmain. The defendant's counsel argue that a will cannot impose a rent charge, and that there should be a "specialty", that is, a written grant, but the court accepts the mortmain licence as good evidence in support of the will, and the Prior wins the case.

Rent Charges had also been bestowed by pious donors on the Priory of Merton,[3] Surrey, and, in the City, on the Priory of Clerkenwell[4] and on St. James's hospital,[5] all of whose representatives bring suits in the eyre, whilst the Master of St. Giles's Hospital[6] for lepers claims a rent that his house had purchased in the days of Henry III.

The cases where both parties are laymen illustrate the transfer of Rent Charges from one person to another. In *Crofton v. Hoddesdon*[7] a certain William Flory had granted a rent of 40s. to John of Hoddesdon for the life of Agnes Potter. John in his turn

---

[1] By the custom of London a man might enter a house through the window in order to distrain, but apparently this was not practicable here.

[2] Assize Roll 546, m. 2.

[3] Assize Roll 546, m. 25d. The report includes a discussion as to the interpretation of the statute of 1285.

[4] Assize Roll 546, m. 4d, m. 19d.

[5] Assize Roll 546, m. 15d.

[6] Assize Roll 546, m. 9.

[7] Assize Roll 546, m. 2.

had granted it to Richard Crofton, a clerk in the service of the City officials,[1] with the right to distrain for it. The rent was charged on Hoddesdon's tenement and when Crofton had distrained on it for arrears Hoddesdon had taken back the distress. Crofton now charges him with disseisin. The judge quashed the writ because he said Flory should have been named in it as the original grantor of the rent; if Crofton had recovered the rent from Hoddesdon by the assize he could then have brought a writ of Annuity against Flory and so have secured the money twice over.[2]

In the case of the Prior of Blackmore the defendant's counsel had said that since what was owed was not Rent Service the plaintiff would have to prove that it was Rent Charge. He argued that since a tenement could not be charged by a testament, the rent must be a Rent Seck, that is, as we have seen, a rent which could not be distrained for.[3] This seems to be a very early use of the term. We have seen that the justice accepted the evidence of the will, as reinforced by the mortmain licence,[4] but the same issue was raised in two other cases. In *The Prior of Merton* v. *Roger le Blund*[5] the deed granting the rent to the Priory made no mention of power to distrain, and there was some argument as to whether the assize would lie in such a case. The justice indicated[6] that the statute of 1285 would apply, since that extended the protection of the assize to "profits arising" from land, and rent was such a profit. This issue however was not decided, as the writ was quashed because the property was inadequately described.

In the case of *Dovecote* v. *Lok and Atte Cok*[7] the rent in question had originally been Rent Service, but had then been granted to a third party who had in turn granted it to the plaintiffs, a man and wife. Again the question is raised if it is a Rent Seck. Counsel for the defendants raise a number of points, insisting chiefly that no

[1] E. Ekwall, *Two early London Subsidy Rolls* (Lund, 1951), p. 244, n. 26.

[2] Brit. Mus. MS. 1602, fo. 4d. Crofton did in fact get a second writ of Novel Disseisin naming Flory as well as Hoddesdon (Assize Roll 546, m. 3), but the record does not give the outcome.

[3] See above, p. 100. *Claver.* "Vous demandez cest rente e ne ditez nient qe les tenemenz sunt de votre fee, par qei il covent qe ceo sait une sek rente, e vous ne moustrez nient fet de cely qei les poait charger." Brit. Mus. MS. Egerton 2811, fo. 24.

[4] See above, p. 102.

[5] Assize Roll 546, m. 25d.

[6] Brit. Mus. M.S. Egerton 2811, fo. 29.

[7] Assize Roll 546, m. 12d.

deed shows that the holders of the tenements on which the rent is alleged to be charged are liable to pay, and that therefore the assize does not apply, for "this is not rent service nor rent charge".[1] The plaintiffs' counsel refers to the case of the Prior of Blackmore, but the judges say that in that case the assize was held by the consent of both parties. On the other hand, by the custom of London, they understand, a man can distrain for a rent of which he is seised without showing specialty, and "nous chargoms mout la usage de la ville ou ceo qe entent qe comune lei meintint soun estat".[2] So they put the case to the jury, who ask to see all the deeds, and having seen them, find that the plaintiffs were not seised of the rent in such a way that they could be disseised of it. So Dovecote and his wife lose their case.[3]

Lastly we have the case of *Newman* v. *The Warden of St. Katharine's Hospital by the Tower*.[4] Margaret, the widow of Edward I, had granted to John Newman a rent of twopence a day for life with 14s. 8d. annually to buy himself a gown, to be paid to him by the Warden of the hospital, whose patroness was the wife of the reigning king. Newman showed Queen Margaret's charter of grant and charged the Warden with disseisin. The rent was in effect a corrody, and as such recoverable by the assize of Novel Disseisin under the statute of 1285. The Warden said that he was not bound to pay, since in the first place the Queen's charter did not mention the Warden of the hospital, and in the second place he had sworn to maintain the wealth of the hospital for the relief of the poor brethren there, and to pay out such a rent would be to diminish its assets. As Queen Isabel, the wife of Edward II, was the patroness in 1321, the justices felt that they must walk warily. "Ceo qe touche la rayne, ceo touche le roy meime."[5] The case is adjourned so that the king may be consulted, and the

---

[1] Brit. Mus. MS. Harl. 453, fo. 21d. From the arguments in this and the two preceding cases it would seem that the use of the assize to recover a Rent Seck was not yet fully established in 1321, in spite of Maitland's observations in Pollock and Maitland, *op. cit.*, II. 130.

[2] MS. Harl. 453, fo. 22.

[3] This is a good example of the constantly recurring insistence on written evidence of which Maitland speaks (*op. cit.*, II. 132). Wills, indentures, deeds of grant or sale are all produced in court.

[4] Assize Roll 546, m. 37.   [5] Brit. Mus. MS. Egerton 2811, fo. 30.

plaintiff is advised in the mean time to sue to "Madame la Rayne". According to Newman's counsel, Isabel had confirmed Margaret's grant, so that we may hope that John Newman secured his pension.

It will be seen that the cases reported in the eyre of 1321, besides illustrating the development of the use of the assize of Novel Disseisin, throw light on various aspects of the social and economic life of the City of London in the early fourteenth century.[1] They also illustrate the relation of the custom and courts of the City to the common law and the common-law courts of the kingdom. In the chronicles[2] the unpopularity of the eyre of 1321 is especially associated with the pleas of Quo Warranto, which seemed the threaten the ancient liberties of the City and kept the mayor and other city officials on tenterhooks. But the ordinary citizen had good reason to dislike it for personal reasons. Whilst the City's jusridiction in criminal matters was strictly limited—it was only in 1327 that it was granted by charter the right to hang thieves[3]—on the civil side the justices in eyre had actually less to offer London litigants than they could normally have in their own courts. In the Hustings of Common Pleas they could bring cases under writ of right and in the Sheriffs' Court the assize of Fresh Force served precisely the same purpose as the assize of Novel Disseisin, and had the advantage of setting a time limit of forty weeks instead of eighty years. The suspension of all the City courts during the session of the eyre, from January to July 1321, must have been a considerable annoyance to the ordinary citizen, compelled to go to the Tower in place of the Guildhall to pursue his pleas of trespass, debt, detinue, covenant and disseisin. But the justices, as we have seen, respected and maintained both the custom of London in private law and the established liberties of the City so long as they conflicted neither with Common nor Statute law.

[1] Two cases give evidence of recent building on vacant sites. Cf. Olivier-Martin, *op. cit.*, I. 458.

[2] *Chronicles of Edward I and Edward II* (Rolls Series), II. 63.

[3] Thieves were sent to the King's prison of Newgate, and tried before the Justices of Gaol Delivery, until on 6 March 1327 the Charter of Edward III appointed every mayor for the time being a Justice of Gaol Delivery, and specifically granted Infangthief and Outfangthief. A. H. Thomas, *Cal. of Early Mayor's Court Rolls* (1924), p. xii.

VII

From Witness of the Shire to Full Parliament[1]

TWENTY-EIGHT YEARS ago Professor Pollard, in a short note in the *English Historical Review*,[2] gave a seemingly definitive explanation of the meaning of the phrase *in pleno parlamento*. His explanation has not, however, satisfied some later writers; there are still a number of different interpretations of the phrase current, and it seemed worth while to attempt a fuller statement. In seeking to establish a sound definition, however, a fresh problem was encountered, which remains unsolved after application to a wide circle of authorities, historical, legal and linguistic,[3] and the following essay, which is in broad outline an elaboration of Professor Pollard's thesis, is therefore neither original nor complete.

The various interpretations of the phrase should first be noted. Stubbs, though quoting from contemporary sources the expressions *magnum* and *generale parlamentum* to distinguish the more generally attended political assemblies of Edward I's reign from the business sessions or "singular" parliaments of the king's court,[4] described the assembly of October 1297 as "a full and perfect parliament like that of 1295", and spoke of laws enacted in

---

[1] Read to the Royal Historical Society, January 1943. Reprinted, by their permission, from the *Transactions of the Royal Historical Society*, 4th Ser. Vol. XXVI.

[2] *E.H.R.*, 1915, pp. 660-2. The occasion for the note was J. H. Round's article in the same volume on the St. John peerage case of 1914, in which the expression *plenum parliamentum* had been variously interpreted as "a full meeting of the assembly, whatever be its constitution" (Parmoor), "a legislative representative assembly with full powers" (Atkinson, Finlay and Cozens Hardy), "a great pow wow" or "a formal sitting" (Simon). See *Minutes of evidence taken before the House of Lords committee of privileges in the St. John peerage claim* (1915), pp. 55, 72, 189, 209, 218.

[3] I should like especially to thank Professors Buckland, Deanesly, Holland, Prévité Orton, and Stenton, Miss E. S. Procter, Miss Inez Macdonald and Mr. L. C. Harmer for their kind answers and help.

[4] *Constitutional History*, § 230.

"full parliaments" containing representatives of all the estates.[1] In like manner he identified the "full" county court with the sessions for which a special summons was issued, as distinct from the ordinary monthly sessions attended only by litigants and "jurors", saying it was impossible that an election carried out by a mere fraction of the county could be described as the act of the whole community, or as being held *in pleno comitatu*.[2] In effect he echoed the sentiments of Selden, who asked, "How can it be said in full parliament when the Commons, one of the States, are absent?"[3]

Later writers have gone further than Stubbs. Mr. Wilkinson commits himself to the statement that "the phrase *plenum parliamentum* was used in 1305 and in 1332 to describe an assembly",[4] whilst Miss Clarke says that by 1320 "prelates and magnates alone were no longer deemed to contitute a full parliament"[5] Both these statements disregard Pollard's observation that the expression occurs only, apparently, in the ablative case:[6] medieval official documents do not speak of "*a* full parliament" but only make use of the adverbial expression "*in* full parliament". We are reminded of Maitland's remark that Latin lacks the definite article. It also lacks the indefinite article. If any king's court is *curia regis*, it is equally true to say that we ought no more to insert either an *a* or a *the* in translating *in pleno parlamento*, than to say "proceedings were in a full swing when I arrived", or "the enemy was in the full flight".

The expression *in pleno* is not, of course, confined to parliament. In England we find in the twelfth century *in pleno synodo*,[7] *in pleno comitatu*,[8] *in pleno capitulo*,[9] *in pleno hustengo*,[10] *in plena curia*,[11] in

---

[1] *Ibid.*, §§ 180, 224.   [2] *Ibid.*, §§ 203, 216.

[3] *Of the judicature in Parliament*, p. 158. See also pp. 42, 161.

[4] *Studies in the constitutional history of the thirteenth and fourteenth centuries* (1937), p. 1. For a later and fuller exposition of Professor Wilkinson's views, see his *Constitutional History of Medieval England, 1216–1399*, Vol. III (1958), pp. 279–80.

[5] *Medieval representation and consent*, p. 170.

[6] loc. cit., p. 660. Exceptions to this generalization will be noted later.

[7] C. R. Cheney, *English Synodalia*, p. 126 (*c.* 1100).

[8] *Chron. monasterii de Abingdon* (R.S.), ii. 226 (1158?).

[9] Brit. Mus., Add. Charters, 1045 (1180).

[10] Deeds of dean and chapter of Windsor, xi.G.II, No. 14 (1174–88).

[11] Madox, *Formulare Anglicanum*, No. 660 (after 1180).

pleno wapentagio;[1] in the thirteenth century *in pleno folkesmot,*[2] *in pleno hundredo,*[3] *in pleno scaccario,*[4] *in pleno consilio;*[5] in the fourteenth century *in playn consistorie;*[6] in the fifteenth century *at the pleyn shire,*[7] *in playn sessions,*[8] *in his plain parliament.*[9] Abroad we find *in pleno mallo* in Lorraine in 957;[10] *in plena curia* in Castile in 1188[11] and in France in 1269;[12] in Jersey *in plena parochia* in 1284;[13] in Scotland *in pleno colloquio* in 1255,[14] *in pleno parliamento* in 1293,[15] *in plane parliament* in 1375.[16] And, *pace* Mr. Wilkinson who regards it as "an elementary blunder" to translate *en playn parlement* by *in pleno parliamento,*[17] we also find the contemporary parallel expression *en plein cour,*[18] *en plein conseil,*[19] *en plain chapitre,*[20] *en plein countee.*[21] The earliest appearance of the expression *en plein parlement* that I have noted occurs at Paris in 1273;[22] the earliest appearance of *in pleno parlemento,* also in Paris, in 1274.[23] The earliest instances in England are found in the records of the much discussed parliament of 1290.

I propose first to examine the occurrence of the expression *in pleno parlamento* in the official records, then to seek its origin, and lastly to estimate its significance in its historical contexts.

As it has been possible to search practically no other source

[1] *Chronicon de Melsa* ((R.S.), I. 309 (1197–1210).

[2] Liebermann, *Gesetze der Angelsachsen,* i. 656 (*c.* 1212).

[3] *Bracton's Notebook,* case 754 (1233).   [4] Madox, *op. cit.,* No. 689 (1274).

[5] *Rot. Parl.* i. 84 (1292).   [6] Higden (R.S.), VI. 337 (1387).

[7] J. Wedgwood, *History of Parliament, Register of Members, 1439–1509,* p. ciii (1451).

[8] Pollard, *Reign of Henry VII,* ii. 56 (1487). For parallel usages, such as *in plain battle,* see *New English dictionary,* vii. 936, 938.

[9] *Rot. Parl.* v. 356.

[10] Thévenin, *Textes relatifs aux institutions . . . carolingiennes,* No. 132.

[11] Rodrigo of Toledo, *Historia de Rebus Hispaniae, lib.* vii. 2, 24, ed. Lorenzana, *Opera Patrum Toletanorum,* iii. 166 (1188). A late thirteenth-century rendering is "ante todos, la corte llana". Another instance in 1202 is translated *en cumplida corte,* but this is a later rendering. *Cortes de los antiquos reimas de Leon y de Castilla,* i. 43, 45. I owe this reference to Miss Procter's kindness.

[12] Langlois, *Textes relatifs a l'histoire du parlement,* p. 78.

[13] *Cartulaire des îles normandes* (Société Jersiaise), p. 141.

[14] *Acts of Parliament of Scotland,* i. 426.   [15] *Ibid.,* i. 444.

[16] Barbour, *Bruce,* xix. 49.   [17] Wilkinson, *op. cit.,* p. 2, n. 3.

[18] Langlois, *op. cit.,* p. 186.   [19] *Rot. Parl.* II. 254 (1354).

[20] Cited Littré *Dictionnaire,* I. 558, from Garnier de Pont Sainte Maxence (twelfth century) For copious illustration of the general statement that *en plein = au milieu de,* see *ibid.,* III. 1161.

[21] *Stat. R.* i. 180 (1320).   [22] Langlois, *op. cit.,* p. 86.

[23] Boutaric, *Actes des Parlements,* i. 179; Beugnot, *Les olim,* ii. 54.

than printed parliament rolls, the results can only be tentative, and too much importance must not be attached to variations in the use of the term that may simply reflect the idiosyncrasies of particular clerks.[1] With these reservations, it can be stated that the expression occurs most frequently in the fourteenth century, that it is used very sparingly during the minorities of Edward III, Richard II and Henry VI; that it is not found at all under Henry V; and that from 1450 to 1502 it is used fairly consistently, though not invariably, in connexion with the formal proceedings at the beginning and end of parliamentary sessions.

The business described as being done *in pleno parliamento* falls under five main headings—judicial, legislative, financial, political and formal.

Under Edward I the judicial business preponderates. Pleas are held, judgements pronounced, attorneys appointed and accords registered in full parliament. Both the private concerns of subjects, such as a claim for dower, and public concerns such as the treason of Nicholas of Segrave or the "usurpation of royal dignity" by the archbishop may be the occasion of judgements *in pleno parliamento*,[2] and the consultations leading to such judgements may be between the king and his council,[3] the king, the justices and other lieges,[4] or between the king and all the magnates,[5] or before king, earls, barons, justices and all his council.[6] In a number of instances, however, the presence of the king alone is mentioned, as when the peace between the men of Yarmouth and those of the Cinque Ports is recited and recorded in full parliament at Westminster in the presence of the lord king on the eve of the Ascension 1290.[7]

Besides giving judgement, Edward I ordains, establishes or provides new laws in full parliament, one such piece of legislation in 1292 arising from discussion in full parliament between justices and others of his council on a point of law in a parliamentary

---

[1] It should perhaps be made clear at this point that I do not hold that the non-use of the phrase is evidence that the conditions described by it were non-existent. The use of the phrase implies an emphasis on the solemnity of the occasion and the validity of the deed; the validity and solemnity do not depend on the use of the formula.

[2] *Rot. Parl.* i. 19, 146, 186, 172. [3] *Ibid.*, 104. [4] *Ibid.*, 19, 181.
[5] *Ibid.*, 104, 214. [6] *Ibid.*, 172. [7] *Ibid.*, 32.

plea,[1] while another, as Maitland pointed out, is enacted at the petition of the earls, barons and community of the realm in the parliament of 1305.[2] Money grants are made in full parliament in 1290 and 1302.[3] It is in full parliament that orders are given to the justices of the Bench in 1292, that the bishop of London is sworn of the king's council in 1307, and that the king commands the chancellor, in 1305, not to issue any more letters of protection in Ireland.[4]

Only scanty records survive of the thirty parliaments of Edward II, and according to these the business done in full parliament between 1307 and 1327 was mainly on the borderline between jurisdiction and legislation, with a strong political flavour. In 1318 prelates, earls and barons and the whole community ordained in full parliament that all gifts to Gaveston and his wife should be revoked.[5] A petition put forward in full parliament next year by his widow and her second husband for the restitution of the county of Cornwall was rejected after discussion among the magnates and community.[6] In 1322 the judgement on Hugh le Despenser given in the previous year was revoked by the king "in full parliament, by his royal power and by the assent of the prelates, earls and barons, knights of the shire and the community of the realm".[7] Petitions from the earl of Atholl about his confiscated lands, and from Abingdon abbey about the allocation of its revenues between abbot and convent, were read and dealt with in full parliament in 1315 and 1320.[8] Letters patent were granted in full parliament to the earl of Warwick providing that his executors might hold his lands during the minority of his heir.[9]

The ordinances of 1310, though providing that various political and administrative matters must be done "by counsel and assent of the baronage, and that in parliament", only once make use of the formula, when they provide that Henry of Beaumont is not to be allowed access to the king henceforth unless by the common consent of bishops, earls and barons, "et ceo en plein parlement".[10]

---

[1] Ibid., 79.   [2] Ibid., 178.   [3] Ibid., 25, 266.
[4] Ibid., 79, 219, 177.
[5] H. Cole, Documents illustrative of English history, pp. 2-3.   [6] Ibid., 49.
[7] Stat. R. i. 188.   [8] Rot. Parl. i. 294, 365. And see below, p. 135, n. 3.
[9] Stat. R. i. 183.   [10] Ibid., 163.

An interesting unofficial use of the phrase occurs, however, in Lancaster's letter of 1317, cited by Miss Clarke, in which he protests against business being done at a council which ought to be treated "en plein parlement et en presence des peeres de la terre". This, he declares, is contrary to the oath sworn by himself and others to observe the ordinances.[1] Further, the *Vita Edwardi Secundi* relates that in 1320, when summoned to a council at York, Lancaster refused, as often before, to come. "Non enim decebat habere parlamentum in cameris, ut dixit."[2]

In the long reign of Edward III the rolls of parliament continue to record all manner of judicial, legislative and financial business as done in full parliament. Judgements are given, trials for treason held, pardons granted and personal petitions handled there. In 1330 the archbishop of York, arraigned before the council for aiding and abetting the earl of Kent, is acquitted *par plein parlement*.[3] Trials take place in full parliament, both in 1330 and 1332, after the commons have gone home.[4] In 1341 the archbishop makes his famous demand that since he is defamed notoriously throughout the realm he may be arraigned in full parliament before the peers.[5] Common petitions are put forward and answered,[6] statutes enacted[7] and grants of money made in full parliament,[8] and that the importance of the qualification is recognized by all appears from the demands that grants of the tax on wool shall only be so made,[9] and that statutes so enacted shall be enforced.[10] But over and above this recurrence of the phrase in familiar connexions, a new use of it, to which Professor Plucknett has been the latest to call attention,[11] seems to be emerging. It is applied especially to the formal proceedings with which parliaments open, and it emphasizes a distinction between the formal or plenary session and the less formal and less public proceedings of smaller groups.

In the parliament of York in 1318 it had been agreed in full

---

[1] Murimuth (R.S.), p. 273. The Latin summary of the letter in Bridlington merely says *in parliamento*, omitting the *pleno*. *Chron. of Edward I and Edward II* (R.S.), ii. 50.

[2] *Vita Edwardi II*, ed. N. Denholm Young, p. 104.

[3] *Rot. Parl.* ii. 31.   [4] *Foedera* ii; i, 643; *Rot. Parl.* ii. 65.

[1] *Rot. Parl.* ii., 127.   [6] 1332, 1339, 1352.   [7] 1330, 1331, 1373.

[8] 1339, 1352.   [9] 1340, 1351.   [10] 1372, 1373.

[11] Willard and Morris, *The English government at work, 1327–1336*, I. 108.

parliament by king, prelates, earls and barons, and commanded by the king, that the said prelates, earls and barons should go together to discuss and consult on the other business and report their opinion.[1] In the same parliament Walter Langton's petition, delivered in full parliament, is then taken *ad ipsum regem*, and discussed by him and certain magnates of the council.[2] In the parliaments of 1331, of March and December 1332, of 1333 and of 1334, the opening statement as the the causes of summons is made, *en plein parlement*, and counsel is asked of those assembled.[3] In 1332, three days after the request has been made, answer is given *en plein parlement*, first by the prelates, then by the earls and barons and last by the knights and commons.[4] In 1341 a subcommittee of twelve lords reports in full parliament on the question of trial of peers;[5] and when the answers to the petition of lords, clergy and commons, reported in full parliament before the king, the magnates, and the commons are considered unsatisfactory, another committee of twelve is appointed.[6] In 1352 the commons deliver to the king in full parliament a roll containing the grant of aid agreed upon, as well as petitions touching the community of the land.[7] Preliminary work has, in each case, been done by a smaller body in a less formal way, and is reported and recorded publicly and formally.

Matters of national policy are also discussed and counsel given, on foreign policy especially, *in pleno parliamento*. The shortage of currency,[8] the project of a voyage to the Holy Land by the king,[9] a journey to France to treat in person with the king of France,[10] the seeking of friends and allies by the king for the recovery of his rights,[11] his resumption of the title of king of France[12] are all matters on which counsel is said to have been given in full parliament, sometimes by the magnates only,[13] sometimes also, expressly, "by the community of the land",[14] or "by the knights of shires and commons of cities",[15] or "by knights, citizens and burgesses".[16] The

---

[1] Cole, *op. cit.*, p. 3.
[2] *Ibid.*, 4 f., 17 f.
[3] *Rot. Parl.* ii. 61, 64, 67, 69, 150.
[4] *Ibid.*, 67.
[5] *Ibid.*, 127 (6).
[6] *Ibid.*, 129 (17).
[7] *Ibid.*, 237.
[8] *Ibid.*, 62 (14) (1331).
[9] *Ibid.*, 65 (9) (1332).
[10] *Ibid.*, 65 (10) (1332).
[11] *Ibid.*, 127 (5) (1341).
[12] *Ibid.*, 300 (8) (1369).
[13] *Ibid.*, 64 (4), 65 (10).
[14] *Ibid.*, 127 (5) (1341).
[15] *Ibid.*, 67, 69 (6) (1332, 1333).
[16] *Ibid.*, 147-8, 150 (14) (1344).

peace of Bretigny, we are told, was confirmed and sworn to "in full parliament by the king, the prelates, the magnates and the communities of the realm".[1] On the other hand, the expression does not occur at all in the long narrative of the proceedings of the Good Parliament.

Under Richard II the usage is similar, save that up to 1384, as in the opening years of his grandfather's reign, the phrase is almost entirely confined to records of judicial proceedings. In a treason trial of 1377 it recurs constantly. The accused are led before the lords in full parliament, sitting in the white chamber; a witness gives evidence against them in full parliament, their written defence is read in full parliament and sentence is given by the lords sitting in full parliament.[2] It is expressly stated that the king is not present at the proceedings; execution of the sentence is respited until he has been informed. In the same session, however, the king "in his own person, with his own mouth by common assent and advice of the prelates, dukes, earls, barons and magnates, in full parliament" grants the petition of the commons for the pardon of the Bishop of Winchester.[3] In the accounts of the impeachments of 1383 and 1386, the appeals of 1388 and 1397, and the other political trials, the phrase occurs constantly, though at times where it might be expected a more general expression is used, such as "the commons came before the king, prelates and lords in the White Chamber, accusing de la Pole by word of mouth as follows".[4] One incident in 1388 is noteworthy. In the marvellous parliament of that year the clergy, according to Favent, made protestation in full parliament that they would take no part in capital trials. Word was then sent to the *plebeia communitas* sitting in the chapter house, who came and had the protest read to them.[5]

Twice the phrase is used, as in 1369, when a military undertaking is sanctioned; in 1383 Despenser's crusade and in 1385 John of Gaunt's Castilian expedition are approved in full parliament,

---

[1] *Rotuli parliamentorum . . . inediti* (C.S. 3rd Ser., No. 59), p. 276.
[2] *Rot. Parl.* iii. 10-12. [3] *Ibid.*, 24 (99). [4] Ibid., 105.
[5] *Historia mirabilis parliamenti*, p. 15. Camden Miscellany, xiv, cf. *Rot. Parl.* iii. 236. A similar protest in 1397 is described on the parliament roll as being made *overtement en Parlement, Rot. Parl.* iii. 341.

the presence of the commons being specifically mentioned, no doubt because both ventures were being financed by a grant.[1]

The suspicion that the occurrence of the phrase depends to some extent on the idiosyncrasy of clerks is strengthened by the inconsistency with which it is used in recording the formal proceedings at the beginning of parliaments. From 1377 to 1385 it does not occur in this connexion, but in the parliament roll for that year, though there is no innovation in procedure, the phrase recurs constantly. It is *in pleno parliamento* that the king presides, that the opening speech is made, that the wool subsidy is granted, that the receivers of the tenth and fifteenth are appointed, and that the stately ceremonial accompanying the creation of two royal dukes, a viscount and an earl takes place.[2] Nor is the formula used consistently after this date even for the formalities. In 1390 it occurs in the closing proceedings when lords and commons thank the king in full parliament for his good governance;[3] in 1394 for the first time the commons are said to present their speaker in full parliament.[4] Two interesting incidents thus qualified occur in the parliament of 1393. One of the members for Devon comes to the king on the third day of the session asking to be released from his position as knight of the shire until such time as he is cleared of shameful charges brought against him. As his request seems fair to the king and the lords he is discharged *en plein parlement*, and five days later at the prayer of the commons he is reinstated by the king, and later restored to his good fame in full parliament.[5] And it is in full parliament that Richard is authorized, with the assent of the commons, to modify the Statute of Provisors as may seem best to him, reporting fully to the commons in the next parliament.[6]

[1] *Rot. Parl.* iii. 148, 204.

[2] *Ibid.*, 203-10. In 1389 and 1397 other creations take place in full parliament (*ibid.*, 263, 264, 355), but the phrase is not invariably used in this connexion. It is not, for instance, used in the instance of John Cornwall, created baron of Fanhope in 1422 "in the presence of the three estates of the same parliament" (*Rot. Parl.* iv. 401) and created baron of Milbroke "in parliament" in 1442 (*Rot. Parl.* v. 40), though G.E.C. describes him as having been made a peer "in open parliament". *Complete Peerage*, v. 254. See also *Calendar of Close Rolls*, 1432, p. 247.

[3] *Rot. Parl.* iii. 283 (38).   [4] *Ibid.*, 310 (6).   [5] *Ibid.*, 300 (6).

[6] *Ibid.*, 301 (8). In 1391 the commons in full parliament had asserted that the king might suspend the statute by the advice of the lords. *Ibid.*, 285.

With the accession of Henry IV the formula suddenly becomes rare in the parliament rolls. Between 1399 and 1436 it seems to occur five times only; in connexion with money grants in 1399 and 1404,[1] in the record and process of the Percy trials of 1403 and 1406,[2] and in 1425, when the earl of Norfolk, having vindicated his right to that style, does homage to the king in full parliament and takes his seat.[3] When we read of proceedings taking place "in the presence of the king, the lords spiritual and temporal and the commons assembled in parliament"[4] or "in the presence of the three estates of the realm in this present parliament",[5] it is difficult to believe that any significant change of procedure has taken place; it is the formula that seems to be dying a natural death. But off the parliament roll a record of 1431 informs us that on 24 January 1431 it was agreed and granted in full parliament that the dean of Salisbury should have royal license to accept the papal provision to the see of Chichester, in the presence of the duke of Gloucester and eight other lords of the council whose signatures follow.[6] Is the temporary absence of the formula from the parliament rolls, now as in 1377-84, in any way to be associated with the royal minority? In 1436 we read once more of the commons making a grant in full parliament,[7] and from 1439 to 1454 the formula is in frequent use both in reporting grants and in describing the formal proceedings at the beginning and end of sessions, which now include not only the chancellor's opening speech and the presentation of the speaker, but also the prorogation of parliament, generally by the chancellor, and, after the king becomes insane, by letters patent read by the chancellor in full parliament.[8]

Under Edward IV the formula is used fairly consistently when parliament is prorogued, especially when the king's letters patent are read in his absence.[9] It is used four times of the presentation of

---

[1] *Ibid.,* iii. 415, 545. [2] *Ibid.,* iii. 526, 604. [3] *Ibid.,* iv. 275.
[4] *Ibid.,* iv. 94 (1416). [5] *Ibid.,* iv. 419 (1433).
[6] Nicolas, *Acts of the privy council,* iv. 76.
[7] *Rot. Parl.* iv. 502. [8] *Ibid.,* v. 141-2, 143, 172, 228, 238.
[9] Of the five successive prorogations of the parliament of 3 Edward IV, that on 4 November 1463 is read in full parliament by the archbishop in the presence of the lords and commons (*ibid.* v. 498 f.), that on 5 May 1464 is by royal letters read in the great hall of the archbishop's palace at York before lords and commons in full parliament (*ibid.* v.

the speaker,[1] thrice of a loyal address to the Crown by the commons,[2] six times of a money grant[3] and once only for the reading of the answers to the common petitions.[4] The exhibition of a bill of attaint by the commons in full parliament[5] seems to be the last echo of its judicial use.

In Richard III's one parliament and under Henry VII it is used for the presentation of a speaker and for a money grant, though not invariably. Finally it occurs once more on a great political occasion. On 10 December 1485 the commons, appearing by their speaker in full parliament, beg Henry to marry Elizabeth of York, and the lords, rising from their seats and standing before the king seated upon his throne, bow their heads and make the same request in a humble voice; to which request the king assents.[6]

It would seem then that whilst the formula is used in the fourteenth century to qualify the record of a wide variety of transactions, judicial, legislative, financial and political, it is by the end of the fifteenth century restricted to those formal occasions, at the opening or closing of sessions, when king, lords and commons are all present. The expression "in full parliament" by this time does appear, as Selden held, to imply the presence of all the estates of the realm.

If this is clear in 1485, it is equally clear that when the phrase first appears in the thirteenth century it has no such connotation. Under Edward I, of twenty-one occurrences on the parliament roll, only three make any reference to the community of the realm, and that expression cannot at this date be taken to indicate a representative element. In only six cases is the presence of magnates mentioned. Two-thirds of the transactions recorded as done *in pleno parliamento* are of a legal or judicial character, and the frequent references to the council and to the royal justices suggest that the phrase when it first comes into use is more appropriate

---

499 f.). The formula is not used for the prorogations of 17 June 1463 or 26 November 1464 (*ibid.* v. 500), and on 20 February 1464 the bishop of Lincoln reads the king's letters in the presence of the lords and commons in the great hall at York "palam et coram omnibus" (*ibid.* v. 499).

[1] *Ibid.* v. 497; vi. 4, 168, 197.　　　　[2] *Ibid.* v. 462, 618; vi. 197.
[3] *Ibid.* vi. 39, 111, 149, 153, 197 (*bis*).　[4] *Ibid.* vi. 153.
[5] *Ibid.* v. 487.　　　　　　　　　　　　[6] *Ibid.* vi. 278.

to the official than to the feudal or political aspect of parliaments. But whether the session be feudal or official it is primarily that of a law court; the phrase is equivalent to *in plena curia*, and a comparison with the parallel usage in France is strictly relevant. There, in 1269, we find a litigant claiming payment of a debt *in hoc parlamento coram consilio regis*,[1] and urging his demand *in plena curia*, whilst in 1273 we have the first instance of the phrase *en plein parlement* when the men of Senlis relate that they have appealed to the *mestres* in full parliament and have obtained a judgement in their favour.[2]

Eight examples of the phrase have been noted in the *Actes des parlements* between 1274 and 1294. Six of these record pleas between subjects—assignments of dower, amends for insulting words, settlement of a claim, giving of security, and recognition of tenure.[3] The other instances are the request of the archbishop of Rouen in full parliament for permission to have an attorney during the king's good pleasure,[4] and the delivery by the butler of France in full parliament of certain letters and seals.[5] Similar occurrences are recorded without the use of the phrase, but whenever it occurs, emphasis seems to be laid on the publicity of the act. To quote Brissaud, "The publicity of the sessions of the royal court was sought for a whole quantity of extra-judicial proceedings."[6]

When we turn to parallel formulas in English courts other than the high court of parliament it is again in connexion with extra-judicial proceedings and private transactions that the expression *in pleno* first occurs. The life-interest to an estate is released *in pleno capitulo* before the archdeacon of Buckingham in 1180.[7] One tenant quitclaims land to another *in plena curia* of William Cumin at approximately the same date.[8] Between 1197 and 1210 land is surrendered *in pleno wapentagio* in Holderness.[9] A gift of land is made, by charter and by seisin, *in pleno hundredo* in Norfolk in 1233,[10] and a Winchester burgess grants land by charter to Reading

[1] Langlois, *op. cit.*, p. 78.   [2] Langlois, *op. cit.*, p. 86.
[3] *Actes du parlement de Paris*, ed. E. Boutaric, i. 179, 201, 205, 206, 277, 283.
[4] *Les olim*, ed. A. A. Beugnot, ii. 191   [5] *Actes*, i. 224.
[6] J. Brissaud, *Hist. de droit français*, i. 882.   [7] Madox, *Formulare*, No. 687.
[8] *Ibid.*, No. 660.   [9] *Chronicon de Melsa* (R.S.), i. 309.
[10] *Bracton's Notebook*, case 754.

abbey *in plena curia* of Burghildebury and Taceham—that is, in Bucklebury hundred.[1] In 1284 an arbitral award in a dispute between the monks of Mont St. Michel and Philip le Breton is published *in plena parochia* of St. Broelard in Jersey, so that all may hear.[2] This phrase, to which Mr. le Patourel has called attention,[3] occurs only once in the *Cartulaire des îles normandes*, the normal formula, recurring from 1286 to 1500, being *en l'audience de paroisse*, or *en ouie de paroisse*.[4]

In London the court of husting was in some respects the equivalent of the county court elsewhere, and its publicity was sought or required for a variety of transactions. A tenement is leased (1188) and a grant of land is made (1202) *in pleno hustengo*.[5] Rights to churches are quitclaimed there (1182) and the last penny for a sale received (1193-4).[6] An agreement between the citizens of London and three French towns is *done en plein husting de Loundres* in 1237.[7] The articles of the cappers are read and granted *in curia tenta de placitis terrae in pleno hustengo* in 1270.[8] The attorneys of the earl of Cornwall claim two fugitive bondmen in full husting 1288.[9] A leading citizen has it publicly proclaimed in full husting that he has lost his seal, and will no longer be bound by it (1301).[10] The king commands the *custos* and sheriffs of the city to proclaim in their full husting that no clipped coin is to be imported (1291).[11] According to a custumal of about 1327, outlawries were promulgated *en pleyn husting*.[12] In 1321 the Justices in Eyre, inquiring into outlawries since 1276, were told of an outlawry pronounced in the folkmoot in 1277,[13] but it would seem that the folkmoot was a mere memory by 1321, and the recent coroners' rolls recording outlawries pronounced in the husting of pleas of land do not use the formula *in pleno hustengo*.[14] But as late as 1368 wills are still being proved in full husting.[15]

[1] Brit. Mus. M.S. Harl. 1708, fo. 70b. I owe this reference to Sir Frank Stenton.
[2] *Cartulaire des îles normandes* (Société Jersiaise), p. 140.
[3] *Medieval administration of the Channel Islands*, p. 100.
[4] *Cartulaire*, pp. 444, 450, 453, 455, 457.
[5] Deeds of dean and chapter of Windsor, xi. G.11, No. 14, *Early Charters of St. Paul's* (C.S., 1939). p. 56.　　　　[6] *Early Charters of St. Paul's*, pp. 139, 83.
[7] *Liber Custumarum* (R.S.), p. 66.　　[8] *Ibid.*, 101.　　[9] Letterbook A fo. 80.
[10] Letterbook C fo. 56.　　　　[11] *Liber Custumarum*, p. 188.
[12] *Liber Albus* (R.S.), p. 190.　　　[13] *Liber Custumarum*, p. 334.
[14] *Ibid.*, 337.　　　　[15] Madox, *Formulare*, No. 336.

All these examples, which could be multiplied, go to show that at first the formula *in pleno* is most often used when publicity is sought to assure the permanence of private transactions. The collocation *in pleno comitatu* is, however, the oldest, the most frequent and the most important for our purpose, and though its use has been well illustrated already by W. A. Morris in his *Early English county court*,[1] I propose to examine it more closely.

The earliest occurrence that I have noted is about 1158, in the Chronicle of Abingdon abbey, where it is related that a royal writ concerning the jurisdiction of the abbey is read out by the sheriff *in pleno comitatu* of Berkshire.[2] Round about 1180 the Burton Cartulary records a litigant's surrender of a claim by handing to the sheriff the writ by which he had impleaded St. Mary's church, that it might be destroyed *in pleno comitatu* of Nottinghamshire.[3] The register of Malmesbury abbey preserves the record of a final concord made in 1189, *in pleno comitatu* of Wiltshire, before the sheriff, seven knights who are named, and other unnamed knights who were present.[4] Madox's *Formulare* gives a deed recording demise of land and payment therefor before the county court of Leicestershire in 1193, witnessed by the sheriff, thirteen named persons and many others *in pleno comitatu*.[5] These are four twelfth-century examples; there are a number of the same kind in the early thirteenth century dealing with family arrangements as to transfers of land, admeasurement of dower, acknowledgement of suit, letting of land to farm, and so forth. But as the thirteenth century advances, the character of the business so qualified changes. Except for the delivery of litigants' writs to the sheriff in full county, a practice long used before it was made compulsory by statute in 1285,[6] and for the reading out in full county of charters of local franchises granted or confirmed by the king,[7] men are

---

[1] University of California publications in History, 1926. Note especially pp. 163 ff.

[2] *Chron. mon. de Abingdon* (R.S.), ii. 226.

[3] *Burton Cartulary*, William Salt Archaeological Collections, v. i. 48-9.

[4] *Reg. Malmesburiense* (R.S.), i. 459-60.

[5] Madox, *Formulare*, No. 221. For transactions in full county of Cheshire, 1189-1222, see *Cheshire Sheaf*, 1923, pp. 9-12.

[6] Stat. Westm., II. c. 39.

[7] *Close Rolls*, 1227-31, pp. 23, 46, 58; ibid., 1231-4, pp. 369, 403, 411, 427, 432, 477, 478, 499; ibid., 1234-7, pp. 34, 51, 62, 132, 140, 203 (and ten more examples).

more and more coming to prefer the greater publicity and security of the king's court for registering their property rights.[1] An instance of making assurance quadruply sure occurs in 1271, when the deed giving the advowson of Austrey church to Burton abbey is read and acknowledged in full county of Warwickshire, in the hundred of Humbleyard, and in full chapter of Arden, whilst a fine respecting the advowson is also levied in the king's court.[2] The local court whose publicity survives longest for private transactions is, as might be expected, the court of the palatine county of Cheshire, where, as Mr. Stewart-Brown showed, there existed a special roll, the Domesday Roll, for recording such transactions.[3] His calendar of the surviving portion of the roll contains examples of the reading of charters, the acknowledgement of debts, agreements as to dower, final concords, records of emancipation, and so forth, all done in full county of Cheshire between 1208 and 1281, whilst the surviving rolls of the county court give further instances.[4] The last occurrence of the phrase is in 1310, when the *Baga de Domesday* itself is produced in full county of Cheshire and search is made in it for a fine which is found and produced in the presence of knights and other lieges there present.[5]

If the transactions between subjects recorded as done *in pleno comitatu* are dwindling in the thirteenth century, the king's business is on the increase. W. A. Morris' examples,[6] borne out by other instances, fall roughly under five heads: first, business connected with crime, such as exactions and outlawries and proclamation of pardons, appeals of murder, showing of wounds to the coroners, production of pledges, handing over of accused persons, even delivery of a complaint of trespass. Secondly, all manner of inquests are ordered to be held *in pleno comitatu*, relating to litigation in the king's courts and to crimes, and also to matters affecting royal interests, such as inquests *ad quod damnum*, inquests into liability to knighthood, or inquests into debts owing to the

---

[5] Compare C. R. Cheney, *English Synodalia*, p. 33, for a similar development in the diocesan synod.

[2] *Burton Cartulary*, loc. cit., v. i. 178.   [3] *E.H.R.*, 1922, pp. 481-500.

[4] *Cheshire Sheaf*, 1923, pp. 1-58; *Calendar of county court rolls of Chester* (Chetham Society, 1925), pp. 13, 23, 53, 95, 109, 134.

[5] *Cheshire Sheaf*, 1923, p. 66.   [6] *Early English county court*, pp. 131-42.

exchequer. Thirdly, from 1233 on, there are orders for the proclamation of royal administrative orders, as for the keeping of watches or concerning clipped coin, the proclamation of the Great Charter and the Charter of the Forest, and the proclamation of statutes, at least from 1288. Fourthly, there are orders for officials to be sworn in full county—hundred bailiffs, franchise bailiffs, escheators, and sheriffs' serjeants.[1] Lastly, elections are ordered to be held in full county from 1220 onwards, of collectors of taxes, of coroners and of knights of the shire for parliaments.

Broadly speaking, then, it would seem that private transactions cease to be registered in full county early in the fourteenth century, though the publicity of the court is still essential for out-lawries, for the proclamation of statutes and for the elections of coroners and members of parliament long after that date.

How far did the value and validity of this publicity depend on the number and quality of the persons present? Stubbs believed that the expression "in full county" indicated the "special fullness" to which the *Leges Henrici* refer in describing the six-monthly sessions of the hundred court[2] and which the thirteenth-century hundred rolls attest when they refer to the "great" or "general" county courts held twice a year.[3] Morris produces ample and convincing evidence that in the thirteenth century the phrase *in pleno comitatu* indicates rather one aspect of any session than a special session, and refers to the publicity of proceedings, not to the fullness of attendance.[4] He notes the contrast drawn in the Statute of Westminster II, echoed by Fleta, between the delivery of a writ *in pleno comitatu vel in retrocomitatu*, (the rere-county held the following day at which financial, but not, it would seem, judicial business could be transacted).[5] The government's commands that proclamation should be made in full county court four times a year at once disposes of Stubbs's interpretation, as does the command that elections be held in full county, at the

---

[1] Besides Morris' instances, the notification by the Lord Edward in full county court of Cheshire of the appointment of a warden of forests and escheats in 1259 is of interest. *Calendar of county court rolls of Chester*, p. 2.

[2] *Constitutional History*, §§ 128, 203; *Select Charters* (9th ed.), p. 124.

[3] Pollock and Maitland, *History of English Law*, I. 526.

[4] *Op. cit.*, p. 100.

[5] Morris, *op. cit.*, p. 151; *E.H.R.*, 1924, pp. 401-3.

next county court after the receipt of the writ.[1] But Morris has his doubts as to the meaning of the phrase in the reign of John: and there are a few instances between 1150 and 1220 when the expression "full" does seem to allude to the number of those present. In 1212, for instance, in the Gloucestershire case famous for its reference to the *buzones*, proceedings are postponed to another session of the county "quoniam comitatus non fuit plenarius . . . propter afforciamentum comitatus", and the proceedings at the next court are described as taking place *in pleno comitatu*.[2] Again, in connexion with the outlawry of FitzWalter in the same year, we meet the statement that in Essex a man must be exacted in four *plenarios* or *plenos comitatus* before he can be outlawed.[3] In 1158 the sheriff of Berkshire assembles a *plenum comitatum* at Farnborough,[4] and in 1220 sheriffs are ordered to hold an election *convocato pleno comitatu*.[5]

If publicity is essential to regularize proceedings, it follows that there must be present a sufficient number of persons whose witness is valid at law, and moreover the court must be properly constituted and held. For judicial proceedings it is fully recognized that in a case of special difficulty and importance a court may be adjourned to secure a larger number of judges. But a session may be useless for purposes of record and registration not only if inadequately attended but also if irregularly held, and in the case of the county court I have noted two indications that the time of day might have some bearing on the validity of proceedings. In a case recorded in Bracton's Note Book under the year 1225, Agnes of Histon appears with her champion in the county court of Cambridge, but her opponent claims an essoin. Both parties are ordered to withdraw *quousque comitatus plenius conveniret*; and when the county has assembled Agnes again offers to prove her

[1] Morris, *op. cit.*, p. 98.

[2] *Curia Regis Rolls*, VI. 229-30. For other instances of the use of *plenarius* at this period to mean, apparently, the fully afforced court, see *Monasticon*, I. 44; II. 281; VI. i. 598; Madox, *Formulare*, Nos. 64, 195; MSS. of dean and chapter of Windsor, xi.G.11, No. 32 ; A. C. Lawrie, *Early Scottish Charters*, p. 166.

[3] *Rot. Lit. Cl.* i. 165-6.

[4] "Vicecomes comitatum plenum apud Ferneburgam congregans." *Hist. mon de Abingdon* (R.S.), ii. 228.

[5] *Rot. Lit. Cl.* i. 437. Note also *coram pleno comitatu* in 1221 (*Rolls of Justices in Eyre*, vol. 59, Selden Society, p. 367).

case, and her opponent's attorney again fails to appear. Agnes waits almost to the end of the county and beyond the hour of noon, and then offers herself a third time, and the county finds in her favour, on the grounds of her opponent's default.[1] Here it looks as if certain business had to wait to a certain hour—possibly for the practical reason of the leisurely arrival of the suitors who were judges. The other instance comes from 1444 when the commons, citing the statute that provides that elections be held *en pleyn countee*, petition for the penalizing of every sheriff who does not hold the election "en temps convenable cest assaver en son plein countee parentre le hour de huit et le hour de onze devaunt el noone".[2]

In pleno comitatu, then, would seem to imply, first, publicity "in open court", in the face of all; secondly, the presence of an adequate number of persons to make the publicity effective in fact and law, by securing a sufficiency of judges or witnesses, according as to whether the proceedings were judicial or extra-judicial; and thirdly, the due constitution of the court, the time of day being that required by custom, and the proper procedure having been observed in declaring the court open.

The expression *in pleno comitatu* is unquestionably older than *in pleno parliamento*. It appears simultaneously with the expression *in plena curia*, used of Anglo-Norman feudal courts and of the royal courts of England, France and Spain. A similar usage is found in contemporary records of ecclesiastical courts, in fact the oldest dated occurrence in England that has been pointed out to me is *in pleno synodo, c.* 1100.[3] The appearance of the phrase *in pleno mallo* in the two Lorraine charters of 957 and 958 seems to be completely isolated, though their authenticity is accepted.[4] Neither linguistic nor legal authrotities are prepared to risk a conjecture as to its origin, or to pronounce on the question whether the Latin or

---

[1] *Bracton's Notebook*, case 1672. [2] *Rot. Parl.* v. 116.

[3] *Liber vitae ecclesiae dunelmensis* (Surtees Society), i. 46*v*. I owe this reference to the kindness of Mr. C. R. Cheney.

[4] *Histoire générale de Metz* (Metz 1775), III. *Preuves*, pp. 70-73. The two grants, made by one donor to two different religious houses and preserved in their archives, were recorded by one scribe. The *mallum* was that of the *pagus salinensis*. At the donor's request, the charters were read *in pleno mallo*, confirmed and sealed by the count and fourteen *scabini* whose names are given, and subscribed *actum in pleno mallo*.

French form is the older. Its appearance in England coincides so closely with the beginnings of Angevin rule as to suggest that it is imported from the Continent; if on the other hand the usage is ecclesiastical in origin, it ought perhaps to be associated with the closer ecclesiastical relationships with the Continent of Stephen's reign. The question as to the origin of the phrase does not seem to have been asked before; and as was stated at the outset, no answer has been found. But there is another and a more important question: does the sudden appearance of the formula indicate an innovation either in legal history or in legal practice?

Here there is an abundance of evidence to prove the negative. The early laws and customs of the peoples of Western Europe emphasize the importance of publicity for securing the validity of a number of private transactions, above all, transfers of land, from the ancient Scandinavian laws, where the *skirskotning* is the substitute for the written record,[1] to the Italian documents in which the notary records in writing the names both of the judges and of those "both sitting and standing in the court", in whose presence the transaction took place.[2] As the Visigothic laws put it, such things should not be done *absconse sed ante liberos homines*,[3] and a series of Frankish charters, from the eighth to the tenth century, illustrate the practice of using the local courts for this purpose, employing a variety of formulae such as *in legitimo placito*, *in publico placito*, *in conventu publico*, *in mallo publico*, *hiis presentibus*, *multis adstantibus nobilibus*, *isti sunt testes qui audierunt et viderunt*, *plena plebe conjuncta*,[4] and, as we have seen, twice only, *in pleno mallo*.

Anglo-Saxon custom is thus fully in accord with continental practice. The laws which prescribe the publicity of the folkmoot for the registration of alien merchants or the finding of a lord for a lordless man are stray examples of the practice. That the witness of the community may be available for sales, exchanges, emancipations and transfers of lands, Edgar's laws provide for panels of

[1] L. M. Larson in *Haskins anniversary essays*, p. 135.
[2] J. Ficker, *Forschungen zur Rechtsgeschichte Italiens*, iv. 14, 53, 74.
[3] Cited Brissaud, *Hist. du droit francais*, ii. 1278.
[4] Thévenin, *Textes relatifs aux institutions . . . carolingiennes*, Nos. 62, 69, 80, 81, 85, 90, 110, 134. See also Zeumer, *Formulae* (*Mon. Germ. Hist.*), pp. 189, 214.

trustworthy men in hundreds and boroughs.[1] In the early ninth century we read of transactions *coram omni synodo* or before the king and his witan.[2] And in the tenth century we get specific reference to the witness of the shire—the witness of "all the thegns of Worcestershire, Danish and English", of "all the good men of the moot", of "all those of East Kent and West Kent", of "the king's reeve and the other good men of Berkshire"[3] and in the eleventh century, *aetforan ealra scyra—coram omne scyra.*[4] And so it continues after 1066. The juries of Domesday attest the production of the king's writ in shire and hundred court as evidence of seisin,[5] and a multiplicity of private charters refer to the witness of courts of all kinds. As Madox writes, "sometimes the feoffor would come into one or other of the king's high courts and sometimes into a county court, hundred court, halimote, burghmote or other court and there would perform the act of enfeoffing in presence of many witnesses".[6] Such deeds are witnessed by so and so *cum toto hundredo*[7] or by *totus halimotus eiusdem ville*[8] or by *totus comitatus Notingham et Derbiee*[9] or by *tota curia*[10] or, again, *his testibus et multis aliis videntibus et audientibus,*[11] or *in presentia et audientia comitatus Gloucestrie,*[12] *coram comitatu Oxenford,*[13] *vidente toto comitatu Berkescire,*[14] and, finally, *residente plenarie scira.*[15] Glanvill does not make use of the expression *in pleno comitatu,* but in laying down the proper procedure for the sheriff to follow in appointing summoners, he says that the order should always be given in the county court so that the party may be fully or openly summoned —*plene fiet summonitio.* "Huiusmodi enim publici actus ... publice debent celebrari."[16] Finally, for the central court, this transitional formula is to be found on the close roll of 1248: *in curia nostra, coram nobis et toto Parliamento nostro.*[17]

An unbroken chain of precedents has been found, linking up the

[1] IV Edgar 3-5.
[2] Kemble, *Cod. Dip.,* No. 186, 1034.
[3] Kemble, *op. cit.,* Nos. 923, 693, 998, 1288.
[4] Kemble, *op. cit.,* No. 789.
[5] Dd. i. 36.
[6] Madox, *Formulare,* p. xxiv.
[7] Madox, *Formulare,* Nos. 322, 329.
[8] H. E. Salter, *Oxford Charters,* No. 52.
[9] Jeayes, *Derbyshire Charters,* No. 1397.
[10] *Ibid.,* No. 134.
[11] Madox, *Formulare,* No. 316.
[12] J. H. Round, *Ancient charters,* p. 73.
[13] D. Royce, *Landboc de Winchelcumba,* p. 188.
[14] *Chron. mon. de Abingdon,* ii. 160.
[15] *Ibid.* ii. 119.
[16] Glanvill, *lib.* i. ch. 30. See also Bracton *De legibus, lib.* iv. ch. 15.
[17] *Close Rolls,* 1247-51, p. 107.

usages of the thirteenth century with those of the early English folkmoots. Whatever the origin of the phrase *in pleno comitatu*, the continuity of the practice which it stands for is established. What bearing have these antecedents upon our interpretation of the phrase *in pleno parliamento*?

In the first place they reinforce the indication given by the French parallel usage and by the association of the phrase in the records of Edward I's parliaments. It is to courts of law that the expression *in pleno* is appropriate, and it is by virtue of the judicial functions of the king's highest court that it comes to be linked with the word *parliamentum*. And in the second place, the story of the transition from the witness of the shire to the full county bears out the contention of Professor Pollard, Mr. Richardson, Mr. Sayles, Professor Baldwin and Professor Plucknett that the essential notion behind it is that of openness, of publicity. The connotation is of a court where the most solemn proceedings must be done in the sight of all men—*palam et coram omnibus*, as the rolls of parliament say of a prorogation in 1464,[1] *publiquement* or *overtement* as they say in 1376, 1383, 1388, 1389, 1397.[2] The Irish rolls use the expression *en overte parliament* about 1480.[3] This publicity is requisite for the validity of legal proceedings, as in the shiremoot and in the Parlement de Paris, but it is also desirable for public and political transactions, and this accounts for the extension of its use in the fourteenth-century parliament rolls. If an aid is granted *in pleno parliamento*, the grant is registered legally and cannot be receded from. If an ordinance or provision is proclaimed *in pleno parliamento*, it is put on record; though a wider publicity may be gained by proclamation in full county, by being issued in full parliament it will be registered on the roll of the king's parliament.[4] Similarly the swearing in of a councillor or the issuing of orders to a chancellor will be made more sure and solemn by such publicity, and its sanction will be sought by Lords Ordainers and other critics of

[1] *Rot. Parl.* v. 499.   [2] *Ibid.*, ii. 323; iii. 153, 241, 257, 258, 341.

[3] *Statute rolls of the parliament of Ireland, 12-13 to 21-22 Edward IV*, p. 56. (I owe this reference to the kindness of Mr. Richardson.)

[4] Note the Irish version of the *Modus*: (of obtaining license to depart from parliament) "Et hoc in pleno parliamento ita quod inde fiat mencio in rotulis parliamenti." M. V. Clarke, *Medieval representation and consent*, p. 389.

the administration. Legally speaking the record of the king's court is unshakeable witness; the memory of living witnesses is not requisite here as in the shire court. "None can deny the record of the king's court", but "if anything done in the shire court is denied, reference must be made to the men who were present."[1]

But the king's highest court is also a feudal court, and for political reasons the presence of the magnates as witnesses and judges may be desirable. Thus the publicity of the parliament is invoked for the trials of great men, for judicial decisions affecting the status of tenants in chief, for common petitioning, and for legislation of national importance like the Statute of Carlisle. It was for publicity of this kind that Lancaster was contending when he protested against holding parliaments *in cameris*; it was on publicity of this kind that the writer of the *Modus* was insisting when he said that if the king and council wished to revise the ordinances made by the special procedure for "difficult cases" they should do so *in pleno parliamento et de consensu parliamenti et non retro parliamentum*.[2]

Mr. Richardson sums up this conception as the contrast between business in public and business transacted behind closed doors.[3] Professor Plucknett, writing of the period 1327-36,[4] stresses rather the antithesis between a united session and the sectional meetings of groups or committees which, as we have seen, are traceable from 1318 at least. Some such contrast may have been in the minds of the men of Lowestoft in their plea in 1379 during the long-drawn-out struggle with Yarmouth. They asserted that the charter granted to Yarmouth in 1372 had been revoked (in 1376) "solemnly, by good deliberation of all the lords and commons in full parliament", while the new charter (of 1378) "had not been granted by so great advice and deliberation".[5] But the parliament rolls for 1376 and 1378 hardly bear out the suggested contrast. Perhaps a better instance of such a distinction occurs in 1388 when

---

[1] *Leges Henrici*, 31, 4; 48, 5.

[2] *Modus tenendi parliamentum*, ch. xvii (M. V. Clarke, *op. cit.*, p. 381).

[3] *Rotuli parliamentorum . . . inediti*, p. xi.

[4] Willard and Morris, *English government at work*, 1327-36, i. 108.

[5] Baldwin, *Select cases before the king's council* (S.S.), pp. 63, 69; cf. Introduction, p. xc, and *Rot. Parl.* ii. 330.

all the lords and commons petition the king and council that all the special bills which cannot be endorsed or answered before the departure of parliament be dealt with by certain lords, whose decision shall be as effective as if done *in pleno parliamento*.[1]

The expression is certainly used when a contrast between a group and a plenary session is intended, but I do not believe that, even in the period 1327-36, its use can be so limited. We have seen that it is applied to sessions of only a section of those attending a parliament. This is true not only for 1305, when business is done *in pleno parliamento* in the presence of the council only,[2] but in 1377, when a trial is conducted *en plein parlement* by the lords in the king's absence, and in 1388 when the protest of the clergy is made *in pleno parliamento* in the absence of the commons. It may be that it is so used as late as 1431, when it seems that the decision *in pleno parliamento* that the dean of Salisbury might accept the papal provision to the see of Chichester was taken merely by those lords of the council whose names are appended to the record.[3] However this may be, in the fourteenth century it wou.d almost seem as if the presence neither of king[4] nor of lords nor of commons was indispensable for what Professor Plucknett calls a plenary session of parliament. In 1333, on the first day of the parliament at York, arrangements were made for the delivery and trial of petitions, and the mayor of York was charged in the presence of the king in full parliament to see to the keeping of the peace. But because the prelates and other magnates had not yet fully (*pleinement*) arrived, it was not until the morrow that the speech declaring the cause of summons was delivered, also in full parliament.[5]

Business, then, can be transacted in full parliament with what might be regarded as very inadequate publicity. The absence of important persons does not destroy, nor does their presence

[1] *Rot. Parl.* iii. 256 (19).

[2] *Memoranda de Parliamento de 1305* (R.S.), pp. 4, 293. I accept Maitland's interpretation of the passage (*ibid.*, pp. xxxv-vi) rather than that of Wilkinson (*Studies*, pp. 8-9) or of Cozens Hardy (*Saint John peerage claim*, p. 154) which I cannot regard as warranted by the French text.

[3] Nicolas, *Proccedings of privy council*, iv. 76.

[4] It might be argued that the absence of the king in 1377 was due to Richard's minority, bnt in 1318 Edward II was absent when Langton's petition was read in full parliament. See *E.H.R.*, 1932, p. 201, n. 5.

[5] *Rot. Parl.* ii. 68.

assure, the necessary conditions. A parliament was an occasion on which many groups of people might assemble, and much business, ranging from interdepartmental consultations[1] to informal discussions between individuals, might be transacted. Such activities might take place at a parliament or during a parliament, but not in full parliament, any more than the routine business transacted at the *retrocomitatus* was done in full county. For matters to be done *in pleno* the court must have been properly constituted by the holding of the due formalities. It is for this reason that the translation "in open county" or "in open parliament", used by Stewart Brown, Sayles, Richardson and Baldwin does not altogether satisfy me, although it escapes the ambiguities and false associations of the adjective "full". There is fifteenth-century warrant for the latter rendering; the locution "in full and plenary council" is used officially in 1482,[2] just as "in plain sessions" occurs in 1487[3] and "in open sessions" in 1504.[4] Selden, it may be noted, used both adjectives, discriminating between their sense. "At this day", he says, speaking of parliamentary jurisdiction, "the practice is to swear the witnesses in open house",[5] and though, in commenting on fourteenth-century precedents, he commits himself to the statement that "the words in full parliament signify the lords and commons"[6] he seems to be speaking of contemporary legal doctrine when he says "in cases capital the judges must be present, otherwise it is not a full court".[7] In this last statement he approaches very nearly to the author of the *Modus* when he says "licet aliquis dictorum quinque graduum post regem absens sit, dum tamen omnes premuniti sint per rationabiles summonitiones Parliamenti, nihilominus censetur esse plenum",[8] and both of them are thinking of the legal constitution of the court rather than of its publicity. A parliament, in fact, must be not merely open, it must be, like a charity bazaar, declared open, and its regularity

---

[1] See Jolliffe, "Some factors in the beginnings of parliament", *Trans. R. Hist. Soc.*, 1940, pp. 101-39.

[2] Baldwin, *Select cases before the king's council* (S.S.), pp. 117-18.

[3] Pollard, *Reign of Henry VII*, p. 56.   [4] *Ibid.*, p. 73.

[5] *Of the Judicature in Parliament*, p. 120.   [6] *Ibid.*, p. 42.

[7] *Ibid.*, p. 164. Compare the distinction in ch. 18 of the Irish *Modus* between *in pleno* and *in aperto* (M. V. Clarke, *op. cit.*, pp. 389 f.).

[8] M. V. Clarke, *op. cit.*, p. 384.

will depend not only on its publicity, which turns largely on its composition, but also on its constitution. In the discussions on the St. John peerage claim in 1914, while Raymond Asquith doubted whether the words *plenum parliamentum* were "in any sense a term of art",[1] and Cozens Hardy maintained the now discredited view that *plenum parliamentum* was only used of parliaments which contained representatives of the commons, and Lord Parker of Waddington's notion was that it was "a full meeting" in the sense that it was not a transaction by a committee,[2] the attorney-general, Sir John Simon, came nearest to the truth, as it seems to me, when he said, "If you turn it into suitable modern English *plenum parliamentum* means 'a formal sitting'," which Lord Stanley of Alderley, following him, paraphrased as "a competent assembly".[3]

As in so many other instances in our constitutional history, it is our conservatism, it is the continuity of our institutions which has enriched our language and perplexed our law and politics with so many ambiguities. In the process of changing from high court to sovereign body the forms of words have been preserved by the fiction that no change is taking place, yet between Fleta and Selden the significance of the phrase *in pleno parliamento* has inevitably been modified by changing ideas as to what constitutes due forms of sitting, and what assemblies are competent. Proceedings at a duly constituted session of the council are done *in pleno parliamento* in 1305 and it may be still in 1333; by 1377 it seems probable that the presence of the magnates has come to be regarded as a *sine qua non* for the constitution of a competent assembly, though if the ordinance of 24 January 1431 were indeed drafted, and not merely promulgated, *in pleno parliamento*, a session of the council only might still be so described.[4] By 1485, however, it seems as if the formula was reserved for joint meetings of the lords and commons, and we have arrived at Selden's position: "How can it

---

[1] *Minues of evidence in the St. John peerage claim*, p. 197.
[2] *Ibid.*, p. 183.   [3] *Ibid.*, p. 72.
[4] Nicolas, *Acts of the privy council*, iv. 76. The discussion by A. R. Myers and W. H. Dunham of the record of 1449 preserved in MS. Harl. 6849, fo. 77(*John Rylands Bulletin*, October 1938; *Speculum*, July 1942) illustrates the obscurity, at present, of the relations of the council and parliament at this date.

be said in full parliament when the Commons, one of the States, are absent?"

In the history, then, of this phrase we have a picture in little of the evolution of English national institutions. To begin with, the witness of the shire is the guarantee of men's private rights and public status; and as the king takes it upon himself to safeguard those rights, so the publicity of the shire comes to be used more and more for the enforcement of the king's peace and the promulgation of his letters and decrees, while conversely the king's court becomes the surest guarantor of private rights and its role supersedes the oral testimony of the shire as legal record.[1] But the established association between publicity and permanence, and the deeply rooted habit of judgement by the suitors of the court, combining with the political traditions of feudalism, react in their turn upon the practices of the king's highest court. The kings who seek to bind their subjects by having grants of money recorded in full parliament before their justices and councillors are succeeded by the kings whose subjects demand a fuller publicity and a more active co-operation, and as first the peers and then the commons establish their position as members of the political public and therefore effective members of parliament, the meaning of the phrase expands, until *in pleno parliamento* does in truth mean "in public and formal session of an assembly of the three estates of the realm".

---

[1] Note, for instance, the development of the fine.

VIII

The Legislators of Medieval England[1]

THERE HAS been so much discussion, and that so learned, of the nature of law in the Middle Ages, that it will be well for me to begin with a disclaimer. What I am concerned with is not so much law as laws, not so much theory as practice, not so much forms as forces. The great American school of legal historians may be right in saying that none save God could *make* law in the Middle Ages, but the student of medieval English government is confronted with assizes, establishments, provisions, ordinances, proclamations, and statutes that men observed or infringed and that judges enforced. They existed, and they mattered; they are both a monument to human activity and an indication of human intentions and opinions. In asking how and why they came to be there I am seeking the originating impulse for legislation rather than investigating its technical validity or the authority and status of the legislator.

In Dr. Ivor Jennings's book on parliament in the twentieth century[2] there is a chapter headed "Who makes the laws?" For one who seeks the substance rather than the form, he says, the answer to this question "The King in Parliament" will not do. Even if you admit that the responsibility for all legislation today rests with the government, you have still to find the government's source of inspiration. He appends to his discussion an analysis of the legislation of one year. Seventy acts were placed on the Statute Book in 1936-7, and he traces each of them to its originating agency—King Edward VIII, the Dominions, the Cabinet, the various Government Departments, Government Commissions, the Bench, Local Authorities, "public demand" in the Press, and

---

[1] The Raleigh lecture on history, read to the British Academy 13 June 1945. Reprinted from the *Proceedings of the British Academy*, vol. xxxi.
[2] Cambridge, 1939.

what he calls associated interests, such as the Society for the Prevention of Cruelty to Animals, the National Union of Teachers, the Central Council for Rivers Pollution, the National Farmers' Union, the Trade Marks, Patents and Designs Federation, and the Salvation Army. Finally, there is Mr. A. P. Herbert.

Who made the laws in medieval England? That is the question that I want to put, limiting myself to the last three centuries of the Middle Ages, to which the bulk of the enacted laws belong. There can be little hope of obtaining results comparable with Dr. Jennings' from such remote records, but the question is worth asking. Though, as he says, the law knows nothing of the legislative process,[1] the historian of civilization must be concerned with it. By and large, we are a law-abiding people, approximating to Burke's ideal of a disposition to conserve with an ability to improve. Our legislative machinery is the oldest in Europe, and if it has stood up to a good deal of criticism from outside in the last twelve years and survived more serious menaces from within, it has been mainly by virtue of its contacts with the opinion of the country at large. At the moment when it is about formally to renew that contact by our customary rough and clumsy methods it is not irrelevant to consider the earlier, experimental period in the evolution of the legislative process, and the nature of the contacts of law and opinion in the thirteenth, fourteenth and, fifteenth centuries.

There are three main sources of legislative activity in medieval England: the directive or planning urge in the ruler, the need for clarifying and defining experienced by the judicature, and the demand from the ruled for redress of grievances.

To the first source, the desire of the executive for order, we can attribute a large part of the legislation of the thirteenth century —such measures, for instance, as the police code built up by Henry III and Edward I from the Assize of Arms to the Statute of Winchester, the order for the holding of hundred courts in 1234, the succession of decrees on the coinage, the series of exchequer ordinances down to Stapleton's of 1323, and Edward I's great Statute of Wales, the first colonial constitution. We have a glimpse

[1] *Parliament*, p. 232.

of one of the departmental discussions, which produced such regulations in the preamble to the *Provisio super vicecomites et clericos suos* of 1298, which shows how three bishops, the king's treasurer, the barons of the exchequer, the justices of the Bench, and others of the king's council, being assembled in the exchequer on the feast of St. Valentine, had before them the problem of the literate but dishonest clerk who made out writs for levying excessive dues, and thus involved his illiterate but innocent chief, the sheriff, in penalties for extortion. They took counsel for a remedy and provided that henceforth the clerk should share his master's responsibility to the exchequer.[1] Official decrees of this sort might or might not need wide publicity, and a large proportion of them were not promulgated in parliaments. I do not propose to discuss them at length; administrative legislation is with us today and we know all about it and its sources. But the directive impulse of the administration, and above all of the council, is a continuing influence throughout the Middle Ages, originating, selecting, and amending the measures that become laws, not least in the period when the forms of legislation would seem to suggest a receptive rather than constructive attitude on the part of the government.

The second source, the judicature, is most important in the first of our three centuries. The judgement in a particular case, formally recorded as a precedent for the direction of future judges and litigants, belongs to the period when parliaments are still pre-eminently judicial occasions, and there are several instances of such *ad hoc* legislation on the rolls of Edward I's parliaments. The Statute of Waste of 1292, as is well known, is the judgement in the case of *Butler* v. *Hopton* after long discussion among the king's justices in full parliament.[2] The two "explanations" attached to the Statute of Gloucester, in effect revisions of a clumsily drafted enactment, have been traced by Mr. Sayles to two lawsuits, of 1278 and 1281, in which Eleanor Percy and the mayor and bailiffs of London, respectively, were involved.[3] The Ordinance *de Proteccionibus* in 1305 arose out of the particular

---

[1] *Stat. R.,* i. 213.   [2] *Stat. R.* i. 109 f.; *Rot. Parl.* i. 79.
[3] *Eng. Hist. Rev.,* 1937, pp. 468 ff.

grievance of the prior of St. Oswald's, who could not get redress from a defendant who was wrongfully pleading the king's protection.[1] In 1315 the *specialis petitio* of Katharine Jordan as to some sharp practice in a plea of Novel Disseisin produced a *generalis responsio* imposing penalties to be enforced by the justices in all such cases.[2] The transition from judicial to legislative remedy is perhaps indicated in a petition of 1318, when, in response to Robert of Mouhaut's complaint as to the penalizing of an attainted jury, the council reply that to change the laws of the realm requires the greatest deliberation, and that in full parliament.[3] Aside from judgements, it was, of course, in the great statutes of Edward I from 1275 onwards, modifying and defining the operation of the Common Law, that the judges made their greatest contribution to the statute book.

But the most abundant source of law-making is the third: public demand, direct or indirect, implicit or explicit; and parliaments were at once the field in which such impulses could work and, as time went on, the institution by means of which men could assert and enlarge their claims to law and justice. It is mainly, though not solely, with legislation in parliaments that we shall be concerned.

It is only possible to attempt such a survey by standing on the shoulders of others. The field opened up by Maitland in 1893 and McIlwain in 1910 has since then been explored by so many scholars on both sides of the Atlantic that the history of parliamentary legislation has been completely transformed. G. B. Adams, W. S. Holdsworth, M. V. Clarke, Eileen Power, Professors Plucknett, Morris, and Gray, Mr. Edwards, and Mr. H. G. Richardson are only a few of those on whose work I have relied in attempting to examine the processes of legislation from Magna Carta to the Reformation.

We all know that Magna Carta is the first statute on the statute roll, but we should not find it a perfectly simple matter to answer the question who made the charter enrolled there, for it took

---

[1] *Memoranda de Parliamento* (R.S.), p. 59; cf. p. 17, petition no. 15.
[2] *Rot. Parl.* i. 289.   [3] Cole, *Documents of English History*, p. 26.

twelve years to make, and there were many hands employed. We begin with its only begetter, Stephen Langton, holding up the Coronation Charter of Henry I to the assembled barons at St. Paul's, if the St. Albans' Chroniclers tell the truth, in August 1213;[1] we go on to the unknown framers of the "Unknown Charter of Liberties", to the equally unknown "men of the school of Glanvill and Hubert Walter" who, as Professor Powicke tells us,[2] must have helped to draft the carefully worded clauses of the articles submitted to John in May 1215,[3] to the barons who took part in the "Parliament of Runnymede", to the faithful supporters of John's young son who cut out the revolutionary clauses in 1216 and incorporated the amendments and additions of 1217. By now we have run through the whole gamut of baronial and official opinion, from the extreme Left-wing views of the five-and-twenty overkings (though even these have been recently rehabilitated by Mr. Richardson)[4] to those Right-wing moderates who stand out as the first English statesmen to catch the Whigs bathing and steal their clothes. The final version of the Charter, issued "freely and spontaneously" by the young King Henry in 1225, the statute cited in the courts and enforced by the judges from 1226 to 1920, owes perhaps less to him than to any of the other legislators, known and unknown, whose ideas and endeavours it incorporates.

Of the fifty or sixty other legislative acts of Henry III's reign only two have achieved anything like fame, and the first of these, though studiously noted in their handbooks by generations of medieval lawyers, is chiefly notorious today for the clause that is not there. In the Council of Merton in January 1236 all the learning and all the arguments from natural and divine law, from canon and civil law, and even, as he asserted, from the ancient custom of the land were on the side of Robert Grosseteste in urging

---

[1] The reliability of Roger of Wendover, the sole authority for this incident, is very doubtful, and there is good reason to credit the barons with independent initiative in demanding a charter. See V. H. Galbraith, *Roger of Wendover and Matthew Paris* (1944) and J. C. Holt "The Barons and the Great Charter" *Eng. Hist. Rev.*, 1955.

[2] *Stephen Langton*, p. 122.

[3] Accepting Mr. Holt's dating in *Eng. Hist. Rev.*, 1957, pp. 407-8.

[4] *John Rylands Bulletin*, 1944, "The Morrow of the Great Charter".

the simple and humane proposal to bring the common law of England into line with canon and civil Law by providing that children born out of wedlock should be held legitimate after the marriage of their parents. The bishop of Lincoln and the reform party were just about 700 years ahead of their times; but the diehards who declared "We will not change the laws of England" clearly implied that they could have changed them if they liked, in this agreeing with Grosseteste when he wrote to Justice Raleigh: "I am not so inexperienced—*nec tam idiota sum*—as to imagine that you or anyone else can make or change laws without the king and the magnates being consulted."[1] Then, as now, the reformer had to have the public opinion that counted on his side if he was to get anything done.

The other statute that is in all the law-books, the Statute of Marlborough, is also the product of discussion and compromise. It began with the Petition of the Barons, presented at the Parliament of Oxford in June 1258, containing the grievances both of great men like the earls of Gloucester and Hereford, of their tenants, and of the communities of the shires. The agenda of the *ad hoc* council of reform noted that the justices and other learned men were to consider the amendment of the laws before the next parliament.[2] Dr. E. F. Jacob[3] has traced the evidence of their labours in the various drafts of the document, which, after being held up by the obstructionist tactics of the greater men and forwarded by the publicity given by the heir to the throne to the protests of the middling men, was solemnly promulgated as the Provisions of Westminster by Henry III in October 1259. Of its twenty-four clauses, ten are based on the petition presented at Oxford fifteen months earlier. Though, as Mr. Jolliffe has said,[4] it was a document of the opposition, and a revolutionary opposition at that, it was enforced in the courts, reissued by Henry III in 1263 as a conciliatory gesture,[5] and reissued again by Simon de Montfort's government after Lewes, though it may have been

---

[1] Grosseteste, *Epistolae* (R.S.), Ep. 24, p. 96.
[2] *John Rylands Bulletin*, 1933, Richardson & Sayles, "The Provisions of Oxford".
[3] *Baronial Reform and Rebellion*, Oxford, 1925.
[4] *Constitutional History of Medieval England* (London, 1937), p. 335 n.
[5] Jacob, *Baronial Reform*, pp. 76 ff.

suspended by his defeat and death. Finally, two years after Simon de Montfort had fallen at Evesham and his followers had been disinherited at Winchester, "The lord king wishing to provide for the betterment of his realm and for such administration of justice as the royal office entails, having called together the more discreet men of the realm, both greater and lesser, provided, established and ordained" at Marlborough a set of enactments which incorporated the whole of the "revolutionary" legislation of 1259, with eleven additional clauses.[1] The concerns of the great men for their feudal dues, the complaints of the countryside against the oppressions of sheriffs, of magnates, and of royal justices, the grievances of tenants against their lords, the skilful devices of the legal experts, who may even have included Bracton himself and, at the latest stage, the pacific influence of the papal legate—all these interests and agencies went to the making of the Statute of Marlborough.

A hundred years later we shall find out best examples of the interplay of interests and agencies in the processes of law-making in the field of economic affairs. All England, from the king to the agricultural worker, is out to make money, and the tussle between high politics and local jealousies, associated interests and class antagonisms is informing the experimental and occasionally amateurish legislation of council and parliament. Eileen Power has depicted the interplay of motives among the different parties concerned in the establishment of parliamentary control of the wool taxes. I should like to glance at two other examples of economic legislative experiment involving various interests, and consider the Statute of the Staple of 1354 and the Ordinances and Statute of Labourers of 1349-52.

The staple for English merchants set up by Edward I had been at Bruges, Antwerp, and St. Omer by turns when, in the Parliament of York in 1318, the question of the establishment of home staples was mooted, and a conference was arranged in the following year between the merchants and the exchequer officials with others of the council, which reported in favour of the establish-

---

[1] *Stat. R.* i. 19-25. Professor Powicke considers that the hand of Ottobuono is traceable in the drafting of this preamble.

ment of home staples.[1] Political factions in the council, it seems, held up action till 1326 when, under the influence of the younger Dispenser,[2] ordinances made "by us and our council for the common profit and relief of the people of all our realm and power" set up the fourteen home staples and laid down regulations for native and alien merchants, purchasers, and manufacturers.[3] In 1328, however, the matter was reopened and the different towns were asked to send delegates to an assembly of merchants at York. The London delegates, writing back to the city for further instructions, indicate the difficulties of the assembly; the towns cannot agree, the merchants of the staple want a foreign staple, and they are all afraid of incurring the enmity of the king and council if they fail to make a recommendation.[4] The compromise suggested by the city fathers in their reply was in fact accepted, the ordinances of 1326 were repealed in the Parliament of Northampton, and free trade "after the tenor of the Great Charter" was established for the time being. A petition from the good folk of the community in the Parliament of York of 1334 for the restoration of the home staples was rejected and in 1340, the war with France having begun, Edward III established an overseas staple at Bruges in the lands of his continental ally. In the April parliament of 1343, in response to an inquiry from the council, the merchants put forward a long and reasoned statement in favour of home staples,[5] but foreign policy still outweighed their arguments and it was not till 1353 that they had their way. In September of that year a Great Council was held, expressly to deal with the maintenance and good government of the staple. A set of carefully drafted ordinances, drawn up by the king's council at least three months earlier, according to Mr. Richardson,[6] was read aloud to the prelates, magnates, and commons assembled in the White Chamber of Westminster Palace; any amendments proposed to be given in writing. The commons demanded a copy of the ordinances; one was given to the knights and another to the burgesses,

---

[1] *Eng. Hist. Rev.*, 1914, Bland, "Establishment of Home Staples".
[2] *Cal. Pat. Rolls, 1324-7*, p. 274.
[3] Bland, Brown, and Tawney, *Documents*, pp. 181-4.
[4] A. H. Thomas, *Cal. of Plea and Memoranda Rolls, 1323-64* (Cambridge, 1926), p. 52.
[5] *Rot. Parl.* ii. 143.   [6] *Bulletin Inst. Hist. Research*, No. 25 (1931), p. 13, n. 4.

and after great deliberation had amongst themselves they gave their opinion in writing. The magnates having read and discussed this written statement, the ordinances were issued in their final form. Only one amendment of the commons is recorded; they proposed to add eight more towns to the list of staples, bringing the number up to seventeen. The king accepted the suggestion only as far as regarded Canterbury "in honour of St. Thomas". The commons further petitioned that the articles of the ordinances should be recited at the next parliament, and entered on the roll of parliament, so that ordinances and agreements made in council should not be on record as if they had been made in common parliament, and to this the king assented.[1] Thus in the following April the chief justice expounded to the lords and commons in parliament how the king had established the staple in England, and how no staple could be maintained without fixed laws and customs, and therefore he had deputed the wise men of his council and the prelates, dukes, earls, barons, justices, serjeants, and others of the commonalty to ordain and make such laws and ordinances; and because he wished them to endure for ever he now caused them to be recited in parliament to endure for ever as a statute. Once again the knights of the shire were invited to get written copies and study them and, if they wished, propose amendments in writing. And after good deliberation the commons found the ordinances good and profitable for king and people and prayed that they might be confirmed, putting forward a number of supplementary proposals, most of which were accepted, and the ordinances, being confirmed, with these additions, by the king and the magnates, were finally placed on the statute roll.[2]

So much for the genesis of the Statute of the Staple of 1354, the fruit of thirty-five years of bargaining, diplomacy, and compromise between king, merchants, burgesses, knights of the shire, magnates, and council. The history of the Statute of Labourers, as traced for us by that great American scholar Bertha Putnam,[3]

[1] *Rot. Parl.* ii. 246-53; *Stat. R.* i. 332-43.

[2] *Rot. Parl.* ii. 254, 257, 261 f.; *Stat. R.* 348 f.

[3] *Toronto Law Journal*, 1944, pp. 251-81. See also *Enforcement of Statutes of Labourers*, New York, 1908; and *The Place in Legal History of Sir William Shareshull* (1950), pp. 51, 53, 68-72.

opens up another window on the processes of law-making. She appears to have caught the architect of the law in his workshop. It begins with the first ordinance "against the malice of labourers" issued by the council in June 1349 while the Black Death was still raging, a hastily drafted emergency measure designed to check the rise of wages and prices and to prevent labourers from breaking their contracts. Its ineffectiveness was soon evident; grievous complaints reached the council of the black market in labour which made it impossible for the employers of labour to pay any taxes. In November a second ordinance was issued, providing that all excess wages might be levied from the recipients and applied to the reduction of the taxpayers' burden, and a new commission to the justices of the peace charged them with the enforcement of both ordinances. By 1351 the government felt it was safe to summon a parliament again, and in this petitions were put forward by the commonalty for the better enforcing of both ordinances. The statute purporting to be a reply to these petitions betrays the hand of the expert lawyer as well as the experienced administrator; and the subsequent petition of the commonalty[1] laid down the terms of the grant of the next triennial subsidy with such skill, closing all the gaps through which the over-paid labourer might escape, the tax collector cheat, or the locality be unduly penalized or favoured in the matter of tax-relief, that Miss Putnam again detects the expert adviser. The parliament roll speaks of long treaty and deliberation by the commons, and of magnates sent to advise with them, so there is evidence to bear out her contention that the inspiration of the measure comes from the council.[2] Miss Putnam goes farther and names the specific councillor who she believes devised the ingenious financial and legal details of the whole scheme, if not the original plan of a nation-wide regulation of wages. Her legislator is William Shareshull, justice of the peace, justice itinerant, junior judge in Common Pleas, Exchequer, and King's Bench, and chief justice of King's Bench from 1350 to 1361, in which capacity he opened

---

[1] *Stat. R.* i. 327.
[2] *Rot. Parl.* ii. 237. Elsewhere it is referred to as "an ordinance made by the king's council". Putnam, *Enforcement of Statutes of Labourers*, p. 268.

five successive parliaments during his term of office. He attended the councils which drafted the first and second ordinance; he was himself an employer of labour in Oxfordshire; he was holding sessions in the summer of 1349 which could have brought him in close touch with the *popularis conquaestio* of the taxpayers; he enforced the ordinances as justice of the peace, and in opening the parliament of 1351 he told the lords and commons that the matters chiefly needing amendment were the failure to keep the peace and the refusal of labourers and servants to work as they used to do. Whether his share in the legislation of 1349-52 was great or small, we cannot mistake the combined action of the views of the employing and taxpaying class, the policy of the government, the experience of the administrator, and the skill of the legal expert in producing the first labour legislation of this country. It is noteworthy also that there were channels by which public opinion could speedily reach the government when parliaments were temporarily suspended.

What were these channels? Stubbs, seeking the origins of the importance of the commons in parliament, found it in the local juries, whose knowledge of their countryside was ascertained for the use of the central government, and in the ancient communal responsibilities of township, hundred, and shire blending naturally with the newer chartered responsibilities of the urban communities to produce the representative element in parliament. Along this line, reinforced as Dr. Post is teaching us,[1] by canonist doctrines of corporate responsibility imposed from above, we might arrive at the commons' share in taxation, but hardly at their share in legislation. It is true that the grievances of the countryside presented by a jury or elicited by inquest might, and did, issue in legislation—witness the relation of the first Statute of Westminster of 1275 to the Hundred Rolls inquest of the previous year—but a more spontaneous means of expressing the subjects' plaints and prayers was needed for parliament to become the national tribunal for righting nation-wide wrongs. That means was the petition or bill, and it is above all in the study of the process of petitioning

---

[1] *Speculum*, 1943, pp. 211-32; *Traditio*, 1943, pp. 355-408.

that the most valuable additions to our knowledge of parliamentary evolution have been made in recent years. The trail was blazed by Maitland in 1893, but only in the last twenty years has exploration been seriously undertaken, notably by Mr. Richardson[1] and Professor H. L. Gray,[2] but also most usefully by Mr. G. L. Haskins, Miss D. Rayner, and Mr. A. R. Myers. The petition, by its freedom from set forms and by its deferential method of approach, offered opportunities for the spontaneous expression of opinion; down to 1914 it was recognized as the natural vehicle for requests from the unenfranchised.[3] We have already noted its close verbal relation to legislation in the history of Magna Carta and the Statute of Marlborough: the same point has recently been made by Mr. Edwards in connexion with the Confirmation of the Charters in 1297.[4] A less close but highly significant relationship is traceable in the preambles to a whole number of statutes, beginning with those of that great autocrat Edward I. A king cannot be coerced, says Bracton, but you can always supplicate him. *Locus erit supplicationi.*

In the Tudor *Discourse upon the Understanding of Statutes* recently edited by Dr. Thorne,[5] and ascribed by Professor Plucknett to Sir Thomas Egerton, later Lord Ellesmere,[6] the reader is warned against taking the preamble to a statute too seriously.[7] This is a very sound warning for Tudor times, but as regards the medieval statute there is a good deal to be said for Dyer's description of the preamble to a statute as "a key to open the minds of the makers of the act and of the mischiefs they intend to remedy". I will quote some of Edward I's alleged reasons for legislation in chronological order. "Because our lord the King greatly desires to redress the state of the realm where it needs amendment, and that for the common profit of Holy Church and of the realm" (1275); "the king providing for the fuller administration of right as the

---

[1] *Bulletin Inst. Hist. Research*, 1927-34 (Nos. 15, 17, 18, 23, 25, 33); *Eng. Hist. Rev.*, 1931, 1932; *Rotuli Parliamentorum Anglie hactenus inediti* (Camden Series), London, 1935; *Select Cases of Procedure without Writ* (Selden Society), London, 1941.

[2] *The Influence of the Commons on Early Legislation*, Cambridge, Mass., 1932.

[3] See P. Fraser, "Public Petitioning and Parliament before 1832". *History*, 1961, pp. 195-211.

[4] *Eng. Hist. Rev.*, 1943.   [5] San Marino, California, 1942.

[6] *Law Qaurterly Review*, 1944, pp. 246-7.   [7] *Discourse*, ed. Thorne, p. 114.

royal office demands" (1278); "because merchants have fallen into poverty through failure to recover their debts" (1283); "to make good the oppressions and defects of former statutes" (1285); "of his special grace, and for the affection that he bears towards prelates, earls, barons and others of his kingdom" (1290); "since the Abbots of Fécamp and St. Edmunds and divers others suppli-cated in parliament" (1290); "at the instance of the magnates of his realm" (1290); "on the grievous complaint both of religious and of others of the kingdom" (1292); "understanding by the public and frequent complaint of the middling folk . . . we have decreed in parliament for the common welfare" (1293); "having diligently meditated on the defects in the law and the many grievances and oppressions inflicted on the people in time past we wish to provide a remedy and establish the certainty of the law" (1299); "in favour of the poor workmen of this city who live by the work of their hands, lest they should lack meat and be impoverished" (1302); "since those who have been put out of the forest by the perambulation have made request at this parlia-ment"[1]—that is, the parliament of 1305, on whose rolls four such petitions are recorded.[2]

If these preambles give the key to Edward's mind, we seem to see a benevolent and order-loving legislator, passing from concern for a complete and coherent system of law to a growing conscious-ness of personal and class grievances calling for redress. Without any intention of calling the nation into partnership with him, it is clear that Edward was to some extent permitting his subjects to suggest, if not dictate, matter for legislation. He was making his parliaments, held twice or thrice a year "for the providing of new remedies for new wrongs, and for the doing of justice to all according to their need", the occasions for receiving petitions from all and sundry.

It used to be assumed that one of the functions of elected repre-sentatives was to hand in such petitions on behalf of their consti-tuents. It may have become their function at a later date, but

---

[1] *Stat. R.* i. 26, 47, 53, 71, 107; *Rot. Parl.* i. 35, 41, 79, 117; *Stat. R.* i. 128; *Rot. Parl.* i. 147, 177.

[2] *Memoranda de Parliamento* (R.S.), pp. 18, 67, 89, 155 ff.

Mr. George Haskins[1] has proved conclusively that it was not so in Edward I's reign, for petitions were presented in large numbers in parliaments to which no representatives came, and it can be shown occasionally that special delegates were appointed by a community to present a petition when other men had been chosen as its representatives. In its origins, petitioning was a direct approach by the subject or group of subjects to the king. If the grievance alleged was a personal or local one, concerning the petitioner alone, it was most likely to demand executive or judicial action on the part of the crown, though judicial action might in a test case, as we have seen, produce legislation. Not until the fifteenth century, it seems, were the answers to requests for special or for localized favours for individuals, groups, or localities cast into legislative form. The main source of legislation was not the special but the general or common petition, which, as defined in 1346, was a petition "that might turn to the common profit",[2] as distinct from one that concerned special or private interests. Such a petition might be presented by one or by many; it would be worded in such a way as to suggest that it had widespread support. From a letter of Edward's printed by Stubbs we know that the petition of twelve articles that purported to express the demands of the whole community of the realm,[3] was presented in the parliament of Lincoln in 1301 by Henry of Keighley, one of the knights of the shire for Lincolnshire; Edward himself later described Keighley as acting for the Archbishop of Canterbury and other magnates of the realm who had pressed the king outrageously at that parliament.[4] In 1301 the "community of the realm"—the medieval equivalent for "public opinion", that is, the body of those politically conscious and politically active—was still predominantly aristocratic. But from 1297 onwards the lesser folk, both knights and burgesses, were being drawn more and more into the vortex of politics, and the reign of Edward II established both the political value to the magnates of co-operation with the "knights and the folk of the boroughs who came to the king's

[1] *Eng. Hist. Rev.*, 1938, "Petitions under Edward I".
[2] *Rot. Parl.* ii. 160.   [3] Palgrave, *Parliamentary Writs*, i. 104 f.
[4] Stubbs, *Const. Hist.* ii, at § 181 (p. 151, 2nd ed.). See also Powicke, *The Thirteenth Century*, 1953, p. 704.

parliament at the king's command for themselves and for the people", as they described themselves in 1309,[1] and also the practical uses to which the petitioning technique could be put. As the fourteenth century advanced, the lords were claiming a share in the hearing and answering of petitions, and it suited them well to inspire and promote petitions which purported to be in the common interest and which were presented by those who were not of their order.

Thus, early in the reign of Edward III, though parliament was still the tribunal where remedies were sought for private wrongs, the tide of petitions of national scope calling for political or legislative action had mounted so high that deliberate classification became necessary. Miss Doris Rayner, in a close and careful study of the technique of petitioning,[2] has shown how between 1324 and 1334 the chancery clerks who kept the records of parliaments were working out a solution of the problem. By 1339 the two categories are officially recognized; the singular or private petition is that which concerns the individual or private interest, and it must be delivered to the auditors and triers, who will pass it on to the appropriate authority for judicial or executive action. The common petition is that which concerns the common interest, and it must be delivered to the clerk of the parliament for reference sooner or later to the king and the lords of the council, with or without the endorsement of the commons as a body. Their endorsement or avowal certainly gives it a better chance of being accepted and becoming the basis of a statute or ordinance.

As Stubbs said long ago, nearly all the legislation of the fourteenth century is based upon parliamentary petitions. According to Professor Gray, this is equally true of the first half of the fifteenth century: then the tide turns, and a growing number of statutes omit all reference to the popular request. With the accession of Edward IV the bulk of legislation shrinks markedly, and under Richard III and Henry VII only a small proportion of the acts of parliament originate formally with the commons.

[1] *Rot. Parl.* i. 444.
[2] *Eng. Hist. Rev.*, 1941, "The Machinery of the Commune Petition".

Whereas under Henry V sixty-nine of his seventy statutes were based on petitions, of the 114 public acts of Henry VII, only seventeen purport to be passed at the request of the commons.

Professor Gray, following Stubbs, interprets this whole movement as the rise and decline of popular power as contrasted with that of the king, the council, and the lords. There is admittedly still much to be done in clearing up the relations of lords and commons in the fourteenth and fifteenth centuries,[1] on which it may be hoped that the *History of Parliament* launched by Lord Wedgwood will throw further light, but I think we are already in a position to say that a petition purporting to come from the commons in the fifteenth century, like a petition presented on behalf of the community of the realm in the fourteenth century, might in fact have originated in a variety of sources. The petition of the magnates and community which produced the Statute of Carlisle in 1307 almost certainly was inspired by Edward I. We saw that the act prescribing the technique for applying labour fines to the relief of taxation was based on a petition that was probably dictated by a member of the council. Indeed the roll of parliament refers specifically to the advice given on this occasion by certain great men "both with regard to the aid and for the making of petitions touching the common people of the land".[2] In the parliament of 1401 a petition touching the Cistercian order was referred to the commons by Henry IV for their consideration, and they approved it. From another entry on the roll it appears that the petition was originally handed in by Archbishop Arundel, but the statute formed on it is described as being granted at the instance and request of the commons.[3] Anyone who could make out a good case for his particular demand being in the common interest might claim or allege the backing of the commons. As far back as 1327 the commons were protesting against having bills put forward in their name without their endorsement or "avowal",[4] and this practice of backing or avowing a bill put forward by an individual, or originated by the lords, or put into their mouths by king or council, is traceable

[1] See above p. 57, note 4.   [2] *Rot. Parl.* ii. 237.
[3] *Rot. Parl.* iii. 457, 464; *Stat. R.* ii. 121.   [4] *Rot. Parl.* ii. 10-11.

throughout the period when Professor Gray is crediting them with something like the monopoly of initiative. Much of the autocratic legislation of Richard II's last parliament was formally petitioned for by the commons. To name a few instances from 1382 to 1423, petitions from the Lombard Merchants in England, from the mayor and aldermen of London, from the dean and chapter of Lincoln, from the poor commons of Northumberland, Cumberland, and Westmorland, from the captains who had served in the French wars under Henry V, from the master of the mint and from magnates like Henry Prince of Wales or John Duke of Bedford are put forward on their behalf by the commons and bear fruit in legislation.[1] In 1423 the lords referred to the commons a petition which they had received from the merchants of the Staple, "to have their opinion", and the commons sent it back to the lords "as one of their common petitions.[2]"

One result of this practice is that in the fifteenth century it becomes usual for outside bodies to address their petitions to the commons, in the hope that they will present them to the king and the lords. The development of this technique has been fully described by Mr. A. R. Myers.[3] A pictorial representation of the process is to be found in the muniments of King's College, Cambridge. On the Parliament Roll of 1444[4] is a petition from the Provost and Scholars of the College Royal of our Lady and St. Nicholas addressed to the "right wise and discrete Commons of this present Parliament" requesting them to pray the king to establish, by the advice of the Lords Spiritual and Temporal and by authority of parliament all the articles annexed, and grant to the college his letters patent to that effect. The charter based on the resulting act of parliament is preserved at King's College, and on its first sheet are a series of miniatures arranged like a flight of steps: in the left-hand margin kneel the commons with the speaker, bearing a roll, at their head. He says: "Priount les Communes." Above are the lords headed by the chancellor who

[1] *Rot. Parl.* iii. 138, 429, 581; iv. 74, 143, 177 f.
[2] *Ibid.*, iv. 250; cited by Stubbs, *Const. Hist.* iii, at § 440 (footnote).
[3] *Eng. Hist. Rev.*, 1937, "Parliamentary Petitions in the Fifteenth Century"; *Toronto Law Journal*, 1939, "The Commons in the Fifteenth Century".
[4] *Rot. Parl.* v. 87.

says: "Nous le prioms aussi." In the centre kneels Henry VI himself, saying "Fiat" and adoring the Virgin and St. Nicholas depicted above him to the right.[1]

Legislation originating in a petition may give the petitioners something different from what they requested. Henry V's promise in 1414 not to enact statutes whereby the commons might be bound contrary to their asking was, as has been pointed out by several scholars,[2] no security that a statute would conform to the terms of the request, nor did it assure to the petitioners the chance of discussing and rejecting amendments. Nine years later a council minute instructed the clerk of parliament to show the acts that had been passed in the last parliament to the justices of both benches, so that they might be rendered into clear language;[3] the final wording of the statutes was not controlled by parliament. Thus the device of "the bill containing the form of the act desired to be enacted" which is coming into use from the middle of the fifteenth century is an important development in legislative procedure. It probably originated in private demands for royal grants like the King's College bill; it was used for measures promoted by the Crown before it was employed for the common petition originating *bona fide* with the commons. It not only led, if Professor Plucknett is right,[4] to more exact drafting and to stricter interpretation of statutes, but it also involved parliament itself more actively and intimately in the legislative process. Legislation was no longer "the government's vague reply to vaguely worded complaints, but rather the deliberate adoption of specific proposals embodied in specific texts emanating from the crown and its officers". More than that: though the formal initiative might be temporarily lost to the commons in the Tudor period, their discussions and criticisms of measures would have a more practical effect on the form and content of the statutes to which, having ceased to be petitioners, they were more truly assenters than when they had claimed that function in 1414. If

---

[1] *Proceedings of Cambridge Antiquarian Society*, 1931-2, p. 87.

[2] S. B. Chrimes, *English Constitutional Ideas in the Fifteenth Century* (Cambridge, 1936), pp. 161 ff., citing Dr. Pickthorn.

[3] Nicolas, *Proceedings and Ordinances of the Council*, iii. 22.

[4] *Law Quarterly Review*, 1944, pp. 248 ff.

Professor Plucknett is also right in his suggestion that the change in attitude towards the statutes evinced in Egerton's *Discourse* is the product of procedural change rather than political theory, we should have an admirable illustration of Dicey's thesis that laws create opinion almost as much as opinion produces laws.

In scrutinizing the channels by which public opinion was conveyed to the legislative agencies we have lost sight of the sources of that opinion. "The connexion between legislation and the supposed interests of the legislators is obvious", says Dicey.[1] Almost every interest in medieval society, almost every element in its make-up, has left its trace on the legislation of council and parliament.

Take first the legal profession. "We made the statute and we know what it means", said Hengham, speaking for the Edwardian bench. Judges, according to Dicey, aim rather at securing the certainty than at amending the deficiencies of the law,[2] and Magna Carta and the Petition of Right exemplify that attitude. The *Quo warranto* legislation of Edward I, embodying the Bractonian theory that all governmental functions exercised by a subject must expressly be delegated by royal act or sanction illustrates well the policy of definition applied in the royal interest. The Treason Law of 1352, assigned by Miss Putnam, like the labour legislation, to Chief Justice Shareshull,[3] also extends by defining. The judges who were instructed to put the good points of the Ordinances of 1311 into the statute of 1322[4] were the forerunners of those who were charged a hundred years later to clarify the wording of the acts that had just passed through parliament.

As for the common lawyers, they were undoubtedly pursuing their own interests in seeking to limit the scope of equitable jurisdiction, both in council and in chancery, by those fourteenth-century statutes to which seventeenth-century enemies of the Star Chamber were to appeal. The attack on the lawyers' membership of parliament in 1372, from whatever quarter it came, was

---

[1] *Law and Public Opinion in England during the Nineteenth Century* (London, 1905), p. 13.
[2] *Ibid.*, p. 362. [3] See above, p. 140, n. 3.
[4] J. Conway Davies, *Baronial Opposition to Edward II* (Cambridge, 1918), p. 583; cf. p. 492.

unsuccessful.[1] Possibly their help in formulating and presenting petitions was making it as useful to others as it was profitable to themselves to be elected to the common house.

The interest of the clergy is easily detected. Their hand is traceable in a series of measures, from *de Bigamis*, recorded before clerics and lawyers and accepted and published by the king's council in 1276, down to the statute for the clergy based on their *querimonia* in 1316.[2] In 1401, besides the statute about the Cistercians promoted by archbishop Arundel, there is the famous *de heretico comburendo*, which corresponds closely clause by clause to the long Latin petition of the clergy, drafted presumably in Convocation, up to the point when the statute replaces the petition that the lay authorities shall deal with the convicted heretic "as is incumbent on them" by the direction "that they shall cause him to be burned before the people in some public place".[3]

The share of the lay magnates in legislation is constant and obvious. To take one field where their interests conflicted with that of the Church, Edward I's statement that he passed the Statute of Mortmain at their instance is borne out by the fact that the first attempt to limit the acquisition of land by an ecclesiatical corporation was made by the barons at Oxford in 1258. In all the anti-papal protests and enactments from 1307 onwards, as in the anti-clerical proposals of the fifteenth century, the voice of the lay landlord and patron is clearly heard. How far the magnates pulled wires in the fifteenth-century House of Commons is a matter of debate, but, as we have seen, there is no question that many of the petitions addressed to the king and the lords of the council in the fifteenth as in the fourteenth century had been inspired by some of those who had the considering of them. "They procure petitions in the name of the commons which touch the commons not at all." The law against poachers of 1293 and the ordinance on maximum prices of 1315 were instigated by the magnates and can fairly be ranked as class legislation.[4] So, in a different sense, was the *Provisio per milites* of 1292—a code of rules for tournaments drafted by knights who

[1] *Eng. Hist. Rev.*, 1931, pp. 377-81. [2] *Stat. R. i.* 42-3, 175 f.
[3] *Rot. Parl. iii.* 466-7; *Stat. R. ii.* 125-8. [4] *Rot. Parl. i.* 101, 295.

took a part in such exercises, which was approved by the earls and other magnates who then requested the king to ratify them. Edward, himself an ardent jouster in his younger days, approved them as being for the common good, confirmed them by letters sealed, and ordered the sheriffs to co-operate in enforcing them.[1] It is as if the cup-tie regulations were issued by order in council.

There was, of course, no hard-and-fast line in England between the greater and the lesser baronage, the nobility and the gentry. Magnates and knights of the shire were at one, for instance, in supporting the Statute of Labourers. But in one legislative episode to which Miss Putnam has introduced us[2] there is a tug of war between magnates and county gentlemen. For some sixty years of the fourteenth century various experiments were being tried to solve the problems of keeping the peace in the counties. The magnates advocated the appointment of one or two great men to "keep the counties" and act as local justices, and got their way three times (in 1328, 1330, 1332); in the commons petition after petition reiterated the demand that those smaller men who since 1307 had been entrusted with the police duties of inquiry and arrest of suspects should be given judicial powers also, so that they could try and sentence peace-breakers. Such powers were given and taken away time after time; but in the end the commons had their way; the justices of the peace were to be local knights and squires, and plenty of them; not one or two great lords with estates in half a dozen counties.

A longer and less conclusive tug of war concerned another office held by country gentlemen—the sheriffdom. The tussle of the sheriffs and the exchequer reveals something like a vested interest working in the House of Commons. The sheriffs, who were responsible to the exchequer for the profits of local government, made up these profits in large part from the sums paid to them by their subordinates, the hundred bailiffs to whom they sublet the hundreds. Under the Statute of Lincoln of 1316, which purported to remedy the grievances of the magnates against oppressive and extortionate sheriffs, they were forbidden

[1] Ibid., 85.　　　　　　　　　　[2] Trans. R. Hist. Soc., 1929.

to charge too high a rate.[1] But the kings found the office of hundred bailiff a useful piece of royal patronage,[2] and in the early fourteenth century they were constantly separating hundreds from their shires by giving them to protégés who kept all the profits of office for themselves and paid nothing to the sheriff, who was nevertheless expected to pay in the same sum to the exchequer as before. Naturally he tried to recoup himself from those parts of the shire which were still in his control, so that the practice was justly described as being "to the great damage of the people and the disherison of the sheriffs". The Statute of Northampton for 1328 provided that all hundreds thus granted away should be rejoined to their shires, and that no such grants should be made in future.[3] A few grants were rescinded "according to the form of the agreement of the common council of the realm made in parliament at Northampton",[4] but the number of petitions from sheriffs and ex-sheriffs in the next few parliaments shows how little had been effected.[5] The terms of these petitions, incidentally, indicate a growing reliance on parliamentary legislation. In the parliament at York in 1333 a petition from all the sheriffs of England evoked an order to the exchequer to enforce the statute of 1328,[6] and steps were taken in ten counties;[7] but in the following year counter petitions from the ousted bailiffs produced a reversal of policy.[8] In 1336 the sheriffs had further backing from the knights of the shire and the commons, and the prelates and magnates agreed that the statute should be enforced.[9] During the years 1328-36, according to Miss Wood Legh,[10] some seven to ten sheriffs had been elected to every parliament. In 1339 a common petition demanded that they should

[1] *Stat. R.* i. 174-5.

[2] See *Fine Roll Calendars, passim.*

[3] *Stat. R.* i. 259, cap. 12.

[4] *Fine Roll Calendar*, 8 July 1328 (p. 97); *Close Roll Calendar*, 28 October 1328 (p. 346).

[5] *Rot. Parl.* ii. 33 (No. 11); Ancient Petitions, No. 548; C. 202/C. 28, No. 229.

[6] *Fine Roll Calendar*, p. 348.

[7] *Close Roll Calendar, 1333-7*, pp. 63, 65, 72, 106, 114, 116, 117, 121, 125, 127, 174, 175, 176.

[8] *Rot. Parl.* ii. 73-84; cf. Richardson, *Rotuli Parliamentorum*, pp. 232-9; *Close Roll Calendar*, pp. 210, 215, 216, 221-2; *Fine Roll Calendar*, pp. 364, 395, 443.

[9] *Stat. R.* i. 277.

[10] *Eng. Hist. Rev.*, 1931, p. 373.

be excluded from parliament. Their numbers dropped markedly, and the agitation in their interest ceased.

With the accession of Richard II the subject was raised again in a slightly different form. The sheriffs asked for an allowance at the exchequer in respect of franchises or hundreds granted out, and, though the minority government demurred at first, in 1381 the concession was made by a statute that sanctioned the rendering of accounts at the exchequer on the accountant's oath.[1] But the exchequer, it would seem, refused to be bound by the act of parliament. Repeated petitions, both from the commons as a whole and from the communities of the shires affected, demanded the enforcement of the statutes of 1316, 1328, and 1381, but the answer was always the same:[2] "Apply to the council, which will consider your case." Henry IV and Henry V in their first parliaments showed signs of yielding, but it was always the same story; the treasurer and barons refused to surrender an inch.[3] By the first parliament of Edward IV the commons had a scheme completely worked out—a bill containing the form of an act[4]—and a committee of lords, according to the Fane fragment, was appointed to "oversee the bill made for the ease of sheriffs" and "thereupon to make report to the king".[5] But, as before, the answer was *le roi s'avisera*, and 150 years after the tussle began the sheriffs were still accounting for their ancient farms, depending upon the good will of the exchequer and not on their own oaths. It is a clear instance of the limitation in practice, rather than in theory, of the effectiveness of parliamentary legislation.

After the country gentry came the merchants, who had been called into consultation by Edward I from 1275 onwards for the fixing of the old and the new customs and for the drafting of the two statutes which regulated the acknowledgement and collection of debts. We have seen their collaboration in the framing of the Statute of the Staple of 1354. Eileen Power has described their

[1] *Rot. Parl.* iii. 45, 116; *Stat. R.* ii. 21.
[2] *Rot. Parl.* iii. 211 f., 247, 266, 280, 290, 305, 330.
[3] *Bulletin Inst. Hist. Research*, xi. 158; *Rot. Parl.* iii. 446, 469, 478, 495; iv. 11 f.
[4] *Rot. Parl.* v. 494 f.
[5] W. H. Dunham, *The Fane Fragment of the 1461 Lords' Journal* (London, 1935), p. 19.

consultative assemblies in the fourteenth century, and their constant influence on fifteenth-century legislation, not only with regard to the changes in the location of the staple, but also in relation to the export of bullion and the minting of coin.[1]

If the burgesses had played their part under Edward III by combining with the woolgrowers against the great financial interests of the merchants, under Richard II we begin to be aware of them as craftsmen. The internecine war between the victualling guilds of London and their opponents is reflected in the legislation of 1383-4—the passing and the rapid repeal of the statutes against victuallers and fishmongers.[2] The regulation of crafts by statute begins with the prohibition of shoemakers from being tanners in 1389 and the statute for girdlers in 1391.[3] The apprenticeship regulations of the City of London are given statutory force in 1430,[4] and with the accession of Edward IV the anti-alien sentiment of the London handicraftsmen is given free vent in legislation prohibiting the importation of a long list of manufactured goods. The first of these must, I think, be the bill "containing the hurts and remedies of merchandises" described in the Fane Fragment as having been put in by the king's own hand;[5] if so it was not carried in that parliament, but in the following one of 1463.[6] It is in connexion with this protectionist movement that a women's interest makes itself felt in parliament, in the petitions of the silkwomen and throwsters of London in 1455 and 1463 against the importation of various small manufactured silk goods.[7] They were a body of domestic workers, less well organized than the crafts of cordwainers, horners, pattenmakers, bowyers, shearmen, and fullers, who also secured protective legislation in their own interests between the years 1464 and 1486.[8]

Lastly there are the special needs of the localities, in which perhaps we get nearest to the voice of the man in the street: the

---

[1] *The Wool Trade in Medieval English History*, Oxford, 1941; Power and Postan, *Studies in English Trade in the Fifteenth Century* (London, 1933), pp. 293-320.

[2] Unwin, *The Gilds and Companies of London* (London, 1908), pp. 146-52; *Rot. Par.* iii. 142-3.

[3] *Stat. R.* ii. 66, 81; *Rot. Parl.* iii. 271, 296.   [4] *Stat. R.* ii. 248.

[5] *The Fane Fragment*, pp. 18-19.   [6] *Stat. R.* ii. 396 ff.

[7] *Rot. Parl.* v. 325, 506; *Stat. R.* ii. 374, 395 f., 493.

[8] *Rot. Parl.* v. 566 f.; *Stat. R.* ii. 414-16, 494, 520.

grievous clamour and complaint of the men of Shropshire seeking protection from the lawless men of Cheshire; those of Tewkes-bury asking that the Severn crossing may be better guarded from the Welshmen and those of the Forest of Dean; the prayer for bridges on the road between Abingdon and Dorchester; the petition of the clothworkers of three Devonshire hundreds; the boroughs of Northampton and Leicester demanding a restriction of their municipal franchise; the mayor and community of Dover praying that their town may be the only exit port for travellers to the Continent; the parishioners of St. Faith's and St. Gregory's by St. Paul's asking for regulations to restrict the slaughtering of beasts in their vicinity "since they have oftentimes been greatly annoyed and distempered by corrupt airs engendered in the said parishes by blood and other fouler things, complaint whereof by the space of sixteen years hath been made as well by the canons of the said Cathedral Church as by many others of the king's subjects of right honest behaviour".[1] Such petitions, promoted by the commons, leave their mark on the statute book alongside the regulations by which the Yorkist and Tudor kings are restoring order to a polity broken by the civil war.

Where, in all this, we may ask, is the ordinary citizen? Is there any legislation which reflects anything more general than a class or a sectional interest? Mr. McFarlane has called the politics of the fourteenth and fifteenth centuries a joint-stock enterprise,[2] and the same description might well be applied to their legislation. The king and council undoubtedly were the guiding spirits throughout the Middle Ages, and towards the end of them the initiative was almost entirely in their hands; but that did not mean that the king's will alone was involved, nor did men think so. Egerton, writing in the early years of Elizabeth's reign, points out that it is difficult to be sure of the intent of a statute because of the number who have had a hand in it: "So manie hedes as there were, so manie wittes; so manie statute makers, so manie mindes."[3] "The public opinion which finds expression in legisla-

[1] Rot. Parl. iii. 440; iv. 156, 345; vi. 431 f.; Stat. R. ii. 417, 421, 527.
[2] Trans. R. Hist. Soc., 1944, p. 73.
[3] Discourse on the Understanding of Statutes, p. 151.

tion is", as Dicey says, "a very complex phenomenon; often a compromise resulting from a conflict between the ideas of the government and the feelings and habits of the governed."[1]

I suggested that the medieval equivalent for "public opinion" is "the community of the realm" and at the Oxford Parliament of 1258 "le commun de la terre" is precisely equated with the baronage.[2] By 1509 it takes two words to say it in English; the *commonalty* is an estate of the realm of long standing, taking its share, but having its place beside the lords spiritual and temporal; but there is a larger whole, a *commonwealth* of England which includes all the orders of the realm, and which is defined by Sir Thomas Smith as "a society or common doing of a multitude of free men collected together and united by common accord among themselves".[3] Not the least important of the common doings that had brought the commonwealth into being had been common action in legislation.

This common action was forced on them partly by the Crown, partly by their own interests. It is perhaps unfortunate that it takes a common danger or a common enemy to evoke a common consciousness and common action. The dislike of the king's foreign servants in the thirteenth century, the anti-papal and anti-clerical feeling of the fourteenth, the jealousy of the alien merchant and craftsman in the fifteenth were probably truer expressions of community feeling than any constructive zeal. But the common action they they provoked was itself an education; the habit of anti-clerical legislation was preparing the ground for an ecclesiastical revolution. And the common action was creating the new entity—the parliament by whose authority laws were made, to whose authority as legislator the individual would appeal.

Moreover the legislative process was familiarizing men with the notion of a common weal. The conception paternalistically expounded in the preambles of Edward I's statutes had been taken over by the fourteenth-century members of parliament

[1] *Law and Public Opion*, p. 10.

[2] Stubbs, *Charters* (9th edition), cf. pp. 381 and 383 on the election of the twelve to treat at parliaments.

[3] *De republica Anglorum* (Cambridge, 1906), p. 20.

who accepted the distinction between the singular needs of the individual and proposals that might turn to the common profit. All those who, in forwarding their own interests, were alleging the common welfare as their motive, were helping to build up the tradition—the magnates conferring with the commons, the councillors and civil servants who drafted the petitions for them, the over-mighty subjects, the merchants, and the poor folk of the shires alike.

Again, through the practice of making the commons the channel by which the ordinary citizens' petitions are transmuted into laws, the doctrine of the electors' responsibility for their representative's financial undertakings has been extended to legislative activities also. "Every man is bound by every act of parliament," says Catesby in 1481, "for every man is privy and party to parliament, for the commons have one or two representatives for each community who can bind the whole."[1] They not only accept the authority of parliament; they see themselves as constituting that authority. "Every Englishman is intended to be there present."[2] By whatever road it had travelled, parliament had come to be the embodiment of national unity.

By common action, in pursuit of a dimly realized common good, and by acceptance of a common responsibility, parliament had come to be at once the school and the expression of common consciousness. The machine and the power to drive it had developed together; the ship had found herself and was ready for the Tudor captain. If the public opinion of the sixteenth century was more truly national than that of the thirteenth, one at least of the causes had been the combined endeavour of so many sorts and conditions of men over 250 years to make and mend the laws of the land.

---

[1] Year Book, Mich. Term, 21 Ed. IV, cited by Thorne, *Discourse on the Understanding of Statutes*, p. 20, n. 37.
[2] Smith, *De republica Anglorum*, p. 49.

IX

The Theory and Practice of Representation
in Medieval England[1]

THOUGH REPRESENTATION is an old, not to say, hackneyed subject, we can never get away from it. It is the basis of our Anglo-American assumptions about democracy, though little used by the Greeks who invented the word democracy and repudiated by Rousseau, the prophet of modern democracy. Representative institutions are the background of Stubbs' great book. His design of the growth of the English constitution proceeds from the history of the things represented to that of the series of events by which the principle and practice of representation were incorporated in the national assembly. I use the word *things* (which we are at such pains to eliminate from the undergraduate essay) advisedly, for the problem, as I should like to pose it, is "*What* is represented, and why?"

In the last twenty years the study of this ancient subject has been reinvigorated from two new sources, each of them originating outside England. The first is the one with which I am most intimately concerned, since it is embodied in an international commission of which I have the honour to be president. In 1933, at the International Congress of Historical Sciences held at Warsaw, a Belgian scholar, M. Émile Lousse, whom we are happy to have with us today, propounded to the assembled historians a project for a concerted study of the formation of assemblies of estates. The *Ständestaat*, the *état corporatif*—the realm of estates—had long been a subject of study in Germany; two articles by Otto Hintze, published in the *Historische Zeitschrift* in 1929 and 1931,

[1] A paper read at the Anglo-American Conference of Historians, 11 July 1952. Reprinted from *History* i. 1953, pp. 11-26, with some revision of the references to Professor Post's work.

had set forth the theory that the evolution of estates was the clue to the later medieval history not merely of Germany but of all Western Christendom. This view, in tune with the new corporatism which Italy and Germany were translating into fact and which La Tour du Pin had been preaching in France for many years, appeared to the historians at Warsaw worthy of scientific investigation; and in 1935 the international commission for the study of assemblies of estates came into being, with M. Coville as its president and M. Lousse as its secretary and driving force.

Conferences were held year after year, mostly under the auspices of the French *Société d'Histoire du Droit*; volumes of studies by French, Swiss, Belgian, Hungarian, Italian and English scholars were published, on various aspects of the history of estates,[1] and the first volume of Professor Lousse's own book on corporative organization and representation came out in occupied Belgium in 1943.[2] It was followed in 1949 by Signor Marongiu's book, *L'istituto parlamentare in Italia dalle origine al* 1500,[3] and two months ago by Mr. Richardson's and Professor Sayles' book on *The Irish Parliament in the Middle Ages*.[4] Owing largely to Professor Lousse, the commission on estates, unlike some other children of the *Comité International des Sciences Historiques*, justified its existence by its activity and it was reconstituted at the Paris conference two years ago. With representatives of fourteen nations involved, it can fairly claim to be an international undertaking.[5]

This digression is not altogether irrelevant. In our study of English medieval history, we are, perhaps, too ready to stay on our island. Considering the very close relations between England and Rome, and England and France during the greater part of the Middle Ages, our reluctance to look overseas and study parallel developments for enlightenment, is rather less than scientific. If English and American scholars have been roused to protest by some of the statements made about English institutions in the

---

[1] *Études présentées à la Commission Internationale pour l'histoire des assemblées d'états;* I., Paris, 1937; II-VIII, Louvain, 1937, 1939, 1940, 1943, 1949 (henceforth cited as *Études*.)

[2] *La Société d'Ancien Régime*, Louvain, 1943.

[3] Rome, 1949.   [4] Philadelphia, 1952.

[5] By 1962 twenty-four volumes of the *Études* had been published, and the membership included representatives of twenty-one nations.

volumes I have mentioned, the result has, I think, been only beneficial; but I have the impression that considerably more attention has been paid to them in the United States than in England. The outcome should be, I think, first, a stimulus to the use of the comparative method; secondly, a re-examination of our own views. It is attack that compels one to define and justify assumptions that may never have been formulated.

Some of Professor Lousse's criticisms in detail can be answered fairly readily. He does very much less than justice to Stubbs, whose learning stands on a rock, however much his interpretations may be affected by the ebb and flow of circumstance. M. Lousse went so far as to say that Maitland, "who taught at Cambridge", did not think much of Stubbs (an Oxford professor) and published a course of lectures in opposition to him, where he showed his knowledge of Western Christendom (in opposition to Stubbs' insularity), by referring to the idea of the three estates of those who pray, those who fight and those who work. The fact is that Maitland expressly referred his Cambridge students to Stubbs' fifteenth chapter, not only for the phrase he quotes but also for a fuller discussion of the history of estates in France, Germany, Sicily, Aragon, Castile, Naples, and the Netherlands, than he, Maitland, had time to give.

The conception of estates of the realm is indeed not a new one to American and English students of history, for whom McIlwain's chapter in the seventh volume of the Cambridge Medieval History has amplified Stubbs' sketch. The classification of society into those who pray, those who fight, and those who labour, is a medieval commonplace, to be found in Alfred the Great and Aelfric, in Langland and Wyclif, in Gerson and Nicholas of Clamangis; it is familiar in Germany in the three categories of *Lehrstand, Wehrstand, Nährstand.* Dumézil[1] indeed would say that it goes back to the origins of the Indo-European peoples and is one of their basic social and religious conceptions, being reflected in the three Hindu castes of priests, fighters and cultivators—Brahmans, Kshatriyas, Vaisyas; in the Druids, warriors and agriculturists of primitive Celtic society, in the three tribes and

[1] Georges Dumézil, *Jupiter, Mars, Quirinus.* Paris, 1941.

three deities of primitive Rome—Jupiter, Mars, Quirinus; in the three Scandinavian deities, Odin, Thor and Freya. A cruder but more recent expression of it is in the inn-sign of the Four Alls, on which are depicted side by side, the parson saying "I pray for all"; the soldier saying "I fight for all"; the labourer, "I work for all", and the king, "I rule all."[1]

Such a view of society is functional, vocational; it does not of itself indicate the common consciousness or common action that goes with the idea of estates of the realm, or the *Ständestaat*. There may well be division of function in the lord's household or the king's realm; but so long as the functionaries are the tools of their lord, as Alfred called them, and so long as the horizontal principle of the associations of like with like has not yet triumphed over the vertical principle of loyalty to and dependence upon the lord, so long society is still in the feudal stage. It is changing economic conditions, what we used to call "the rise of the middle class", that produces the sense of common interest with one's equals, common aims, common action against one's enemies (often one's superiors), and that leads to the formation of associations and the organization of societies by estates. To take one instance: such a stage is reached when the English bishops begin to regard themselves, and be regarded primarily, as members of the clerical estate, rather than as tenants in chief, owing service at the king's court "like the other barons"—*sicut barones ceteri*, as the Constitutions of Clarendon phrase it. Stubbs notes the corresponding moment in Aragon as occurring in 1301.

For Professor Lousse the process of association is clear cut and deliberate. It follows a regular pattern of mutual oaths—*conjurationes* or *communiones*; of pacts like that of the citizens of London in 1193 or of the community of the baronage of Oxford in 1258. M. Petit-Dutaillis in his last book[2] insisted that it is in this mutual oath that the *sine qua non* of the French commune consists, not in any specific privilege or status. For M. Lousse, however, there is a second stage; the *corporation*, whether urban, mercantile, or noble, that has been constituted by oaths, must secure legal status; it must obtain a charter of privileges from the governmental

[1] Cf. *La société d'Ancien Régime*, p. 103.   [2] *Les communes françaises*, Paris, 1947

authority in order to become an estate and not merely a group. A number of corporations may combine to appeal for privileges and thus establish themselves as an order. He has a rich collection both of pacts and of charters of privileges to bear out his contention. But it is here that the formula begins to look foreign to the student of English institutions.[1]

Confronted with the charge of obstinate insularity and national pride, which M. Lousse hurls against him, the English historian examines the tendencies of English social and constitutional evolution to see how they look in the light of the continental formula. Yes, there are gilds; yes, there is at least one sworn commune; yes, there are charters to boroughs, and charters of liberties to the barons, and to the clergy (though the English historian is a little startled to find the Constitutions of Clarendon and the Statute of Mortmain listed among the concessions of liberties to the English church). Yes, there is—but only for a fleeting moment—a *communitas bachelerie*. But the only lasting associations and corporations that we are aware of in England are the gilds and companies, the universities and colleges, and the religious houses and orders. There is no closed or sworn order or fraternity of nobles, and even less of knights; there are no charters to groups of towns. The associations of magnates for the obtaining of privileges are occasional and ephemeral; they are not part of the permanent order of English society. As with Pirenne's formula for the growth of towns, so with M. Lousse's formula for the corporative state; England is the square peg that will not fit into the round hole.

There are two main reasons for this, as it seems to me—the economic and the political—or rather one that combines the two and is even more basic—the chronological. It is the timing in England that differs from that of the Continent. Owing to the circumstances of the Norman conquest, which wedded military efficiency to the fairly advanced institutions of the Anglo-Saxon monarchy, England had something like 100 years' start of France

[1] In the second edition, however, of *La Société d'Ancien Regime* (1952) M. Lousse refers to the *pays*, which he considers has some points in common with the English shire, and indicates that the local community, as well as the social group, has its part to play.

in the evolution of a royal administrative system. Neither the great feudatories who confronted the Capetian dynasty, nor the imperfectly feudalized regionalisms of the Empire, were present to impede the growth of Anglo-Norman and Angevin authority; the beginnings of the *Beamtenstaat*, the bureaucracy, which, on the Continent, came to be the dominant character of the great monarchies and princedoms of the fourteenth and fifteenth centuries, are traceable in England from the twelfth century onwards.

But if England is administratively and politically ahead of the Continent, she is economically behind. She has her commercial and industrial features—we all know about the tribe of foreign merchants in the port of London in the days of Ethelred—but compared with the ferment in the valleys of the Po, the Rhine and the Scheldt, or even in northern France, her urban and industrial developments are on a small scale. Weaker and less institutionalized central authorities on the Continent are confronted by denser populations, with more urgent economic problems and more substantial resources, which in their turn, it may well be, stimulate the nobles into a more class-conscious solidarity. The pacts, the corporations, and the orders of the Continent are the product of conditions that do not obtain in England.

Nevertheless, this new angle of vision is illuminating, and we need be in no hurry to reject the light it may give us. Certain old commonplaces and recent interests take a fresh colour, for instance, the rise to prominence of the expression *communitas* in the thirteen century, commented on by Stubbs, Jolliffe and Powicke, among many others. Tait in his book *The Medieval English Borough*, as he relates the appearance of the mayor in the English borough to the wave of communal sentiment coming from France, points out that John, who had sanctioned the commune of London on his brother's behalf in 1191, appealed fourteen years later to the commune of the realm, the *communa liberorum hominum*, for the defence of the kingdom against a threatened French invasion in 1205. You will remember how the phrase and possibly the sentiment was turned against John in 1215 when the twenty-five guarantors of Magna Carta were empowered as a last resort to grieve and distrain the king *cum communia totius terrae.* When, under John's son, the expression *communitas regni* or *communitas terrae* recurs more and more frequently, it should have for us now overtones evoked by the continental events to which Lousse and Petit-Dutaillis have been calling our attention. The oath taken by the *comune de la tere* at Oxford in 1258 is absolutely in the continental tradition.

Or again there is the petitionary process, so intimately bound up with the judicial and legislative activities of early parliaments, so fruitfully studied in recent years by H. L. Gray, H. G. Richardson, G. O. Sayles, G. L. Haskins, D. Rayner and A. R. Myers. This may profitably be examined afresh in relation to the rich material furnished by Lousse in his fourth chapter. We are still very much in the dark as to the genesis of the petitions, whether singular or common, that were presented to the king and his council in the thirteenth and fourteenth centuries. Who drew up the Petition of the Barons of 1258? and how were the *Monstraunces* of 1297 drafted? or the complaints of the rectors of Berkshire in 1240? In the ninth chapter of *Henry III and the Lord Edward*, Powicke has suggested that "the growing coherence of the clergy probably influenced the *communitas* of the barons and made it more conscious"; it seems not improbable that the clerks who drafted the *gravamina* of their own order had the lion's share in moulding the petitionary technique, with its immense potentialities for the future.

In M. Lousse's attack on the *parlementarisme* of Stubbs he was not in 1943 aware of the formidable allies he possessed. He ignored all the undermining of the seventeenth- and eighteenth-century conceptions of primitive democratic institutions by the erection in 1893 of the high court of parliament as a royal and judicial elder brother who had ousted the younger brother, the embryonic house of commons, from the place of honour. But Stubbs' picture —not quite as black and white as some allege—has had to face criticism from a third quarter.

In the same year that M. Lousse's book came out there appeared two important articles by Mr. Gaines Post of the University of Wisconsin on "*Plena Potestas* and Consent" and on "Roman

Law And Early Representation in Spain and Italy",[1] in which he demonstrated, with a wealth of learning; how great was the contribution of Roman and Canon Law to the theory and practice of medieval representation. Medieval representation, he says, was constructed of heterogeneous materials on a foundation of feudal law, local institutions, royal curias, ecclesiastical synods, and the growth of royal and papal authority, but in both ideas and procedure its architects were greatly aided by the revival of Roman Law in the eleventh and twelfth centuries. In his articles on *plena potestas* Mr. Gaines Post has convincingly linked the early summoning of representatives to assemblies in Spain and Italy with the Roman lawyers' device of the plenipotentiary attorney representing his principal in a court of law: a conception that fits in very neatly with the *persona ficta* of M. Lousse's corporations.

In face of all these attacks, are our English knights of the shire and burgesses to retire meekly into the background, saying, as they did to king and lords in 1348, "As to your war and its array, we are so ignorant and simple that we know nothing about it nor can give any counsel in the matter"?

It was a deceptive reply and a pregnant negative; the rolls of parliament show that they took four days of discussion to arrive at it. We also should not be in a hurry to write off the representative element in the English parliaments as irrelevant in the thirteenth and fourteenth centuries. *Sustine modicum*, as the senior clerk said to his junior in the exchequer in 1177 when he asked him a tricky question; *Sustine modicum: ruricolae melius hoc norunt*—"Wait a bit; let us ask the country folk."

There are really two issues: What is represented by the representatives? And what is the origin of the device of representation? M. Lousse alleges that it is a corporation or association that is represented, and one recognized if not created by royal charter, Mr. Gaines Post very rightly emphasizes the authoritarian and legalistic aspects of the device as used by twelfth- and thirteenth-century rulers, and, as Stubbs and other have done before him, points out ecclesiastical precedents. But the earliest reference to representation in England occurs in a slightly old-fashioned record

---

[1] *Traditio*, i. (1943) pp. 355-408; *Speculum* (1943), pp. 211-232.

of local custom that can be dated soon after 1110, whilst the earliest instance of political representation outside England is in the year 1136, in Italy. There is no need to deny the influence of the Church; it must have been operative in England at any date after A.D. 600. On the other hand, "representation" is a far from unequivocal expression, as is made clear, for instance, in de Lagarde's brilliant analysis of its various significations in the days of Ockham.[1] But long before jurists and scholastics began examining into the bearing of the word, representation, the thing itself, was already on the scene as an obvious common-sense solution of constantly recurrent problems. If you want to get the opinion of a crowd, whether of children or of adults, you will in effect say, "Don't all talk at once—who will speak for you?" If an agreement on action has been arrived at by a group of people, one man will naturally be empowered to act for them. If a job has to be done for which a body of persons will be held responsible, it is mere common sense for them to arrange among themselves that one or two shall do it and leave the others free to get on with the work of food production, or business, or whatever it may be. These problems, you will note, arise when there is an active community upon which some external demand is made. That is all that is needed to produce some form of representation.[2] The precise nature of the link between community and representative, and between the community and the source of the external demand will be worked out in practice and defined, as becomes necessary, by custom and, in due course, by written law, and last of all, perhaps, in theory.

So we are driven back to our starting point—what is the community that is represented? This is where Stubbs comes into his own and the obstinate insularity of our "nationalist" historians is vindicated. In English sources, the oldest unit to be represented is the vill, in 1110; the next is the shire and hundred, in 1166; the next is the cathedral chapter, in 1226; the next is the diocesan clergy, in 1254; the next is the "community of the land"—

---

[1] *Bulletin of the International Commission of Historical Sciences*, No. 37 (Paris, 1937), pp. 425-51.

[2] Compare M. V. Clarke, *Medieval Representation and Consent*, pp. 335-47.

otherwise the barons—in 1258; and the next, the borough in 1265.

The representation of the clergy is clearly inspired by canonist doctrine, and can be associated with Innocent III's enunciation of the principle that links representation with consent—*quod omnes tangit ab omnibus approbetur*. In the case of the borough we have a corporation of Lousse's sort; boroughs owe the privileges which make them boroughs to a royal grant; and the practice of summoning representatives of towns to assemblies had precedents in Italy and Spain from 1162 on, representatives who, from 1214 onwards, come as plenipotentiaries with power to bind those who send them, a device which, as Mr. Post has shown, is directly traceable to papal influence.[1]

But with the earlier instances we are in a different world. The vill, the hundred and the shire are not voluntary associations privileged by royal charter, nor is the community of the barons who, at Oxford, have to elect twelve of their number to attend the parliaments that are to meet thrice a year, to treat of common needs and common business with the king's council. (One of the twelve, it should be noted, is a bishop, who on "functional" principles has no business there.) The twelve are to have power to act on behalf of the community of barons; and the *purpose* of the device is to save the pockets of the barons who cannot afford such frequent journeys to court: *Ceo serra fet pur esparnier le cust del commun*—a sound and practical reason.

It is a reason, moreover, that links up with that given in the *Leges Henrici*, in its account of the attendance of the representatives, of villagers at the shire and hundred moots. In theory, it implies, all the village might be expected to come; but either the lord of the village or his steward can discharge the obligation of the whole vill; failing that, the reeve, the priest and four of the better men of the vill should attend in place of (*pro*) all the village. Again, a common-sense delegation to one or two of a common responsibility. Whether this was a new practice under Henry I, or a recording of ancient custom, as Stubbs assumed, there is nothing

[1] Note also the letter of Pope Clement IV to Charles of Anjou in 1267, cited by P. S. Leicht, *Études*, II. (1937), p. 99.

to show; both William the Conqueror and Henry I stressed their preservation of the customs of Edward the Confessor, but we know that they also introduced new practices.

The first reference to representation of the shire, however, does sound like a new practice. In 1166 Henry II provided that if criminals arrested under the new procedure of the jury of indictment could not be brought before a royal justice in their own shire, they should be sent to the nearest royal session in some other shire, and with them, the sheriff was to bring two lawful men of the hundred and township where they had been arrested to bear the record of the shire and the hundred as to why they had been arrested. Neither shire nor hundred court kept a written record of their proceedings; only the oral testimony of "credible men of the court", the ancient "witness of the shire", could be produced to prove what had occurred. And this record, it must be remembered, binds those whom they represent, in the sense that the whole shire may be penalized for the action they report. This is not the same relationship as that of a jury which commits no one beyond itself. Nevertheless, when the jurors give their information to the king's inquisitors in 1086, Domesday Book notes that the "hundred says" so and so, and Stubbs does not seem to be going too far in bringing the jury into his picture of the origins of representation.

We may fully accord to Mr. Edwards the essential importance of the formula of *plena potestas* that rivets the power of the representatives to bind those who send them,[1] we may fully accept Mr. Post's demonstration that that formula is of Roman origin, like the *plene instructi* of the clerical proctors; but it is clear that the conception in England is older than the adoption of the formula. The burgesses summoned to the council of 1268 had to bring with them letters from their community declaring that they would hold as accepted and established whatever these men should do on their behalf; the community of the barons in 1258 had agreed to hold as established whatever the twelve whom they had elected should do; and men who bore the record of the shire might in fact involve

---

[1] See also H. Koenigsberger on "The Powers of Deputies in sixteenth-century Assemblies", *Études*, XXIV. (1962), pp. 211-243.

the shire in an amercement if they reported an irregular action of the shire court.

I do not wish to insist on this point; no doubt the barons at Oxford had clerical advisers and colleagues; Bracton, himself a clerk learned in the Roman law, undoubtedly worked with them. But I wish to recur to my point—*what* was represented?—and to insist on the old standing of the communities of shire, hundred and township.

The districts called the shire and the hundred, as they existed in 1166, were not so very ancient, perhaps not more than 200 or 250 years old. But the communities of shire and hundred succeeded to the traditions of the folkmoots; the assemblies in which, as the tenth century hundred ordinance said, men did justice to each other, and folk right, the law of the people, was declared; the *popularia concilia* whose existence, as Stenton reminds us, is attested in the days of Coenwulf of Mercia. The continuity of the twelfth-century shire and hundred courts from those assemblies of the tenth century in which the men of the court had done justice to each other under the presidency of ealdorman or reeve is unbroken down to that thirteenth-century session when the sheriff of Lincolnshire had to give up the attempt to do business and close the court because the country gentlemen went on strike and refused to do their duty as doomsmen. Neither Stubbs' assumption (based on a mangled text) that Henry I was reviving a moribund institution, nor Mr. Jolliffe's that Henry II recreated it, is warranted by any objective evidence. For business, for justice, and for publicity the shire court maintained its vitality, though it may well have been livelier and more active in a county of many small freeholders, like Lincolnshire, than in a county that contained many large liberties, like Dorset.

This is not to deny that the policy of the Norman and Angevin kings helped to keep the shire and hundred alive. They preserved them not merely by edicts that compelled the sheriffs to observe ancient custom, but even more by giving them work to do. The hundreds had had thief-catching duties; William the Conqueror gave them a concern with homicide by the institution of the *murdrum* fine, besides calling on them for information as to the holding of land, well before 1086. Henry II involved them in the reporting of suspects and Henry III gave them military and police responsibilities, for the keeping of watches and furnishing of armour, and demanded more and more information as to royal rights and private liberties and official misdoing from the hundred juries. The shire found itself involved in the extension of royal justice and the enlargement of the scope of royal revenues: invited by John to send delegates to discuss the affairs of the realm with the king; invited by Henry III to send delegates in 1227 to report on the sheriff's observance of Magna Carta and in 1254 on the willingness of the shire to contribute to the expenses of the king's wars in France.

Who, in fact, ran the shire court? From M. Lousse's angle, it was the *petite-noblesse—de smalre heeren—les seigneurs bassains—the Kleinadel*—though he visualizes them in isolation, each on his own estate, only taking common action in free knightly associations—*Ritterbunde*. The nearest he can get to a shire is a *"localité rurale—une agglomeration plus ou moins dense"*. In the three-fold cord of English traditional institutions, he can distinguish only the royal and feudal, he is not aware of the communal. It is true that, broadly speaking, the thirteenth-century shire is the field of the gentry, the knights, the squirearchy. The magnates have ceased to attend it, probably well before 1259; but, though the knights or gentlemen will undoubtedly take the lead in county doings, they will be working with freemen of ungentle blood, yeomen, *valetti*, who may represent the shire at parliaments if knights are not available. All the freeholders of the shire contribute to the expenses of their representative at a fixed rate. And there are no water-tight class barriers—the burgess may be a squire, the agriculturist may buy a town house, the squire's son may marry a villein's daughter, the same man may represent borough and county by turns. And above all, the locality counts. Devonshire will petition the king to have a Devon-born sheriff; and at Oxford the barons will demand that the sheriffs shall not only be land-holders, but residents in the shire they administer. The *pays*, the *patria*, the *country*, as the county was still called in Jane Austen's days, of the country gentlemen is the dominant *motif*; however he may link up with his fellows in the house of commons as an estate of the realm, it is not an order or estate that he represents, but a locality, and the house of commons, when it finally comes into existence, is not a house of *roturiers*, of the non-noble, but a house of communities, urban and rural.

It is this fact, together with the fluidity of social relations in England, that might lead us to maintain the position that Lousse condemns in Stubbs and in other English historians; to reassert *"le caractère absolument exceptionnel du parlement anglais"*. It is the survival of the shire that is unique; and it is the shire that makes the English parliament absolutely exceptional.

And at the lowest level of all, the community of the vill has still in the thirteenth century a perfectly definite place in the national system as a community that bears joint responsibility, that can and does take common action in its own interests, that is still represented, as it was in 1110, by its priest, reeve, and four men, or something very like it, and that is declared, in a royal document of the year 1255, to be entitled to prosecute its plaints in the courts by three or four of its own men—as the later legal theory of corporations would phrase it, "to sue and be sued".[1] The very fact that this legal status was lost in later days strengthens the case for the antiquity of the tradition of responsibility and representation in the oldest and smallest community.

How far are we justified in maintaining that this relationship of the ancient communities to representation and to the king's court is absolutely unique and peculiar to England?

The latest contributor to the history of the estates strongly disputes the claim of uniqueness. Mr. Russell Major in his book on *The Estates-General of* 1560, published in 1951 by the Princeton University Press, argues that many of the differences alleged between English and continental representative assemblies did not in fact exist. In France, as in England, the different orders co-operated. The same local assemblies gave mandates to the representatives of the different orders, who were not organized as three distinct houses in the estates-general until well on in the sixteenth century. The class antagonism so often insisted on was not, he maintains,

[1] See above, pp. 79-80.

in existence to any degree sufficient to account for the difference in the ultimate fate of the two nations; "the line between noble and non-noble was so vague as almost to defy definition".[1]

"A deputy to the estates-general was usually elected and empowered by all three estates, but even when named by a single order of society, local ties bound him as strongly to the other orders of his community as his class tie bound him to members of his estate from other parts of France . . . he represented a particular region whose privileges and autonomy he was carefully instructed to maintain."

Further, the men elected were very often men of considerable experience in local government; and they were not only instructed but paid by those who sent them to the national assembly.[2]

For Mr. Major the key to the different history of the national representative institutions of France and England lies in the strength, not the weakness of local feeling—the regionalism which prevented effective common action from being taken in a meeting of the estates-general, or even in the estates of the Languedoil, and made the provincial estates, rather than the estates-general, the source of financial supply for the Crown. The explanation of the greater effectiveness and ultimate survival of the English parliament as against the fading-out of the continental estates is to be found, he maintains, in the policy of the monarchy. Everything turned on the question whether a national representative assembly was or was not of use to the king: if it was, he convoked it; if not, he used the provincial estates in France, the provincial *cortes* in Spain. Mr. Major, whether or not we accept the validity of his arguments, drives us back to look at our facts and our arguments once more, and to ask the question, "What is represented and why?" with renewed determination.

Mr. Chrimes, following on the heels of Maude Clarke, has collected instances to show the emergence of the *term*, "estates of the realm" in England in the fourteenth and fifteenth centuries.[3]

[1] This fact is abundantly illustrated in the thirteenth- and fourteenth-century records of Forez, as Professor Perroy has recently demonstrated. See "Social mobility among the French *Noblesse* in the later Middle Ages", *Past and Present*, April 1962.

[2] *The Estates-General of 1560*, pp. 73-5.

[3] S. B. Chrimes, *English Constitutional Ideas in the Fifteenth Century* (Cambridge, 1936), pp. 105-26.

It is most conspicuous in connexion with the depositions of kings —Edward II, Richard II, Edward V. On the occasions when the king's parliament cannot function, the ingredients that go to make a parliament without a king combine to constitute something like a Convention Parliament of the seventeenth century. The lawyers, like Thirning in 1399, see that, legally speaking, a parliament needs a king. The politicians, like the prior of Canterbury in 1326,[1] see that it is desirable to spread the responsibility for revolution as widely as possible, and to involve in the act of changing the succession as many of the elements of society as can be brought in. Preachers will produce texts and similes to underline the conception of a hierarchical order of society; it is a commonplace; but the estates, though they may be a way of thinking, do not seem to be really of outstanding practical significance. Nor can we get away from the fact that the practice of representation does not apply to the two higher estates. However much the Church contributed to the prevalence of the canonist theory, the position of the clergy in parliament does not conform to it. The bishops and abbots are not elected representatives of the clerical order; the diocesan clergy are not in parliament but in convocation. The lay peers of England are not elected by their fellows, they are summoned by the king.

It looks, then, as if we must go back to our traditional formulas, though modified by examination and comparison into something rather different from the Stubbsian pattern. Parliament is both "an assembly of estates and a concentration of local communities", but we couple with this formula the phrase that comes from across the Atlantic: "self-government at the king's command". It was the effective centralization of power under the Angevins that made possible the preservation and utilization of local institutions and local sentiment by the monarchy, which in its turn made possible the growth of the conception of the community of the realm, to which Stubbs directed our attention, and on which Sir Maurice Powicke has so recently insisted. The episode of the villagers of Great Peatling, which Mr. Richardson dug out of the plea rolls

[1] M. V. Clarke, *Medieval Representation and Consent* (London, 1936), pp. 177-8.

for us, with its many-sided social, legal and political implications,[1] may be cited once more in this connexion. In 1265 the villagers of this small Leicestershire township could act as a body to meet an emergency; they could, as a community, enter into a contract and be penalized for breaking it; they could sue and be sued, not only by the magnate whose followers they had mishandled, but by individuals of the community itself, and pay damages to them. But Sir Maurice Powicke[2] links up this local episode with political thought on a national scale when he quotes from the record the words by which the men of Peatling Magna justified their attack on the men of a royalist magnate. It was because "they were against the barons and the welfare of the community of the realm" —*contra utilitatem communitatis regni et contra barones*.[3] The fact that in 1265 peasants could speak like this—that the community of the vill was aware of the community of the realm—gives us in a nutshell the clue to the history of representation in England. From such a beginning there could develop what, by Tudor times, was a political commonplace—the conception that all England was represented in the house of commons. A man was there not only for his own locality but for something much more; he was "a publick, a Councellor to the whole State".[4] Though, as Burke was to say long after, the local units were but "inns and resting places", national consciousness had been bred in the "*patria*", the country, the neighbourhood, and it was there that the foundations were laid which preserved the institutions of representation unbrokenly in the countries of Anglo-Saxon tradition when they perished elsewhere.

[1] See above, pp. 81-82.

[2] *Henry III and the Lord Edward*, pp. 509-10.

[3] As Mr. Post has pointed out (*History*, 1953, pp. 289-90), the phrase *utilitas communitatis regni* indicates the far reaching influence of baronial propaganda, itself reflecting clerical thought. See Powicke, *op. cit.*, p. 387, and cf. above, pp. 157 f.

[4] Quoted by Louise Fargo Brown in "Ideas of Representation from Elizabeth to Charles II", *Journal of Modern History*, xi. (1939), 27.

X

The Study of English Medieval
History Today[1]

A COMMENDABLE custom of the country from which I come
entitles the occupant of a university chair to praise the
famous men who came before him, and permits him to make a
public profession of the academic faith that is in him. Since
Radcliffe College has set me here today, I gladly avail myself of
the opportunity to pay my tribute, before that gracious and learned
society and before the ancient and famous community of Harvard
University which has admitted me to be numbered amongst
the flock of its masters of arts, to the scholars who built up
the tradition of medieval studies in this university, and to attempt
to indicate the claim of those studies upon a student of the
twentieth century.

It is seventy-eight years now since the famous interview in
which the first professor of medieval history at Harvard asserted
roundly that he knew nothing about medieval history, but
admitted, when pressed by President Eliot (on whom we must
believe that Professor Gurney had urged the need of some teaching
on the period that intervened between Constantine and Colum-
bus), that he was unable to point out anyone else who knew more.
Henry Adams was to go further than alleging that in 1870 he
knew nothing; he asserted thirty-five years later that he had "cared
less than nothing for the subjects on which he undertook to lecture,
and that, down to the moment he took his chair and looked his
scholars in the face, he had given, so far as he could remember,
one hour, more or less, to the Middle Ages".

[1] Lecture given at Radcliffe College, Cambridge, Massachusetts, on the occasion of the
installation of the writer as Zemurray-Radcliffe Professor of History in Harvard University, 10 December, 1948.

There is something in Adams of the son in the parable who refused to work in his father's vineyard, and afterwards repented and went. He may have been as ignorant as he professed to be, but he certainly knew something about teaching. "He had," as he says, "no fancy for telling agreeable tales to amuse sluggish-minded boys." And he knew something about historical method. As President Eliot doubtless was aware, he had three years before given evidence, in his article on Captain John Smith and the Pocahontas legend, of his power to apply some of the more important rules of evidence to the handling of original material. It was in approach and technique that he was to open a new chapter in the history of scholarship at Harvard. The syllabus of his course in European History, preserved in the Houghton Library, is little more than a dry catalogue of political items; the only hints of a personal approach are to be found in a few headings cast in an interrogative form, such as, "Did Gregory or Henry profit most by the submission at Canossa?" But we have the evidence of Lodge and Laughlin that they were the only lectures in their four undergraduate years that evoked "anything resemb-line active thought". Possibly the tone which makes the reader of *The Education of Henry Adams* today long to have the writer face to face to answer him back awakened in the more independent of his pupils the impulse of contradiction. However that may be, he could, according to Channing, "draw out from a man the very best that was in him". "He had a genius for starting men to think," says Laughlin, "he stirred up the stagnant mind," so that men came back for more when they had graduated. And it is, of course, in his work with the graduates that Adams has earned the undying gratitude of American scholars, for his was the first true seminar, not only in Harvard but in the United States. The group of young graduates who met in Adams' house in Marlborough Street, to use his own words, "worked like rabbits and dug holes all over the field of archaic society; no difficulty stopped them. They learned to chase an idea like a hare through a dense thicket of obscure facts." It is impossible to accept the detached and cynical estimate of the Adams of thirty years later that the exercise was pointless and the experiment a failure. "Adams was like a colt in tall clover," says Laughlin; and if we turn to Henry Adams' own letters in 1876, when the *Essays in Anglo-Saxon Law* were ready for the press, and Lodge, Young, and Laughlin had achieved the first three Ph.D.'s in history awarded at Harvard, we find clear evidence that he then felt it had been well worth while. "This has been a thoroughly satisfactory piece of work," he says to Milnes Gaskell. "I shall be curious to know whether your British universities think they can do better." And, again: "I am pleased with my scholars, and proud of them; they have shown qualities which I believe to be of the first rank. I look with more hope on the future of the world when I see how good our material is."

Adams had blazed a trail and founded a school of method. The study of medieval history had been fairly launched. It was to be kept going both by its own pupils and by recruits from elsewhere. More than that, the fashion of institutional history had been introduced; and as Emerton and McVane kept alive the tradition of medieval European teaching, so Gross, coming here from Göttingen in 1888, was to take over from Young and establish permanently the study of English medieval institutions. Every student of medieval English history acknowledges an immeasurable debt to that great scholar for his great bibliography, *The Sources and Literature of English History*; and every worker on English local history in this university traces with gratitude his hand in Widener's magnificent collection of the transactions and records of innumerable English county societies. I am proud to acknowledge a further personal indirect obligation. It was one of Gross' early graduate students, Gaillard Lapsley, who gave to generations of Cambridge students, in his ruthlessly logical analysis and brilliant exposition of English medieval institutions, the most valuable intellectual training that a student reading for the Historical Tripos at Cambridge in those days received in his undergraduate years. We became friends, and I shall never forget the glow of satisfaction with which I received Lapsley's commendation of my book on the *Hundred and the Hundred Rolls* in 1930: "It would have pleased my master Gross." It would be an impertinence for me to speak, in the presence of those who knew them, of the teaching of Gross and of his two great successors,

Haskins and McIlwain, but their written work speaks for itself, and is the possession of the Old and the New World alike. From the *Gild Merchant* to the *Coroners' Rolls*, from *Norman Institutions* to the *Renaissance of the Twelfth Century*, from the *High Court of Parliament* to *Constitutionalism, Ancient and Modern*, they have left an indelible mark on the history of medieval institutions. To be entrusted with the task of keeping alight the torch they handed on is indeed a high honour and a heavy responsibility.

What claims has medieval history upon the interest of a young man or woman in the year 1948?

As a subject for study, the Middle Ages have lost the glamour they wore in the days when the Waverley Novels were best sellers. Today they rank rather with Wordsworth's poet:

> "You must love him, ere to you
> He will seem worthy of your love."

That, of course, was what happened to Henry Adams. He fell in love—or, if you like, experienced his conversion—in 1895, when for the first time, for a moment, he knew what humility meant. "I never before felt quite so utterly stood on as I did in the cathedral at Coutances. The squirming devils under the feet of the stone apostles looked uncommonly like me"—but alas! he had to add—"and my generation." And a year later, when he was entering on his long discipleship to Our Lady of Chartres, he compares himself to "a monkey looking at the stars". By 1900 he was becoming bewildered by the astonishing contrast between what he had taught at Harvard in 1874 and what he was now trying to learn; by the contrast between the twelfth century of his thirtieth and of his sixtieth years. He and his pupils had revelled in the detective work of chasing legal details from Frankish laws through Anglo-Saxon codes and charters like hares and rabbits. He had pinned down "the sublime truths of Sac and Soc". He had claimed as his epitaph, "Hic jacet homunculus scriptor, doctor barbaricus, Henricus Adams, Adae filius et Evae. Primo explicuit socnam." Now these pursuits seemed the most barren antiquarianism. "The book on the dreary Anglo-Saxon law was a *tour de force* possible only to youth." Now, by

1901, he had made the discovery that the dead bones were alive, that he was a part of the Middle Ages, and that they were a part of him. "Remember me," he says, in his prayer to the Virgin of Chartres:—

"An English scholar of a Norman name,
   I was a thousand who then crossed the sea,
   To wrangle in the Paris schools for fame . . .

"When Blanche set up your gorgeous rose of France,
   I stood among the servants of the Queen,
   And when St. Louis made his penitence,
   I followed barefoot where the King had been."

But he came to his discovery a tired and defeated man, too tired to make the full surrender; and it may be doubted whether his path into the Middle Ages was more than a beautiful blind alley, never wholeheartedly accepted as an alternative to the sardonic sport of sitting like Jonah under his gourd, waiting for Nineveh to fall; as John Hay described him, "Hustling for a front seat on the verge of the abyss into which all governments are about to plunge, so that he may have nothing to obstruct his vision in the final cataclysm." Henry Adams remains an enigma to the end of the chapter; but he supplies unshakeable evidence of the widely divergent approaches that may be made, even by one and the same man, to the Middle Ages.

Thirty-three years ago that same fact was borne in on me at an historical gathering I attended at Stratford-on-Avon. We were holding our discussions on medieval history in the grammar school where Shakespeare had been a scholar, and the chairman, T. F. Tout, sat on a long-legged schoolmaster's stool which had nothing modern about it. Dr. Coulton, tall, ascetic, with dreamy blue eyes gazing into space, spoke to us of St. Francis, and medieval religion, as one completely at home in that world of simplicity and practical devotion. Then Tout capped him with the picture of Occleve, English civil servant and minor poet of the fifteenth century, with his palm so ready to be greased, his life so filled with dreary red tape and with endless petty shifts for keeping the wolf from the door. Tout knew his medieval Grub Street and Whitehall backstairs as intimately as Coulton knew his saints and social workers. We had the full range from the stars to the gutter, and both were equally medieval and equally real; and what a world it was, that had room and to spare for two such scholars and for their explorations and discoveries!

To Henry Adams, religious art was the key to the Middle Ages, and his own experience led him to the exaltation of the feminine principle as the driving force behind medieval thought. Such a line of approach must be pursued warily, as it runs through emotional bogs. One of Henry Adams' own pupils explored it in his *Classical Heritage of the Middle Ages* and his *Medieval Mind*, to Henry Adams' own somewhat naïve surprise. "I thought myself alone, and suddenly I find you in possession of the whole cloister," he wrote to Henry Osborn Taylor in 1901. "Are there others?" There certainly are others. More recently we have had the subtle and profound interpretation of Cochrane and the warm imagination of C. S. Lewis to illuminate the transformation of pagan thought and the education of pagan emotions by Christianity, and Charles Williams' remarkable exposition of the place of Beatrice in Dante's philosophy. And in the greatest of living English medievalists, Sir Maurice Powicke, we find exemplified the enrichment of the historian's learning by familiarity with the habits of thought and feeling, with the religious and social, as well as the political, assumptions and attitudes of the men of the thirteenth century, so that his writings have as it were a fourth dimensional quality. Of all the approaches to the medieval world, this is the one that calls most stringently for the study of language and literature, as has been very fully recognized by the Medieval Academy of America. Such studies are essential for the collection of first-hand material, those "facts" which had once, according to Laughlin, bored Henry Adams, but which from 1895 to 1902 he was collecting with the industry of an ant. Exacting as are its demands, no more rewarding pursuit could be recommended to those who find in the unity of human nature and the diversity of human personality at once the justification and the fascination of the study of history.

But art, poetry, and autobiography are not the only forms of human self-expression. Men have revealed both their conscious aspirations and their unconscious assumptions in the customs, the laws, and the institutions that they have created. To many today, the forms in which medieval religion expressed itself are so alien as to be meaningless; and medieval morality may seem strange or even repellent. To such the practical and perennial problem of government, the reconciling of order with liberty, and the rights of the individual with the well-being of the community, may be that above all which brings the past to life. The pursuit of justice, the securing to all their due, is a concern we share with the men of the Middle Ages. And the study of law and of institutions is much more than that chasing of antiquarian technicalities which enthralled the first Harvard seminar of 1873. It was to justify itself solidly in the years that followed. In the golden days of the nineties, so Professor Morison tells us, it was the constitutional aspect of history that predominated at Harvard. Of some fifteen historical courses given in the year 1890-91, twelve were wholly or partly concerned with constitutional development. Though, since then, other aspects, social, economic, or philosophical, have come in to change the orientation of historical studies, institutional and constitutional history must make an over-riding appeal to the medievalist. Not only are the practical problems of government and administration common ground with past and present citizens and administrators; not only does the documentary analysis which it involves offer a peculiarly valuable discipline to the student desirous of acquiring the techniques of scholarship; but the study of medieval constituional development is almost indispensable as a foundation for the study of modern history, above all in England and the countries which derive their institutions from England. If it is impossible to understand the methods of Tudor government or the arguments of seventeenth-century politicians and lawyers without reference to the evolution of the medieval council, the medieval justice of the peace, and the medieval parliament, it is equally impossible to understand the institutions and the principles of American government without reference to the growth of the local communities and the common law system of England. John Adams defending the British soldiers after the Boston Massacre exemplifies precisely that tradition of justice which was expounded by the judges of Henry III in 1219: "We were set here to do justice to all like, both rich and poor. It would not befit the honour of our lord the king or of ourselves to make ourselves contemptible in the eyes of those to whom we were sent by revoking the just judgement we have given, and acting contrary to the approved custom of the realm." This is the tradition of even-handed justice, regardless of personal or political considerations or social or racial standards, which is the most precious heritage of our two countries today.

But the story of the growth of the practice, the art, and the science of law has even wider implications. The history of law is not simply the evolution of a technique; it registers the long endeavour of men, by trial and error, over countless generations, to reconcile peace, security, and justice. Diverse conceptions of law have been held by different civilizations and nations at sundry times. To the Chinese it was a model or pattern of the good life, to be set before a people by those who understood the principles of right living; to the Romans a discipline enforced by the supreme authority of the state; to the Hebrews a reflection of the divine justice which rewards every man according to his work; to the Teutonic nations the custom of the people, sanctified by tradition, securing to each man his own rights.

Something of all these conceptions, transmitted and integrated by the Christian Church, can be traced in the code drawn up 1,000 years ago by the greatest of English kings. But how primitive and barbarous do the laws of Alfred the Great seem when scrutinized in detail! "We enjoin upon you as most needful," says the victor of Ethandun, "that every man abide carefully by his oath and pledge." The sanctity of contract, that is, is still optional. "We declare that a man may fight on behalf of his lord, if his lord be attacked." Private war is countenanced by public opinion, and by the law of the land. "A man who knows his adversary is at home shall not have recourse to violence before demanding justice of him. If he has power enough to surround him in his house and besiege him, he shall not fight if his enemy consent to remain inside the homestead. If he has not power enough to besiege him,

he shall ride to the king's ealdorman and ask his help. If the ealdorman will not help him, he shall ride to the king before he has
recourse to violence." That is, the established authorities may be
unwilling or unable to support a man's lawful claims, and self-
help is the accepted manner of vindicating them. These are the
provisions of a society that has built up a code of personal rights
and a procedure for seeking justice, but has not yet evolved an
executive power strong enough to maintain the rights and enforce
the law, nor a public opinion that expects and accepts such an
authority. But from the time when Alfred issued these laws,
which so clearly recognize the evils he was seeking to remedy,
there runs the unbroken chain of institutional development,
enactment, and opinion, advancing along parallel lines, which has
brought into existence the system we take for granted today, that
punishes breach of contract, protects our property, regulates our
relations with each other, helps to form our ideas of right and
wrong, and has established the collective security of our pursuits,
our homes, and our businesses.

In tracing this evolution the historian will find himself fully
occupied in studying the phenomena without seeking, as Henry
Adams did, to frame laws comparable to the Darwinian law of
natural selection, or the second law of thermo-dynamics; nor
need he accept the sweeping summary of Henry's younger
brother: "Law is nothing but a series of regulations imposed on
the strong for the protection of the weak, and, as the work of the
strong, has for the most part favoured their interests at the cost of
the weak." For the outstanding feature of the evolution of the law
of the two great Anglo-Saxon communities has been the co-
operation of the so-called strong and weak in formulating, applying, and enforcing the law. "I dared not thrust myself forward,"
says Alfred the Great, "not knowing how that would please those
who should come after me." Cnut, the Danish conqueror, and
William, the Norman conqueror, promise to the English people
the laws that are already theirs by right and custom. Kings like
Edgar, Henry II, or Edward I, seeking to put an end to disorder,
call upon the men of the countryside to do justice to each other,
to take responsibility for enforcing order, to report to the king's

delegates what the local usages are, so that he may enforce them, to say what their neighbour's wealth is, so that financial burdens may be equitably distributed. A strong ruler, whether he is Henry I or Henry VIII, wishing to do things decently and in order and to have the law on his side, establishes rules and systems which, in process of time, restrict the ruler's own freedom of action. The jury, offered to the subject as a royal gift, becomes the treasured possession and the inherent right of the free man. The king's own servants will tell him that the custom of his exchequer, or the practice of his bench, or the privilege of his parliament precludes the action he wishes to take. But, conversely, the men of the countryside, seeking to secure their ancient and inalienable rights, recognize in a strong central authority the surest means of protecting those rights. Law is the people's; justice is the king's, and he is sworn at his coronation both to respect the laws of his people and to execute justice and mercy. Henry the Lion of Justice will be preferred to Stephen, "the mild man, soft and good, who does no justice", and allows the country to lapse into anarchy; the exorbitant power of the Tudors will be preferred to the saintly ineptitude of the last Lancastrian.

The study of Anglo-Saxon institutions carries with it, I would suggest, a two-fold inspiration for the world citizens of today. The growth of law has been slow and not without grievous setbacks, but it has been sure because it has grown from the bottom upward. Rooted in the habits and assumptions and supported by the public opinion of the community, the responsibility for maintaining it has been accepted by a community able to improve, to use Burke's phrase, because disposed to conserve; a community that has incorporated in its legal system elements from Rome, from Denmark, from Normandy, from Holland, from Switzerland, or from wherever it needed them. What we thought we might require, we went and took; and what we found worked, we adopted, without inquiring too curiously into its origin or its logical relations to the other parts of our hardy hybrid constitutions. What Channing says of the genesis of the Massachusetts towns will apply in wider fields: "They were not based on any model; they grew by the exercise of English common-sense and political experience, combined with the circumstances of the place."

But further, as we survey a lawless world and doubt whether the human race is not slipping backwards rather than advancing forwards, it may encourage us to look back once more at the world of Alfred the Great. When he issued his code, there were ruling in Britain at least another half-dozen kings besides himself. In England proper, at least three languages, English, Danish and Welsh, were current, with what would today be considered their accompanying racial-minority problems. Recrudescent paganism in the eastern part of the island was barely mastered by Christianity; frontiers were constantly being readjusted; older customs were being jealously maintained behind and across those frontiers, and even within his own kingdom the three customary laws of three different peoples were in force. And, as we have seen, the man who broke his contract might be held a sinner and a cad, but might escape punishment as easily as a treaty-breaking power in the twentieth century. The man who was assaulted depended not on the protection of the police but on the loyalty of his friends; like Czechoslovakia in 1938. The highway robber who fortified himself in his homestead might keep his stolen goods, unless the wronged person could get enough active backing to recover them by force; as Japan kept Manchuria, and Italy, Abyssinia.

Who, at that date, could have foretold the rise of a law common to all England and of a government able to enforce it so effectively that the bearing of weapons by the civilian would become an anachronism? Who could have foreseen the development of a working system and science of law which would incorporate the rediscovered legacy of Roman order, the binding code of feudal responsibility, and the Christian assumptions of equality and the sacredness of human personality with the primitive communal sanction of individual rights? What the citizen of today scarcely pauses to contemplate, the medieval historian can watch coming into being; and looking back down the vista of 1,000 years he has a background against which the defeats and disappointments of the last thirty take a juster proportion.

If, then, I feel myself honoured to be speaking to you today from this place, it is not only as succeeding to a great tradition of historical teaching and scholarship in this university and college; not even as forming a link, however insignificant, between our two great free commonwealths; but also because I believe that the subject with the teaching of which I have been entrusted embodies, perhaps more fully than any other aspect of history, the slow advance of erring and straying humanity in its persistent endeavour to subdue chaos to order, discord to harmony, and self-interest to justice.

XI

Stubbs Seventy Years After[1]

SEVENTY-FIVE years ago the Clarendon Press published the first volume of *The Constitutional History of England in its Origin and Developments*, and its third volume came out in 1878. Those of us in Cambridge who have been responsible for the list of books recommended to the attention of the students of medieval constitutional history have of set purpose placed Stubbs' book in the category of those recommended for "study"—a category in which no other secondary history book is to be found. It is our considered view that no student of the early history of our constitution can dispense with reading it, and this article is an attempt to justify that opinion, whilst indicating, as far as may be, the directions in which the results of seventy years' research and reinterpretation have supplemented Stubbs' knowledge and modified our attitude to his judgements. I would say at once, with all the force at my disposal, that there is no nineteenth-century historian towards whom it is less possible to be condescending without condemning oneself as unfit to study history. As one who loves Maitland this side idolatry, I can only accept Professor Galbraith's opinion that Maitland's learning fell far short of that of Stubbs—as Maitland himself would have been the first to declare. "In the augmentation of knowledge", he said, "Dr. Stubbs stood supreme. No other Englishman has so completely displayed to the world the whole business of the historian from the winning of the raw material to the narrating and generalizing."[2]

In his valedictory lectures at Oxford last year, Professor Powicke, citing Lord Acton's saying that every part of history constantly needs new sifting by fresh minds, added: "If so, we can dismiss no great book as definitive; but neither can we ever

[1] Reprinted from *The Cambridge Historical Journal* 1948, (Now *The Historical Journal*).
[2] *Coll. Pap.* III. 498. (*E.H.R.*, 1901, p. 419.)

regard a great book as out of date." I should like to take that as my text in examining Stubbs' *History* from the standpoint of a reader of the year 1948.

The stock criticism of Stubbs is that he is "Victorian" in his attitude to English history. If this overworked and much abused word is used to denote complacency, it would be hard to discover in Stubbs any expression of that temper that could rank with Hallam's, who introduces his chapter on the constitutional history of medieval England with the remark: "No unbiased observer who derives pleasure from the welfare of his species can fail to consider the long and uninterruptedly increasing prosperity of England as the most beautiful phenomenon in the history of mankind. In no other region have the benefits that political institutions can confer been diffused over so extended a population; nor have any people so well reconciled the discordant elements of wealth, order and liberty." Hallam said this in 1818, the year before Peterloo, seven years before the birth of Stubbs. If Stubbs is to be identified with this attitude it must be not as a Victorian but, to use his own words to Prothero in 1894, as one belonging to the reign of George IV.[1] But I don't find Stubbs particularly complacent. After all, he was a Tory.

How far was Stubbs' vision limited by the assumptions and prejudices of the nineteenth century? He was not afraid to pass moral judgements—but then, no more is Mr. Churchill in this twentieth century. He was not immune from the pariotism of insularity, manifested also by Matthew Paris and the writer of the *Song of Lewes*, which assumes that Englishmen are preferable to foreigners in English political life: an attitude which is not peculiar to the nineteenth century. His assumption, on the other hand, that every activity originating in Rome is an unwarrantable interference with English liberties certainly "dates", and it distorts badly his picture of the Church in England after 1066, making the corrections of Maitland, A. L. Smith, Z. N. Brooke and, most recently, Powicke, very needful.[2] When we recall the atmosphere

[1] W. H. Hutton, *Letters of William Stubbs* (1904), p. 362.
[2] F. W. Maitland, *Roman Canon Law in the Church of England* (1898); Z. N. Brooke, *The English Church and the Papacy* (1931); F. M. Powicke, *Henry III and the Lord Edward* (1947).

surrounding the Ecclesiastical Titles Act of 1851 we can, I think, fairly label this attitude Victorian. Its fullest and most learned expression is that historical appendix to the *Report of the Commission on Ecclesiastical Courts*,[1] the preparation of which consumed so much of Stubbs' time from 1881 to 1883, which evoked Maitland's famous article, and which indubitably contributed to Stubbs' elevation to the episcopal bench in 1884.

Again, it may be fairly maintained that to a man who was an alert seven-year-old boy when the first Reform Bill was passed, who lived to see the second and the third become law, and whose maturity was dominated by the great figures of Gladstone and Disraeli, the English parliament might well seem to impose itself as the central theme in constitutional evolution—just as the twentieth-century historians, from Tout onwards, have devoted increasing attention to the study of administrative history. Stubbs was an unrepentant Tory; but if to read institutional history backwards is to be Whiggish, he most emphatically applied a Whig interpretation to history, again and again perceiving the fully fledged bird in the as yet unhatched egg, and this in spite of his own warning of "the danger of generalizing from results and attibuting to men of the past the historian's own formulated conclusions".

And lastly, over and above Stubbs' acceptance of the unconscious assumptions of his age and his subjection to the influence of contemporary circumstances, he was to some extent dominated by the theories of contemporary historians. I do not think he owed much to writers like Hallam, Palgrave, Sharon Turner and Kemble; he cites Hallam occasionally, and he calls Kemble "my pattern scholar",[2] but his essential independence comes out in his words to Freeman in 1866 when he was editing Benedict Abbas. "I am trying to do my Henry II by the light of nature, not reading Palgrave or Lyttelton. You will be shocked at me, I fear, but I find I cannot write without feeling that it is all my own as I go on."[3] But he read the works of contemporary scholars, and he was undoubtedly influenced by German historians, not only, to his

---

[1] I. 21-51. (London, 1883.) See below, p. 224. [2] Hutton, p. 77.
[3] Hutton, p. 104.

and our great benefit, in respect of their sound scholarly method, but also, with less good results, in respect of their Germanistic theories.

One other limitation imposed by the times in which he wrote was the comparative inaccessibility of unprinted record sources. Stubbs was familiar with the diocesan archives, which he visited in the years 1851-8 when he was compiling his *Registrum Angli-canum*, and he visited Lambeth Library twice a week during the years when he was librarian there, from 1862 to 1866. He also hunted manuscripts in the British Museum and the university libraries of Oxford and Cambridge for his work on the *Concilia*, and for his Rolls Series editions. But the mass of records to be seen now at the Public Record Office by the most inexperienced beginner were not available to him, and it results that his use of chronicle material is only checked by such records as had been printed when he wrote. His treatment of the reign of Henry III, for instance, is very much influenced by his dependence on Roger Wendover and Matthew Paris, whose political bias and inaccuracy in matters of chronology have been recently so eloquently expounded by Galbraith.[1] Thus we have to supplement him by reference to the work of R. L. Poole, Tout, Miss Mills, Mr. Steel, Mr. Wilkinson, Mr. Sayles, Mr. Jenkinson and others for the history of the government's administrative departments, the exchequer, the chancery, the household and even the benches, which can only be written from the records. On the other hand, in the great volumes of Rolls of Parliament, Parliamentary Writs and Proceedings of the Privy Council printed in the seventeenth, eighteenth and nineteenth centuries, Stubbs had access to material for the history of Parliament and to some extent of the Council,[2] of a kind that was not available for other branches of the government, and he exploited them to the full.

Before considering certain specific faults of omission and commission that may mislead the student today, it will be as well to note the bibliographical history of the book. The *Constitutional*

---

[1] *Roger Wendover and Matthew Paris.* (Glasgow University Press, 1944.)

[2] Plucknett has pointed out (*Trans. R. Hist. Soc.* for 1918, p. 164) that the *Proceedings* printed by Nicolas represent Sir Robert Cotton's seventeenth-century selection from the records, and give a somewhat misleading impression of the original material.

History was projected in 1868, two years after Stubbs became Regius Professor at Oxford.[1] The first volume, as we saw, appeared in 1873, and it passed through six editions in all; the other two which followed in 1875 and 1878 reached their final form also in their fifth edition in 1896. In 1883 Stubbs left Oxford to become Bishop of Chester. As late as 1885 he was still hoping to produce a second series of the *Select Charters* to run down to 1558,[2] but in fact his edition of William of Malmesbury in 1889, the year of his translation to the see of Oxford, was his last historical work. He wrote to Prothero in February 1889, "So far as I can see now, my history is written",[3] and he wrote to an inquirer in 1899, "I am afraid the book must be left alone."[4] I have compared earlier and later editions, though necessarily not very thoroughly, and I should say there was no modification of any significance introduced after 1887, with the possible exception of some slight alterations in the note on bookland and folkland added to the 1896 edition, which, as Petit-Dutaillis shows, pay deference to Vinogradoff's article in the *English Historical Review* for 1893, but are inconsistent with various passages in the text which have not been altered correspondingly.[5] Petit-Dutaillis is mistaken in thinking that Stubbs could have incorporated the contents of Maitland's *Domesday Book and Beyond*, even if he had had the time to absorb it; the book appeared in 1897, after Stubbs' last edition. Stubbs died in 1901: Petit-Dutaillis' references, therefore, to "the last edition of 1903" are misleading.[6] It was merely a reprint of the final edition of 1896; and that, in spite of a busy man's struggle to keep up with the literature, really bears out Maitland's remark, that Stubbs stopped in 1873,[7] as regards the Anglo-Saxon chapters.

I think then, that we are justified in advising the student to begin his study of Stubbs in 1066. The revolution effected in Anglo-Saxon studies by the philogoical and archaeological

---

[1] Hutton, p. 154. [2] Hutton, p. 359. [3] Hutton, p. 361.
[4] Hutton, p. 366. An "epitome" of the *Constitutional History* had been suggested.
[5] Petit-Dutaillis, *Studies and Notes Supplementary to Stubbs' Constitutional History.* (Manchester Press, 1930), pp. 29 f.
[6] Petit-Dutaillis, p. ix.
[7] Maitland, *Coll. Pap.* III. 507. (*E.H.R.*, 1901, p. 424.)

researches of the last thirty years would alone justify such advice, apart from the failure of Stubbs, noted by Maitland and by his French editor, to eliminate the strong impress of the influence of Maurer's dubious and irrelevant theory of the Mark. Stubbs does not really impose the Mark theory on England; but his constant eking out of imperfect English evidence by reference to continental conditions creates a misleading impression. He also expressly rejects the relevance of Celtic material, the study of which has been so much advanced by Vinogradoff, Jolliffe, and others, and minimizes the importance of the Danish influence of which Stenton and Douglas have taught us so much.[1] His picture of the "evil days of the Mercian supremacy" has been most adequately corrected by Stenton.[2] On the other hand, it is interesting to note that his observations on the appearance of the hundred are in no way inconsistent with Corbett's suggestions, now generally accepted,[3] and Stenton pays a warm tribute to his scholarship in the ecclesiastical field and fully bears out his contention concerning the unifying work of the Anglo-Saxon Church.[4]

Broadly speaking, one could say that the most marked contrast between Stubbs' approach to early English history and that of a modern historian is in his almost complete disregard of economic considerations, which now seem more relevant than "political" or "constitutional" ideas in treating primitive and decentralized communities.

From the Norman Conquest onwards the book becomes indispensable and criticism narrows to specific points. Petit-Dutaillis has shown how Stubbs failed to incorporate Round's work on feudalism, and how he complicated the problem of the introduction of knight-service into England by assuming that it was inseparable from the formation of knights' fees, which he

[1] S[tubbs,] C[onstitutional] H[istory,] i, § 30, p. 68. (The paragraphs are given, as they remain constant through all editions; the page references are to the 6th edition of vol. I, the second edition of vols. II and III.) Vinogradoff, *Growth of the Manor* (1904, 1911); Jolliffe in *E.H.R.* (1926); Stenton, *Danes in England* (British Academy, 1927); Douglas, *Social Structure of Medieval East Anglia* (1927).

[2] *S.C.H.* I, § 86, p. 250; Stenton in *E.H.R.* (1918) and *Anglo-Saxon England* (1943), ch. VII.

[3] *S.C.H.* I, § 45, p. 103; *Cam. Med. Hist.* III, pp. 366 f.

[4] Stenton, *Anglo-Saxon England*, pp. 235 f., 693.

rightly surmised was not completed for a generation or more.[1]

A more fundamental revision that is called for is in his identification of feudalism with anarchy—an error not peculiar to Stubbs. Stenton and Powicke for the eleventh, twelfth and thirteenth centuries have stressed the political education that the feudal system gave to the feudal baron; Maitland has underlined the feudal nature of English Law; and G. B. Adams has elaborated Stubbs' own suggestion of the contribution made by feudalism to English constitutional theory.[2] The value of the conception of the contract, fixing responsibility both ways, is now recognized; it is part and parcel of our constitutional heritage, and though Stubbs' picture of the horrors of feudal anarchy under Stephen would not be challenged, we should not today accept the denigration of the system that his phraseology so constantly implies.

On the side of omissions, we should undoubtedly allot more space in our picture of constitutional development to the growth of the common law and of the royal judicial system under the Angevins, and even more in the age of Bracton, when Stubbs' concentration on the grievances of the barons and the "weakness" of Henry III obscures the legal developments of his reign. Yet he observes in his retrospect over the thirteenth century: "Little as can be said for Henry III himself, there was much vitality and even administrative genius in the system of government and some of his bad ministers were among the best lawyers of the age."[3] I suggested before how the inaccessibility of exchequer records had hidden from Stubbs the thirteenth-century developments elucidated by the researches of Tout and Miss Mills and expounded by Professor Powicke in his great book, where he incidentally rehabilitates the hated foreigners whose corruptness and greed Stubbs accepted from Matthew Paris.[4]

It is Powicke too who, in Stephen Langton and in the sixth volume of the Cambridge Medieval History has set Magna Carta in

[1] S.C.H. I, § 96, pp. 284 ff.; Petit-Dutaillis, pp. 59 ff.

[2] Stenton, English Feudalism (1929), pp. 43 ff., 193 ff., 249-55; Powicke, Stephen Langton (1928), pp. 120-3; Pollock and Maitland, History of English Law (1896) passim; G. B. Adams, Origin of the English Constitution (1920), especially chs. IV and VI.

[3] S.C.H. II, 294, § 244. Bracton's testimony is expressly cited.

[4] Tout, Studies in Administrative History, vols. I, II; M. H. Mills, Trans. R. Hist. Soc. (1925, 1927); Powicke, Henry III and the Lord Edward, ch. III.

its proper perspective. Whilst rejecting Jenks' sensational attack on "The Myth of Magna Carta",[1] he exposed Stubbs' anachronistic picture of a nation, conscious of its own identity and acting as one. This "nation" of Stubbs' recurs at all the great political crises. He puts in provisos and recognizes that the evidence will not bear the weight he puts on it, and he notes the agency of groups and factions, parties and leaders; and yet, all unawares, the nation is back again, forcing the charter on John and the Provisions of Oxford on Henry III, the confirmation of the Charters on Edward I and the taxation statutes on Edward III, deposing Richard II, "at one with itself" behind Henry V and "reduced to silence" under Edward IV.[2] The "English people" was a political fiction long after 1215; in fact, as late as 1796, Burke's account of "the British publick" exposes its unreality.[3] But we talk of "public opinion" today too glibly to throw stones at Stubbs, and if Powicke deprives him of the nation in 1215, he gives him back the coronation oath with interest, vindicating magnificently Stubbs' association of the ancient ceremonial with the coronation charter of Henry I, the archetype of Magna Carta.[4]

We can now consider Stubbs' treatment of his central theme—the evolution of parliament. To him, as to any nineteenth-century Englishman, parliament stood for democracy, and its representative element was its essential feature. He sees the Anglo-Saxon Witan as the assembly of the people; the Anglo-Norman Curia Regis as inheriting its traditions; and feudalism slowly broadening down to admit the representative element, deliberately incorporated by that "buccaneering old Gladstone", Simon de Montfort.[5] Edward I, replacing the feudal by the national principle, arrived at the right formula in 1295; his son in the Statute of York defined the place of the Commons in the constitution; his grandson accepted their control over taxation. Such is Stubbs' picture.

The modern interpretation of the evolution of the medieval parliament, inaugurated by Maitland's edition in 1893 of the Roll

[1] *The Independent Review* (1904).   [2] *S.C.H.* III,, § 321, p. 72; § 373, p. 275.
[3] *Letters on a Regicide Peace* (ed. E. J. Payne), p. 49.
[4] *S.C.H.* I, § 108, p. 329; *Stephen Langton*, pp. 107-16.
[5] Hutton, p. 162.

of the parliament of 1305, and developed at length by McIlwain, Pollard, and, since 1928, by Richardson and Sayles,[1] gives a very different value to the concern of the representatives in parliaments. To begin with, the word *parliamentum*, at first a colloquialism rejected by the stylist, has become by 1250 a technical term in official use, with a predominantly judicial flavour. The king holds a parliament with his magnates to discuss politics and finance; the king's councillors and clerks of the chancery and barons of the exchequer hold parliaments which, Mr. Jolliffe has suggested, are in effect interdepartmental conferences.[2] These assemblies and gatherings of the officials and magnates of the king's court are the occasions on which petitions addressed to the king will be considered by the experts in conference. Richardson and Sayles have argued that the characteristic feature of a parliament is the hearing of petitions.[3]

Where, in all this, does the function of representation come in? No representatives are needed for the presentation of petitions, and when the king orders their election it is not, as Pasquet suggested thirty years ago, for that purpose.[4] In this respect opinion has swung back nearer to Stubbs' opinion and stressed the importance of finance, which Pasquet minimized. Carl Stephenson, J. G. Edwards and Maude Clarke have emphasized the relation of representation with consent to taxation.[5] From 1254 on, it can be shown that the parliaments to which the king summons representatives are those from which he hopes to get a grant of money. Parliaments may be the occasion for such demand; but many parliaments are held where only judicial and political business is done, and down to the end of Edward I's reign, we have no reason whatever to believe that a parliament, either in law or in men's minds, was less a parliament because no representatives

[1] For a survey of the literature, see Lapsley's Introduction to Maitland's *Selected Essays* (Cambridge University Press, 1936), and H. M. Cam, in *Relazioni del x Congresso Internazionale di Scienzi Storiche* (Roma, 1955), pp. 36-48.

[2] *Trans. R. Hist. Soc.* (1940).

[3] *Bulletin Inst. Hist. Research* (1930), pp. 72-7; *Parliaments and Great Councils* (1961), p. 43.

[4] *Origines de la chambre des communes* (1914), translation by Laffan (Cambridge, 1925), pp. 184 f., 201. Cf. G. L. Haskins, *E.H.R.* (1938).

[5] Stephenson in *Haskins Anniversary Essays* (Cambridge, Mass., 1929); Edwards in *Oxford Essays presented to Salter* (Oxford, 1934); M. V. Clarke in *Medieval Representation and Consent* (London, 1936), chs. XII, XIII.

attended it. Thus Stubbs' picture of Edward I as "perfecting the design of a national parliament, composed of the three estates"[1] cannot be accepted. Modern scholarship tends to stress the propaganda value of assembling representatives of the shires and boroughs; kings and lords were bidding for their support.[2] It was the political tension of the fourteenth century, when rival parties competed for the backing of the commons, that secured them their place in parliament, as Richardson points out.[3] But on the other hand, Edward I's use of parliaments for the hearing of petitions and doing of prerogative justice gave the common man an interest in them, and his use of parliaments for the publication of a large proportion of his great statutes established the all-important tradition that was to produce in the fifteenth century the doctrine of the overriding validity of statute law, and in the seventeenth century that of the legislative sovereignty of parliament. In that sense Edward can still lay claim to be the founder of parliament, and if we turn from the narrative of his reign in chapter XIV to the more general survey at the end of chapter XV we find Stubbs once again anticipating his critics. Edward I's work, he says, was "to some extent undesigned"; "the result of a growing policy exercised on a growing subject-matter"; "His view was the strengthening of the royal power"; "the constitution as it ultimately emerged may not have been that which Edward would have chosen"; "He admitted only the council and the baronage to give their consent to legislation."[4] Stubbs even anticipates Tout's comparison of Edward with Philip IV, and though he had not grasped the significance of the Household, which Tout was to establish, he specifically refers to "the importance of the council in all the branches of administration" under Edward.[5] There is very little wrong in his summing up of the contribution of king, baronage, clergy and people to the growth of parliament; "no great names or programmes of great design proceed from the

---

[1] *S.C.H.* II, § 244, p. 291.

[2] See Lapsley, *Crown Community and Parliament*, pp. 231-272, especially p. 271.

[3] *Bulletin Inst. Hist. Research* (November 1928), p. 75. Cf. *S.C.H.* II, § 245, p. 307; "Both sides look to the commons for help, and while they employ the commons for their own ends, gradually place the decision of all great questions irrevocably in their hands."

[4] *S.C.H.* II, § 244, pp. 291, 295, 296.   [5] *S.C.H.* II, § 244, p. 296.

third estate".[1] Imperceptibly Edward the democrat has become
an autocrat who builded better than he knew. For all the finer
shades of Powicke's portrait of the lord Edward, the outlines of
the picture are all there in Stubbs.

With regard to the later developments of the power of the
commons, Stubbs' insistence on the importance of financial
control and the significance of the contest over the wool trade is
fully borne out by the studies of Unwin, Wilkinson and Eileen
Power.[2] The chief change in emphasis today in interpreting parliamentary development in the fourteenth and fifteenth centuries is
in the study of the practice of petitioning, and the all-important
emergence, in the middle of the fourteenth century, of the distinction between the singular petition, the forerunner of the private
bill of today, and the common petition which concerns the
common interest, though it may, like a private member's bill
today, originate in the action of one person.[3] Stubbs was fully
aware of the importance of the petitioning process,[4] and if he took
the "common petition" to mean the petition presented in common
or by the commons, it is an opinion which was shared by Pollard,
H. L. Gray and many more up to comparatively recent times. But
Stubbs knew his parliamentary rolls and writs intimately, and any
unwary historian who thinks he or she has made a new discovery
about parliament had better scrutinize Stubbs' footnotes closely
to escape announcing with trumpets a bright new idea which is
already neatly ensconced in the heart of our classic.

If Stubbs misleads the unobservant reader by citing the account
of parliament written by Sir Thomas Smith in 1565 when he is
discussing the fifteenth-century House of Commons,[5] he makes it
perfectly clear that he is citing it in default of contemporary
evidence, and that it is inseparably mixed with Tudor theory.
Closer scrutiny will, I think, lend support to his argument that the
practices described bear the mark of long standing.

---

[1] S.C.H. II, § 244, p. 304.
[2] G. Unwin, *Finance and Trade under Edward III* (1918), pp. 179-255; B. Wilkinson,
Studies in the Constitutional History of the fourteenth and fifteenth centuries (Manchester, 1937),
ch. III; E. E. Power, *The Wool Trade* (Oxford, 1941), ch. IV.
[3] See D. Rayner in *E.H.R.* (1941).
[4] S.C.H. III, § 440, pp. 461 ff.   [5] S.C.H. III, § 442, pp. 467-76.

It is not in his account of the institutional advance of parliament in the fourteenth and fifteenth centuries that Stubbs had laid himself open to criticism so much as in his more general statements of constitutional theory. The fifteenth century, Stubbs maintained, saw a great constitutional experiment, and this experiment he associated with the Lancastrian dynasty. "The House of Lancaster", he says, "had risen by advocating constitutional principles, and on constitutional principles they governed."[1]

This, perhaps the most pervasive and far-reaching contribution of Stubbs to the interpretation of later medieval history, has been called by Mr. Steel the Lancastrian legend.[2] It is a reading of the events and tendencies of the fourteenth and fifteenth centuries that is at once consistent and comprehensive, but, as far as I have been able to pursue the question, it is, for Stubbs, strangely undocumented.[3] As an interpretation of English history, it identifies constitutional progress with "the Lancastrians"; at first a party, and after 1399 a dynasty. They are described succinctly in one passage as "the anti-royal, the baronial or, as it afterwards became, the Lancaster party".[4] In 1340 they are "the constitutional party".[5] We are told that the house of Lancaster was "the mainstay of right government"[6] until it became the reigning dynasty, and tried "the great constitutional experiment" of parliamentary government.[7] "The constitutional claim of the House of Lancaster was based on a solemn national act, strengthened by the adherence of three generations to a constitutional form of government."[8] The Yorkists, overthrowing the Lancastrians by force, on a claim "justified neither by law nor history"[9] destroyed "all that was destructible in the constitution".[10]

This thesis turns on two main points; the Lancastrian party and Lancastrian principles. For the moment let us leave the principles

---

[1] *S.C.H.* III, § 301, p. 8.

[2] *Richard II* (Cambridge University Press, 1941), p. 92.

[3] The passages cited from speeches made on behalf of the Crown at the opening of parliaments in § 364 are no more than medieval commonplaces which might have been uttered at any period from the thirteenth century onward.

[4] *S.C.H.* II, § 260, p. 418.   [5] *S.C.H.* II, § 258, p. 384.

[6] *S.C.H.* II, § 255, p. 368.   [7] *S.C.H.* II, § 300, p. 5.

[8] *S.C.H.* III, § 363, p. 234.   [9] *S.C.H.* III, § 363, p. 235.

[10] *S.C.H.* III, § 373, p. 273.

and look at the party. There was nothing anti-royal about the first earl of Lancaster, Edmund, the loyal younger brother of Edward I, though he was to be erected posthumously into a symbol of legitimism when a cock-and-bull story that he was really the elder son of Henry III, wrongfully ousted from his due position on account of physical deformity, was put forward first by John of Gaunt in 1394 and then by his son Henry IV in 1399.[1] The territorial fortunes of the house were founded when, after Evesham, the forfeited lands of Simon de Montfort and of Earl Ferrers were bestowed on Edmund; to his earldoms of Leicester, Derby and Lancaster his descendants were to add those of Lincoln and Hereford. Thomas of Lancaster, Edmund's son, led the baronial opposition to his cousin Edward II, procured the death of Piers Gaveston and was himself beheaded in 1322. The Lancastrian lands descended through two Henries, his brother and his nephew, to his great-niece Blanche, Chaucer's heroine, who married John of Gaunt, the fourth son of Edward III. She was the mother of Henry of Bolingbroke, who, returning from exile on his father's death in 1399 to claim the Lancaster inheritance, outmanoeuvred Richard II, contrived his deposition and established the Lancastrian line of kings, the dynasty that reigned in England from 1399 to 1461 and came to an end with the murder of Henry VI and his son in 1471.

The two pivotal events in this story are the execution of Thomas of Lancaster in 1322 for opposition to Edward II, and the deposition of Richard II by Henry of Lancaster in 1399. "As the heir of Lancaster and by taking up the principles for which Thomas of Lancaster was believed to have contended, Henry IV made good his claim", says Stubbs.[2] Once more setting aside the question of principle, how far can the continuity of a Lancastrian party or faction be shown to have existed? An examination of Stubbs' narrative, accepted and filled out by Tout in his *Chapters of Administrative History*, reveals the gap which Mr. Steel comments on. Between 1341 and 1371 no Lancaster is concerned in party politics, and both the second Henry of Lancaster and his son-in-

---

[1] *Eulogium Historiarum* (R.S.), III, 369; *Chron. Adae de Usk* (ed. Thompson), pp. 30 f., 182-6.
[2] *S.C.H.* II, § 269, p. 507.

law, John of Gaunt, are supporters of the Crown against the
baronial opposition. Moreover, Lancaster is divided against itself
when Henry of Bolingbroke, the future Henry IV, is backing his
uncle Thomas of Gloucester, the real leader of the opposition,
against his father John of Gaunt, Richard II's ally.

But I think Stubbs and Tout are justified in maintaining that
there is a Lancastrian tradition or a Lancastrian faction. The idea,
rather scouted by Mr. Steel,[1] that territorial possessions carry with
them a continuity of interest and sentiment, can be supported with
evidence of personal and territorial affinities; the great con-
glomeration of earldoms, which struck the contemporary
imagination as it strikes posterity, meant a vast nexus of dependents. The implications of such associations have been driven
home recently by Mr. McFarlane.[2] The Lancastrian faction, or
the Lancastrian adherents, the tenants and dependents of the four
earldoms held by Thomas, his brother and his nephew, might well
have carried over their loyalties to the second line when Blanche's
husband, John of Gaunt, succeeded to his father-in-law's titles,
castles and liberties.

There is another aspect to the Lancastrian tradition, linking
loyalties, localities and politics. Thomas of Lancaster, like a former
earl of Leicester, Simon de Montfort, who lost his life as a result
of opposition to the Crown, acquired the status, almost at once, of
a martyr, a posthumous worker of miracles and a candidate for
canonization. His brother erected a cross to his memory in the
town of Leicester, miracles were worked before his picture in
St. Paul's, and the crowds and offerings at his tomb at Pontefract
led to an armed guard being put round the church by royal order
to prevent visits.[3] This merely diverted the crowds to the place of
his execution outside Pontefract Castle, which in turn became a
centre of pilgrimage and the site of a chapel built with funds
collected from all over England.[4] In response to a petition pre-

[1] *Richard II*, p. 92.

[2] *Trans. R. Hist. Soc.* (1944), pp. 53-73; *Bulletin Inst. Hist. Research* (1945), pp. 161-80.

[3] *French Chronicle of London* (Camden Series), p. 46; Knighton, I. 426; *Calendar of Close Rolls*, 28 June 1323; *Flores Historiarum*, III, 213.

[4] *Foedera*, II. ii. 707 (8 June 1327); *Rot. Parl.* ii. 84 (1334); *Cal. Papal Petitions*, 1392-1429, p. 271.

sented in parliament, Edward III wrote three times to the Pope requesting an inquiry to be made into the miracles with a view to his canonization.[1] According to Walsingham, he *was* canonized in 1390.[2] Wright prints an office for St. Thomas of Lancaster "Ducum decus, lucerna Lancastrie"[3] and Mr. Kemp tells me that there is a stained-glass window depicting him in a church near Banbury. The cult, however, clearly centred at Pontefract, the great castle under whose shadow Stubbs was born.[4] Blood flowed from Thomas' tomb, we are told, in 1359[5] and again in 1466. Stubbs dug that fact out of the fragmentary annals of John Herryson, chancellor of the University of Cambridge from 1465 to 1468, preserved at Caius.[6] Miracles were still coruscating from the chapel at Pontefract, that is, five years after the accession of Edward IV of York, when Henry VI had just been captured and imprisoned in the tower, four years before his readeption. The martyred and canonized Thomas anticipates the fate of the deposed, murdered and nearly canonized Henry of Lancaster, before whose statue, as Stubbs says, the rough yeoman of York-shire and Durham used to worship.[7]

Tout, Maude Clarke, Mr. Wilkinson, Mr. Steel and Mr. Chrimes all accept the existence of a Lancastrian faction, as the body of adherents whose interests are linked with those of the house of Lancaster;[8] the evidence of the cult of St. Thomas of Lancaster proves that there was a real continuity from 1322 to 1466, and that the Lancastrian tradition did in fact "overleap attainder, reconciliation, the failure of heirs male and a royal marriage"[9] in establishing a continuous claim on local and personal loyalties.

[1] *Rot. Parl.* ii. 7; *Foedera*, II. ii, 695 (February 1327); II. ii. 782 (March 1330); II. ii. 814 (April 1331).

[2] *Historia Anglicana* (R.S.), II. 195. Thomas' name occurs in the *Acta Sanctorum* for 22 March amongst those who are *praetermissi et alios dies rejecti*.

[3] *Political Songs* (Camden Series), p. 270.

[4] Stubbs, *Seventeen Lectures on Medieval and Modern History*, p. 474.

[5] *Historia Anglicana*, I. 288.

[6] *Chron. Abbreviatio* (ed. J. I. Smith, Camb. Antiq. Soc., Quarto Series, 1840), p. 10.

[7] *S.C.H.* III, § 341, p. 131; § 538, p. 211.

[8] Tout, *Admin. Hist.* III. 10 ff., 35, 47, 136, 288, 302; M. V. Clarke, *Fourteenth-Century Studies* (1937), pp. 36 ff.; B. Wilkinson, *The Chancery under Edward III* (1929), p. xxviii and ch. v *passim*; S. B. Chrimes, *Constitutional Ideas of the Fifteenth Century* (1936), pp. 5 f.

[9] Steel, *Richard II*, p. 92.

Half then of Stubbs' thesis is vindicated by the historical evidence he cites; there was a Lancastrian tradition and a Lancastrian faction. It is when Stubbs seeks to identify this faction and this tradition with a constitutional doctrine that the difficulties begin, and he himself once again not only sees but points out the difficulties.

In so far as Thomas of Lancaster stood for a theory of parliamentary authority or representative or democratic principles, one would look for this in the Ordinances of 1311.[1] These, like the Provisions of Oxford, to which Stubbs relates them, do not refer to representative institutions though they mention baronial parliaments.[2] Stubbs' account of Thomas' aims is clearly derived from a more oratorical but less famous source than the Ordinances, namely the St. Albans chronicler's account of the deathbed speech to him of his father-in-law, the earl of Lincoln, who exhorted him to do all in his power "to relieve the oppressions of the church and the people, notably financial oppressions", and to see that the king followed the counsel of his native-born barons.[3] Thomas in fact was not interested in the House of Commons, and Stubbs says so:[4] according to his interpretation of the Statute of York, it was to Edward II that its establishment as an integral part of parliament was due.[5] Thomas cared for nothing but his own interests; "the cause was better than the man"[6] and Tout hardly goes beyond Stubbs in labelling Thomas "that most impossible of all medieval politicians—without dignity, patriotism or common-sense—sulky, vindictive, self-seeking, brutal and vicious".[7]

Nor can any formulation of principle be ascribed to Henry of Lancaster, Thomas' brother, whose influence was exploited by Isabella and Mortimer in overthrowing Edward II and who lent active support to the overthrow of Mortimer himself in his turn. It seems highly probable that his main object in 1326 was to

---

[1] To be found in full in *Rot. Parl.* i. 281-6 or *Stat. R.*, i. 157; abridged in Lodge and Thornton, *Eng. Const. Documents*, pp. 12 ff.

[2] Chs. 9, 14, 22, 25, 29, 40.   [3] Trokelowe (R.S.), pp. 72-3.

[4] *S.C.H.* II, § 254, pp. 350 f.   [5] *S.C.H.* II, § 224, p. 246; § 254, p. 352.

[6] *S.C.H.* II, § 254, p. 349.

[7] *Place of Edward II in English History* (2nd ed. 1936), p. 16.

recover the Lancastrian estates forfeited by his brother.[1] Stratford, who drew up the articles of deposition in 1327, and who played a leading part in the crisis of 1341, has the best claim, as both Stubbs and Tout say, to be considered the mouthpiece of the "anti-royal, baronial, Lancaster party", but he also was an arrant time-server, out for his own interests.[2] If we look for the formulation of constitutional theory in the fourteenth century the doctrines ascribed to the younger Despenser or set forth in the *Modus tenendi parliamenti*, are far more "democratic" than anything we can confidently associate with any Lancastrian party.[3]

The second Henry, Blanche's father, was an entirely loyal soldier and diplomatist. He was a member of one of the two religious gilds that founded Corpus Christi College, Cambridge, and the self-portrait that he left, all unconsciously, in his *Livre de Seyntes Medicines* justifies Froissart's praises and reveals a Christian gentleman who might well have been the original of Chaucer's very perfect gentle knight, but hardly a party leader.[4]

When, after the lull of 1341-71, the constitutional conflict awakes again in the Good Parliament, the Lancastrian faction is on the side resisting reform. Maude Clarke maintains that John of Gaunt was the first to formulate the doctrine of high prerogative developed by Richard II[5] and Stubbs regards him as a traitor to the good cause, "the cause of the Commons", and says it was left to his younger brother Thomas of Woodstock to "re-form the Lancastrian party" and lead the opposition to Richard II,[6] thereby provoking the king to more explicit assertions of the doctrine of prerogative and divine right. But Stubbs admits that this opposition was more concerned with interest than with principle. Richard, as it were, made his opponents constitutionalists *malgré*

---

[1] D. Hughes, *The Early Years of Edward III* (University of London Press, 1915), p. 1; Stubbs, *Hist. Introd. to Rolls Series*, p. 516.

[2] Tout, *Admin. Hist.* III, 40 f.; *Edward II*, p. 209; Hughes, pp. 2 f.; Wilkinson, *Chancery*, pp. 106-9; *S.C.H.* II, § 255, p. 361; § 258, pp. 384 ff.

[3] Lodge and Thornton, *op. cit.*, pp. 18 f.; M. V. Clarke, *Representation and Consent*, pp. 388 f.

[4] E. J. Arnould, in *Bulletin of John Rylands Library* (October 1937); editor of *Le Livre de Seyntes Medicines* (Anglo-Norman Text. Soc. Oxford, 1940).

[5] *Fourteenth-Century Studies*, p. 36. Cf. Armitage Smith, *John of Gaunt* (1904), pp. 146 f.

[6] *S.C.H.* II, § 265, pp. 464, 469.

eux. "They worked out the result almost unconsciously", he says.[1] Even though Henry put forward a fantastic legitimist claim quite inconsistent with a parliamentary title, he could still appear as a champion of the faithful commons;[2] the deposition of Richard, though not "the pure and legitimate result of a series of constitutional conclusions" was yet essentially "an assertion of national right against absolute government".[3]

Thus equivocally is Stubbs' "Lancastrian experiment" launched and his "Lancastrian constitution" inaugurated. The conflict between the historian's honesty and the special pleader's eloquence continues. It was, he practically says, the logic of events that compelled the Lancastrian dynasty to be constitutional rulers. "The reality of their constitutional title was more completely recognized in later times than in the age in which it was practically vindicated." "The theory of parliamentary institutions was advanced and accepted by the different factions in the government" rather than acted upon to a very great extent in the first half of the fifteenth century.[4] He almost tells us that the constitutionality of the Lancastrian experiment is, like beauty, in the eye of the beholder. He anticipates every criticism. He says, in effect, that it is Richard's theory of the prerogative that creates the presumption of a counter-theory; "the growth of constitutional life is stimulated by the growth of royal assumption ... and for every assertion of national right there is a counter assertion of royal authority".[5] It was Richard II, in fact, who created the Lancastrian legend.

What about the constitutional experiment of the fifteenth century, and Stubbs' third volume? Stubbs begins with the remark, "If the only object of constitutional history were the investigation of the origins and forms of parliament, the study of the subject might be suspended at the deposition of Richard II to be resumed under the Tudors";[6] the fifteenth century is for him a period of definition and conservation rather than development. His altogether admirable twentieth chapter, cautious, learned, well-documented, on the organization of the House of Commons

[1] *S.C.H.* II, § 268, p. 500.
[2] *S.C.H.* II, § 269, p. 507.
[3] *S.C.H.* II, § 273, p. 515.
[4] *S.C.H.* III, § 364, p. 237.
[5] *S.C.H.* II, § 273, pp. 513-14.
[6] *S.C.H.* III, § 299, p. 2.

under the three Henries bears out this promise; it is quite indispensable, and in some respect less misleading than the more detailed work of the late H. L. Gray on the *Influence of the Commons on early Legislation*.[1] But in spite of the soundness of his approach to institutional history, Stubbs' narrative continually suggests constitutional advance and the battle of two constitutional theories. He draws the picture of a council nominated by and responsible to parliament, a sort of fifteenth-century cabinet system; he builds up the picture of a Yorkist tyranny which makes the revolutions by which Edward IV and Richard III ascended the throne utterly different from those which displaced Edward II and Richard II. Yet, as he himself shows and as Mr. Chrimes and others have elaborated at length, Richard of York put forward his claim to the succession with every deference to the rights of parliament,[2] and parliament itself declined to pronounce on them; and the accession of Richard III was buttressed with every conceivable form that could do deference to the legislative status of parliament, almost, it would seem, imitating the procedure of 1399. The three estates besought him to assume the Crown as his brother's lawful heir, accepting a cock-and-bull story that bastardized the children of Edward IV, reminiscent of the one trumped up by Henry IV. He occupied the empty throne in Westminster Hall as hereditary and elected king, and it was parliament which, "seeing that the declaration of any truth or right by the three estates in parliament and by authority of the same maketh before all other things most faith and certainty", declared him king and secured the throne to him and the heirs of his body.[3] The terms "extraordinary and clumsy expedient" used by Stubbs to describe the proceedings might equally well have been used of the manoeuvres of 1399, so minutely examined by Lapsley, Richardson and Wilkinson, who, with all their labours, subtlety and skill have hardly done more than fill out the cautiously worded outlines of Stubbs, the perfect hedger.[4] There is, then, no

---

[1] Cambridge, Mass., 1932. [2] Chrimes, *Constitutional Ideas*, pp. 27-31.
[3] *S.C.H.* III, § 360, p. 224; § 361, pp. 228 f.
[4] *S.C.H.* II, §§ 268-9, pp. 502-9; III, § 302, pp. 9-14; Lapsley in *E.H.R.* (1934, 1938); Richardson in *E.H.R.* (1937), and *Bulletin of Hist. Inst.* (October 1939); Wilkinson in *E.H.R.* (1939).

evidence that either in theory or practice the Lancastrians made any break with the past.

Very much remains to be done on the history of the fifteenth century: and I am glad to think that it is not only in Oxford and London that its bewildering records are being closely investigated. I owe to a Cambridge researcher the suggestion that it is Stubbs' quite unjustified condemnation of the Yorkists which throws into such strong relief the Lancastrian legend. Stubbs attributes to spontaneous revival the evident economic advance in the sixties and seventies, when all the evidence goes to show that the general improvement and the economic revival were alike attributable to the energy and firm government of Edward IV.[1] The Yorkists were indeed, as J. R. Green suggested, but as Stubbs was reluctant to admit, the forerunners of the Tudors.

We can thus accept Stubbs' picture of the establishment in the fifteenth century of the tradition of parliamentary practice, whilst looking for more light on the development of the office of Speaker.[2] We can note that Mr. McFarlane agrees with Stubbs as to the importance and independence of the knights of the shire,[3] while observing that Miss McKisack's and Lord Wedgwood's discoveries suggest queries as to the origins and affinities of some of the borough representatives.[4] Institutional progress and social change that was transforming the relations of the different elements in the constitution, we must allow; but on the general issue of an advanced and precocious constitutional theory, closely associated with the functions of parliament, the examples of archaic thought adduced by Plucknett and Chrimes fully justify Galbraith's summary: "The facts had out-run the theory; constitutional practice had outrun constitutional progress."[5]

Plucknett in his essay of 1924 shows that no public law as

[1] I owe these suggestions to Mr. J. R. Lander of Pembroke College.

[2] Such light is now forthcoming from the work of J. S. Roskell. See "The Medieval Speakers for the Commons in Parliament" *Bulletin Inst. Hist. Research* 1950, pp. 31-52 and a succession of later studies.

[3] *Trans. R. Hist. Soc.* (1944).

[4] McKisack, *Representation of English Boroughs* (Oxford, 1932), pp. 45-64; Wedgwood, *Hist. of Parl. 1439-1509* (1938), *Register of Members*, pp. cxvi-cxxvi.

[5] For Plucknett see following note; for Chrimes, *Cont. Ideas*, pp. 196 ff.; for Galbraith, *History* (March 1942), p. 233.

distinct from private law was yet in being.[1] As in 1399, when Richard II's subjects deserted him for Bolingbroke, because as Maude Clarke shows,[2] they felt their private possessions and rights endangered by his attacks upon the law, so in 1470, when Sir John Fortescue wrote,[3] it was the common law, that mass of rules and practices safeguarding private property and private right, that was still the guarantee of English liberty when contrasted with French slavery. The authority of statute law is a lawyer's, rather than a politician's, conception; the alliance of parliament and the common lawyers had little to do with the will of the nation in matters of government. A strong and well-endowed monarch, with an inexpugnable hereditary title, is in Fortescue's eyes no menace to liberty, because he will be the better able to fulfil his age-old task of upholding the law and doing justice. It is true that in the future the established rule that the consent of the representative element in parliament was necessary for extraordinary taxation was to be the purchase for all further acquisition of power by parliament, but to contemporary consciousness not the House of Commons, but the common law was the main safeguard against tyranny bequeathed by the fifteenth to the sixteenth and seventeenth centuries. I believe that to be the main caution that one ought to enter against Stubbs' interpretation of medieval political attitudes. But we must, once and for all, get rid of the Lancastrian label and see our later Plantagenets as one dynasty trying to tackle the problems of government with much the same tools and much the same principles, or lack of principle, whether they are descended from the older or the younger sons of Edward III.

One more point before I conclude. Petit-Dutaillis attacks Stubbs for his character drawing. "Like many Englishmen, he had little imagination, and I wonder whether he fully understood such characters as Henry II, John Lackland, Edward I, Henry V, and what manner of men the chiefs of the baronial opposition were", he says, and he proceeds to characterize Henry II as "neurasthenic",

---

[1] *Tudor Studies* (ed. Seton Watson, London, 1924), pp. 161-81.
[2] *Fourteenth-Century Studies*, pp. 99-114.
[3] *De laudibus legum Anglie* (ed. S. B. Chrimes), p. lxxxviii.

John as "troubled by a psychic excitation which has been defined by our alienists" and Henry III as "ludicrous".[1] Stubbs' best character sketches are to be found in the historical introductions to the volumes he edited in the Rolls Series, and to anyone who has read them the shoe seems on the other foot. Stubbs knows his men most intimately; he knew their times also.

A careful reading of the history of the Angevin kings might tempt one to think that the legend of their diabolical origin was not a fairy-tale, but . . . the mystical expression of a strong historical instinct . . . The long pageant shows us under so great a variety of individual character such signs of great gifts and opportunities thrown away, such unscrupulousness in action, such uncontrolled passion, such vast energy and strength wasted on unworthy aims, such final disappointment in spite of brilliant achievements as remind us of those unhappy spirits who, through the Middle Ages, were continually spending superhuman strength in building in a night inaccessible bridges or uninhabitable castles, or purchasing with untold treasures souls that might have been had for nothing and invariably cheated of their reward.[2]

Does neurasthenia or psychic excitation take us much further? I think I prefer the vocabulary of the nineteenth century.

But of course Stubbs applies the moral measuring rod. His kings are "good" and "bad". In this he is followed today by Powicke, who does not hesitate to call John a "clever, amusing, unreliable, distrustful and thoroughly bad man".[3] Powicke's Henry III, painted on a larger canvas, with a more variegated palette, is recognizably akin to Stubbs' outline sketch, "John and Henry III had in common a certain feminine quality of irresolute pertinacity. Both had a gift of rash, humorous sarcasm."[4] Will anyone maintain that Petit-Dutaillis' "ludicrous" hits the mark better? Galbraith in his brilliant article on "Good kings and bad kings in Medieval English History"[5] suggests that in Stubbs' verdicts the bishop prevailed over the historian, but shows pretty conclusively that the moral standard was the only one used by the medieval chronicler, Stubbs' chief source, as it must be ours.

[1] *Studies Supplementary to Stubbs*, p. 310.
[2] *Historical Introductions to the Rolls Series*, p. 91.
[3] *Cam. Med. Hist.*, VI, 220.
[4] *S.C.H.* II, § 178, p. 99; Powicke, *Henry III and the Lord Edward*, *passim*.
[5] *History* (1945), pp. 119-32.

H

Maitland put his finger on the supreme difficulty that faces the medieval historian; that of thinking the thoughts of a past age. As Galbraith says, the assumptions that the medieval chroniclers are so different from our own that the problem of interpreting their evidence is highly complicated. Victorian standards of morals, like Victorian views of the English constitution, are naturally not those of the 1940's; in the twenty-first century our views will "date" as surely as Stubbs', and we shall be very lucky if our facts are as sound. The historian Stubbs transcends the bishop as he transcends the old Whig.

Most of this article has been devoted to discussing Stubbs' faults of omission and commission. But after all these reservations have been made, a vital and magnificent achievement remains. It is not only the learning, which dwarfs the small-scale recon-structions of modern scholarship and converts his critics into champions (as Lytton Strachey, having flayed the Victorians, was conquered by Victoria) so that even Petit-Dutaillis admits that it is "a fundamental book",[1] and not only Maitland, Maude Clarke, Wilkinson and Eileen Power but Jolliffe, Richardson, Galbraith, even Chrimes, all find themselves coming back to Stubbs, whilst Powicke has almost justified the Stubbsian "nation" by producing the village of Great Peatling to show that in the year 1265 "the peasants of a village community had grasped the idea of the com-munity of the realm".[2] It is not only the scholar whose own weapons we have to borrow if we wish to attack him who con-fronts us; it is the historian with his wisdom, his sense of pro-portion, his far-ranging vision, that sweeps over the whole con-fused field of institutional evolution. May I recall to you his incomparable summary of the effects of the Norman Conquest, his mastery of the Angevin period, his just estimate of the place of both Church and baronage in the story, and above all his insis-tence on the contribution of the local communities of village, hundred, borough and shire to the political education and insti-tutional growth of the English people? As he anticipates the latest school of continental students of the *ancien régime* by defining

[1] *Studies Supplementary to Stubbs*, p. 305.
[2] *Henry III and the Lord Edward*, p. 510; and see above, pp. 81-82.

parliament as an assembly of estates,[1] so he vindicates its continuity from the England of Edgar and Edward the Confessor by calling it a concentration of local communities—a *communitas communitatum*.[2] I suggested that he slighted the economic aspect of history, but, as if to catch his critics out on the last wicket, his final chapter is devoted to the social and economic make-up of medieval England; inadequate by modern standards, but full of suggestive facts, and reflecting an intimacy with English towns and shires in which, I would venture to guess, he has only been surpassed by the Master of Trinity.[3] In his last letters the Yorkshireman is well on top.[4] He knew his England as he knew his Middle Ages. Although we may regret the bishop who ousted the professor, we may be glad of the country parson who made him; who managed to fit in two services a day and 100 sermons a year, and bring up a family of nine while compiling the *Registrum Anglicanum*, translating Mosheim, writing for the *Gentleman's Magazine* and editing the *Itinerarium Ricardi Primi*, Benedict Abbas, Hoveden, and the rest.[5] He was a born scholar; he grubbed in the muniments of Knaresborough Castle before he was nominated to a servitorship at Christchurch;[6] but he learned some things in sixteen years of parish life which are hid from the don in his study. And when he closes his great book by calling on the historian not only "to rest content with nothing less than attainable truth" but also "to base his arguments on that highest justice which is found in the deepest sympathy with erring and straying men", we recognize that it is, in fact, his moral certainty and his religious conviction that impose unity and order on his vast and varied matter and form the rock on which his great structure is based.

[1] See above, pp. 161, 174.
[2] *S.C.H.* II, § 184, p. 161; § 185, p. 166.
[3] G. M. Trevelyan.
[4] Hutton, pp. 378-92.
[5] Hutton, pp. 35 f., 53, 409 f.
[6] Hutton, p. 16.

XII

Maitland—the Historians' Historian[1]

WHEN MAITLAND died, in 1906, one friend noted "the smallness of the ripple on the general consciousness caused by the passing of England's greatest historian since Gibbon and Macaulay".[2] His indignation was shared on the other side of the Atlantic; Americans recalled that when Gardiner, Creighton and Stubbs were still living, Acton had ranked Maitland as the ablest historian in England.[3] Tributes poured in from the scholars of France, Italy, Germany, and the United States, and the University of Oxford sent a special message of condolence on his loss to the University of Cambridge—a gesture, as far as I know, without parallel. But *The Times* only accorded him a third of a column. Spenser has been called the poets' poet; Maitland seems to be the historians' historian. Today when there is talk of history as literature it is the rarest thing for Maitland to be named. Yet the union of grace, wit and humour with the most exacting standards of scholarship and the most exquisite sense of language is not so common that we can afford to forget Maitland.

If we attempt to define the peculiar merits of Maitland as a historian and to estimate his contribution to the interpretation of English history, we shall find, I think, that there is one and the same explanation for his special gifts and for his failure to attract the general public. Law was his guiding light; and the legal approach to history is too impersonal for the average reader, who demands incident and characterization from his historical writers. Maitland came to history by way of law. His sister has traced the stages of the fourteen-year journey; from mathematics (where

[1] Reprinted, with some omissions and alterations, from the introduction to *Selected Historical Essays of F. W. Maitland*, published in association with the Selden Society at the University Press Cambridge, 1957. Their permission to reprint is hereby acknowledged.
[2] T. Seccombe, in *The Bookman* (February 1907), p. 216.
[3] Munro Smith, in *Political Science Quarterly* (1907), p. 282.

he did badly), and moral sciences (where he excelled), by convey-ancing work in chambers (that admirable introduction to the science of diplomatic),[1] and extension lecturing to workmen and others,[2] to his first brilliant essays in legal journalism and the meeting with Vinogradoff, on a Sunday tramp in January, 1884, which "determined the course of his life".[3] He was to be not a legal practitioner, but a legal historian; he had "discovered the work that it was best for him to do".[4]

Of his great services to the study of law others can speak; I am concerned here with his services to history. He brought law to bear on history. The history of law was not a specialized sub-section of the history of England; it was an integral part of it; it was the key to the whole story. Stubbs had traced in masterly fashion the evolution of English self-government from the practices of primitive local communities; Maitland put the com-mon law back in the centre of the picture, and with it the monarchy. It was the king's court that had made the law common to all England: by making himself the protector of the lawful possessor, great or small, the king had bound together the rights of ruler and subject. And the work of Henry II was carried on under his grandson. By dwelling on the great constructive work of the great judges, Bracton's masters, Maitland restored the reign of Henry III to its proper position in English history, taking the eyes of the student off the wearisome involutions of the struggles between king and barons.

Later historians were to pursue in detail the amazing story of the branches thrown out by that central trunk—"the trans-formations of the Curia Regis"; but even before the great *History of English Law* had appeared Maitland had fitted parliament into the picture. As he had said of the jury, "it was not popular, but royal"; as his American disciples were to emphasize, it was judicial before it was legislative.

[1] H. A. L. Fisher, *Frederic William Maitland* (Cambridge, 1910) (henceforth cited as Fisher), p. 17.

[2] His lectures on "The Cause of High and Low Wages" at the Artizans' Institute, Upper St. Martin's Lane, when he was twenty-four, seem to have anticipated W. E. A. technique. See H. Solly, *These Eighty Years*, II. 440.

[3] Letter to Vinogradoff, 15 November 1891 (Fisher, p. 51).

[4] Mrs. Reynell in *Cambridge Law Journal* (1951), p. 73.

But if Maitland brought law to bear on history, he brought history to bear on law. Again and again he emphasized the danger of imposing legal concepts of a later date on facts of an earlier date—a common fault, before his time, of the majority of legal historians and of many constitutional historians. We must not read either law or history backwards. We must learn to think the thoughts of a past age—"the common thoughts of our forefathers about common things". "We must not attribute precise ideas or well defined law to the German conquerors of Britain." It is as if "we armed Hengist and Horsa with machine-guns or pictured the Venerable Bede correcting proofs".[1]

The debt of Maitland's two mistresses was mutual. The technique which makes his exposition of general principles so vivid and arresting is that of the lawyer. Every generalization is seen in terms of the individual, every principle in its application to a particular case. As Vinogradoff said, "what he wanted most was to trace ideas to their embodiment in facts".[2] A brilliant example of his method is the imaginary situation arising from a homicide, by which Maitland drives home the effects of the impact of feudalism on Anglo-Saxon law and the practical reasons for the substitution of amercement for the old *wite* and *bot* system.

Let us suppose that a man learned in the law is asked to advise upon a case of homicide. Godwin and Roger met and quarrelled, and Godwin slew Roger. What must be paid; by whom; to whom? Our jurist is not very careful about those psychical elements of the case which might interest us, but on the other hand he requires information about a vast number of particulars which would seem to us trivial. He can not begin to cast up his sum until he has before him some such statement as this: Godwin was a free ceorl of the Abbot of Ely: Roger, the son of a Norman father, was born of an English mother and was a vavassor of Count Alan: the deed was done on the Monday after Septuagesima, in the county of Cambridge, on a road which ran between the land which Gerard a Norman knight held of Count Eustace and the land of the Bishop of Lincoln: this road was not one of the king's highways: Godwin was pursued by the neighbours into the county of Huntingdon and arrested on the land of the Abbot of Ramsey: Roger, when the encounter took place, was on his way to the hundred moot: he has left a widow, a paternal uncle and a maternal aunt. As a matter of fact, the result will probably be that Godwin, unable to

[1] *Domesday Book and Beyond*, pp. 356, 520.
[2] *E.H.R.*, 1907, p. 282.

satisfy the various claims to which his deed has given rise, will be hanged or mutilated. . . . The old law consisted very largely of rules about these matters; but it is falling to pieces under the pressure of those new elements which feudalism has brought with it.[1]

This descent to the concrete brings us close to the circumstances and ways of life of the dramatis personae, as well as to the rules of law. And the introductions to the Year Books which, he says, "come to us from life", are also introductions to the mental habits of young lawyers learning the law by listening to older lawyers discussing the cases and of judges illustrating their judgements with anecdotes. As G. M. Trevelyan has said, Maitland uses law as a tool to open the mind of medieval man. He never loses sight of the individuals who created and worked the institutions that he is investigating.

Such a technique could only be used by a master of original material. Maitland's first work had been the editing of legal records,[2] as his last years were to be spent on editing law reports. No one has sung the praises of the Public Record Office more eloquently than Maitland, to whom "the whereabouts of the first-hand evidence for the law of the Middle Ages" had come as a dazzling discovery seven years after he was called to the bar[3]—it was "the most glorious store of material for legal history that has ever been collected in one place".[4]

ii

Such an approach to law and history involves intimacy not only with persons[5] but with places. Along with a taste for first-hand evidence Maitland inherited from his grandfather, the ecclesiastical historian, an estate in Gloucestershire. The Downing Professor was

[1] *History of English Law* (2nd ed.), I. 106-7.

[2] *Pleas of the Crown for the County of Gloucester, 1221* (1884); *Bracton's Notebook*, containing 2,000 cases extracted from the rolls of the King's Court, 1217-40 (1886).

[3] Maitland was working at the Record Office as early as February 1884, well before the May conversation with Vinogradoff described by Fisher, pp. 24 ff. For evidence see Powicke, *Modern Historians and the Study of History* (1955), p. 10; and Plucknett in "Maitland's view of Law and History", *Law Quarterly Review* (1951), pp. 85-7. For his familiarity with medieval *printed* court rolls by 1881, see his postcard to Pollock (Fisher, p. 38).

[4] Inaugural lecture, reprinted, *Collected Papers of F. W. Maitland*, 1911. I. 595-6. Cited as *Coll. Pap.*

[5] Maitland's eldest daughter was named after a lady in *Bracton's Notebook*, i, 16, 93-95; iii, No. 1843 (margin).

Lord of the Manor of Brookthorpe.[1] Like Stubbs he comes down to the earth he knows in his picture of his native county in 1221— or rather, as he says, "a photograph of English life as it was early in the thirteenth century in its most vital parts—the system of local government and police, the organization of county, hundred and township". Look again at the two sections of the Ordnance Survey placed between pages 16 and 17 of *Domesday Book and Beyond* to make his point about nucleated villages and hamlets; or at his picture of the open fields of his other home, Cambridge, in the Ford Lectures on *Township and Borough*.[2] Only those who have themselves tried to write the history of the city of Cambridge can justly value the depths of his knowledge of "the town in which I live". But both in his study of Cambridge and in that of the Cambridgeshire village of Wilburton[3] the special local problems are never isolated from the general problems that they may help to elucidate: in the one case the corporation theory, in the other the transformation of villein into copyholder. Maitland's analysis and interpretation of the Wilburton rolls has been the model for and the precursor of many such studies since 1894, but their value is in no sense superseded. Each manor has its own history, and it is as true now as when Maitland wrote that "the time has not yet come when generalities about *the* English manor and its fortunes will be safe or sound".

The court leet of the manor had been constantly mentioned by local historians, but its origin and its functions in relation to the national system of justice had not been fully grasped. In his introduction to *Select Pleas in Manorial Courts*[4] Maitland, after discussing the Quo Warranto investigations of seignorial liberties, showed the relation of the leet to the sheriff's tourn and, for the first time, traced the origin of their presenting juries to the Assize of Clarendon (1166).[5] His description of the double presentment

---

[1] Strictly speaking, farmer of the manor, which the family held at lease from the see of Gloucester. [2] Cambridge, 1898.

[3] *E.H.R.*, July 1894; *Coll. Pap.*, II. 366-406; *Selected Historical Essays*. (Cited as *Sel. Hist. Ess.*), pp. 16-40.

[4] Selden Society, vol. 2, for 1888.

[5] For more recent discussions of the jury of presentment see Van Caenegem, introduction to *Royal Writs in England from the Conquest to Glanvill*, (Selden Soc.), vol. 77, for 1958-59, p. 58, n. 1.

by free and unfree jurors made clear the functioning of an institution intimately bound up with the king's peace and the king's revenue, and not only the king's. To the sheriff's tourn corresponded the courts leet held by lords of manors to whom the functions and profits of such a court had been delegated by the king—or who had annexed them without grant. An essential part of the machinery of justice and police in the twelfth century, courts leet and private views of frankpledge had a solid financial value to their holders long after the justices of the peace had made them superfluous for judicial purposes.

iii

"Pollock and I have mapped out a big work, too big I fear for the residue of our joint lives." So Maitland wrote in November 1889,[1] and *The History of English Law before the time of Edward I* was his principal concern for the next five years. He wrote all of it except the chapter on Anglo-Saxon Law, about which, he told Vinogradoff in May 1892, he was not too happy. "My effort now is to shove on with the general sketch of the Norman and Angevin periods so that my collaborator may have little to do before we reach the Year Book period—if we ever reach it."[2] No student of English history needs an introduction to Book I of the *History;* its four last are indispensable reading for anyone who would understand the origins of our constitution. Less familiar are the articles written for the *Encyclopaedia Britannica* in Las Palmas in December 1899—"the work of a bookless imagination, but dates were brought from England"[3]—a dazzling *oeuvre de vulgarisation,*[4] and the series contributed to *Social England* (1894–98).[5] The last of these is especially valuable as covering the period subsequent to Edward I,[6] and ends with one of Maitland's happiest *dicta:* "Were we to say that equity saved the common law, and that the Court of Star Chamber saved the constitution, even in this

[1] Letter to M. M. Bigelow, 24 November 1889.
[2] C.U.L. Add. MS. 7005 D, No. 14. They did not reach the Year Book period; apart from some fragmentary fore-runners, for which see Selden Society, vol. 60 (1950), the Year Books only begin after 1272.
[3] Letter to Pollock (Fisher, p. 117).
[4] *Encyclopaedia Britannica,* 11th ed. IX. 600–7. *Sel. Hist. Ess.,* pp. 97–121.
[5] *Coll. Pap.,* II. 477–96. [6] *Sel. Hist. Ess.,* pp. 122–134.

paradox there would be some truth." There followed *English Law and the Renaissance*, the Rede Lecture given in 1901,[1] in which Maitland drew a picture of English Law against the background of the sixteenth century, a picture whose colours, critics today agree, are unduly heightened. But nowhere else do we so unmistakably catch the accents of the speaker who "heard his words as he wrote them".[2] Further, it exemplifies its author's saying "History involves comparison, and the English lawyer who knows nothing and cares nothing for any system but his own hardly comes in sight of the idea of legal history."[3] From these luminous surveys of the history of English Law we get a notion of what Pollock meant when he spoke of the transformation that Maitland's genius had accomplished. Twenty-five years ago the early history of the Common Law, he said, had been "obscure, isolated, a seeming chaos of technical antiquities. Maitland commanded the dry bones to live, and henceforth they are alive."[4]

iv

If we were to ask what had been Maitland's chief impact on the teaching of history we should, I suppose, put first his presentation of Henry II as founder of the Common Law, and with it of the English monarchy as the effective guardian of justice to all. But today we should unhesitatingly set alongside this his contribution to the history of parliament in his edition of the Parliament Roll of 1305—The *Memoranda de Parliamento*.[5] Yet when the "trail-blazing" introduction[6] appeared in 1893, it passed largely unregarded. Its wider implications were not perceived. It was a seed cast on barren ground and the germination was slow. Not until McIlwain's *High Court of Parliament* appeared in 1910, three

---

[1] Cambridge, 1901. Reprinted in *Anglo-American Legal Essays*, 1907, and *Sel. Hist. Ess.*, pp. 135-151.

[2] Ermengard Maitland, *F. W. Maitland, A Child's-eye View* (Selden Society, 1957), p. 8.

[3] Inaugural Lecture: *Coll. Pap.* 1. 488.

[4] *Proceedings of the British Academy*, 1905-6, p. 456.

[5] *Records of the Parliament holden at Westminster on the 28th day of February 1305* (Rolls Series vol. 98).

[6] The adjective is Professor Schuyler's. *American Historical Review*, 1952, p. 318. The greater part of the introduction was reprinted in Maitland, *Selected Essays* (Cambridge, 1936), pp. 1-72, and again in *Sel. Hist. Ess.* (1957), pp. 52-96.

years after Maitland's death, was there any explicit recognition of what it meant for parliamentary studies, which had, in effect, marked time for some twenty years.

The genesis of this volume has not, I think, been traced before now. Early in the New Year of 1889, shortly after his election to the Downing Professorship, Maitland agreed to edit a volume of "Petitions to Parliament" for the Rolls Series, and the Treasury formally approved the project in May.[1] In August Maitland confided to Vinogradoff, "I have had a good holiday and am now going to do a little work in the Record Office. I want just to start the edition of the 10,000 odd petitions to King and Council but when it is well started I hope to get out of it."[2] But on 1 October Maitland reported to Maxwell-Lyte that he must suggest a change of plans. It was impossible to produce a scholarly edition of the petitions until they had been dated, and as their original grouping had been disturbed by editors whose identifications must be tested, this would be the work of years. Instead, Maitland proposed to edit "one very early roll of parliament that has not yet been printed" and to "illustrate the enrolments of the petitions and responses by the petitions themselves and by the writs whereby effect was given to the responses . . . thus bringing out the connexion between the different parts of the government machinery . . . I cannot help thinking that one roll of parliament properly illustrated would be of much greater value than a mere collection of petitions conjecturally dated".[3] The change of plan was apparently approved before the end of November 1889, but Maitland's other weighty commitments presumably took precedence. In April 1892, however, "his head was full of it",[4] and by May the printers were receiving the text. Early in 1893 the first part of the introduction was being submitted to Maxwell-Lyte[5] and by the end of November the book was out.[6]

In October, while revising the proofs, Maitland had written to

[1] P.R.O. 8/131, pp. 387, 424. I have to thank the Deputy Keeper of the Records for permission to see this correspondence.

[2] C.U.L. Add. MS. 7005 D, No. 10.   [3] P.R.O. 8/131, pp. 482 ff.

[4] Letter to Round, 10 April 1892, London University Library (henceforth cited as L.U.L.) 653.

[5] P.R.O. 8/212. Letters of 7 May 1892, 30 May 1893.

[6] Information from Director of Publications, H.M.S.O.

Round "I am trailing my coat through many fairs."[1] But no one was moved to tread on it. When, in June 1894, Maitland wrote to thank Round for "an extremely kind review of my parliament roll in the *Athenaeum*" he added "Your praise is the more welcome because no one else out of Scotland has said one word of the book."[2] Apart from Round's review, a negligible note in *Notes and Queries* and an admirable notice by Langlois in the *English Historical Review*,[3] it would seem that critics had failed to react to the provocation insinuated by Maitland. Round and Langlois, like Baldwin later, concentrated on the value of the introduction for the history of the Council; Fisher and Tout stressed the value of the text in illustrating the activities of an early parliament. But Stubbs' model parliament in effect held the field until well after Maitland's death. A.L. Smith in his deeply felt eulogium of Maitland, indeed, went so far as to regret that Maitland should have been put to such hack work. To him it was "a harnessing of Pegasus to a cart . . ." It was "like finding an electric light left on in a cellar".[4]

As late as 1911, Tout, criticizing Fisher for his failure to appreciate Maitland's permanent contribution to the study of English medieval history, makes no reference to it.[5] In 1920 A. F. Pollard declared that Maitland's essay had been generally ignored by English instructors of youth for nearly a generation.[6] Whatever may have occurred in lecture rooms—and Lapsley, in 1936, suggests that it was being recommended to students as a "standard" work before 1910[7]—there seems no evidence in print of the recognition by scholars that it was a turning point in parliamentary studies before McIlwain proclaimed its importance.[8]

[1] Letter to Round, 30 October 1893 (L.U.L. 653).

[2] Letter preserved at Girton College, Cambridge. I have been unable to trace any Scottish notice of the *Memoranda*. George Neilson, or possibly Bain, may have written to Maitland.

[3] *The Athenaeum*, March 1894, pp. 273 f.; *Notes and Queries*, 22 September 1894; *E.H.R.*, October 1894, pp. 755-8. Even Langlois, however, failed to appreciate all the implications of Maitland's essay for English parliamentary history.

[4] *F. W. Maitland: Two Lectures* (Oxford, 1908), p. 38.

[5] *Scottish Hist. Rev.*, 1911, p. 74.   [6] *Evolution of Parliament* (1920), p. vi.

[7] Maitland, *Selected Essays* (Cambridge, 1936), p. 2.

[8] But Baldwin, reviewing *The High Court of Parliament,* observed that the author's views were "current among various writers of the School of Maitland". *Amer. Hist. Rev.*, 1910-11, p. 598. I have failed to find evidence for this.

America and France appear to have been before England. Pasquet in 1914[1] showed a fuller appreciation of Maitland's work than any English writer had so far done. It was not till 1920 that Pollard's lively and readable sketch sent his readers back to the *Memoranda* to discover, as Petit-Dutaillis indicated later,[2] that it was as well to take their Maitland first hand. As Baldwin put it, in his review of *The Evolution of Parliament* in 1921, "The entire history of Parliament must be rewritten;"[3] but it had taken nearly thirty years for that conviction to be generally accepted. The following thirty-five years have seen a laborious and fruitful cultivation of the field that Maitland opened up.[4]

This imperception may in part be attributed to Maitland's modesty[5] and to the seeming tentativeness of his approach. Twice in his introduction he says that it would not be right for an editor in the Rolls Series to propound theories touching debatable matters. In one footnote only does he define a difference from the accepted views. Moreover, much of what he says is to be found in his magnificent but ambiguous master, Stubbs, who was able to cling to his faith in a "Model Parliament" whilst supplying a wealth of evidence that proved that concept misleading. Once again, it is the light of the law that Maitland turns on to history, and in that light the parliaments of Edward I's reign look very different from Stubbs' bifocal vision of them.

What was the new light brought to bear on the history of parliament by what McIlwain has called "the most penetrating of all Maitland's works"? Maitland suggested, only too cautiously, that Parliament was in essence royal, not popular; a court of justice before it was a legislature; an expansion of an aristocratic

---

[1] *Les origines de la Chambre des Communes* (Paris, 1914, translated by R. G. D. Laffan, 1925).

[2] *Studies Supplementary to Stubbs* (English translation, Manchester, 1930), p. 334.

[3] *Amer. Hist. Rev.*, 1921-2, p. 108.

[4] For a brief survey, see Powicke, *The Thirteenth Century* (Oxford, 1953), p. 747; for a more elaborate bibliography, see the *Relazioni* of the Tenth International Congress of Historical Studies (Florence, 1955), vol. I, pp. 36-46.

[5] Even with his reputation established, he could write to Poole, on his election to Ford's lectureship "Didst ever feel like a bubble that was going to be pricked?" *C.H.J.*, 1952, p. 324. (A letter to Round of the same date—23 February 1897—establishes the reference.) And in 1901 he spoke of the Downing Professorship of the Laws of England, which he had held since 1888, as "the chair that I cannot fill".

and bureaucratic council before it had any representative character. But if his observation that things were done in full parliament (a characteristically curial phrase) after both representatives and barons not of the council had gone home was outstandingly significant, the statement that a parliament was "an act rather than a body of persons" was the one most calculated to shake readers out of their established assumptions. Parliament was not an institution, but an event. Things were done *in* parliament, not *by* parliament. "Parliament" cannot, at this stage, be the subject of a verb, nor the object. "One cannot address a petition to a colloquy, a debate."

To whom, then, were the petitions addressed which Maitland had originally been asked to edit?[1] There was in existence in 1305 a body of persons, already an institution, which could be described as taking action; its constitution might be fluctuating, but it could be linked with the king when petitions were addressed to him. "A session of the king's council is the core and essence of every *parliamentum*." In its judicial capacity, reinforced by legal experts, it constitutes the king's highest court, in a supremely solemn session, a tribunal superior to the court *coram rege*, "where judicial doubts are determined, new remedies established for new wrongs, and justice is done to every one according to his deserts".[2]

Starting from the hearing of petitions, Maitland is mainly concerned with the judicial business of a parliament. But the council has executive and advisory functions, and the wrongs for which remedies are sought may have been committed by the king's own agents. The answer to a petition need not be the outcome of a judgement: the writ that implements it may be purely administrative. "The whole governmental force of England is brought into a focus" in a parliament.[3]

---

[1] In writing to Maxwell-Lyte, 6 January 1889, Maitland speaks of petitions *to* parliament; on 7 August 1889, "having made himself familiar with the already printed petitions", he describes them as petitions *in* parliament; on 1 October 1889 he says "though these petitions are said to be heard *at* or *in* a parliament they are addressed to the king or the king and council". P.R.O. 8/131.

[2] Fleta, *Commentarius juris Anglicani, lib.* II. *c.* 2.

[3] "Maitland set himself a definite job—to show how the petitions to the king in council in parliament reveal the relation between various aspects of the administration, and he did this and more very clearly and brilliantly; but, in doing it, I do not think that he com-

A caveat ought here to be entered, necessitated by the results of the research which Maitland's essay has stimulated.

The nature of his record, which is far from giving a complete account of the parliament of Easter, 1305, leads him to underestimate the unofficial or political aspects of a parliament. In this he has had distinguished followers; but the evidence not only of the chroniclers but of Edward's own correspondence is clear.[1] The introduction to the Memoranda was a magnificent attack on "after-mindedness". We were not to interpret the roll of Edward's reign in the light of those of his grandson's or of any later reign. But "Edward I entered into a traditional inheritance".[2] Maitland might justifiably have considered the parliaments of Henry III's reign. It had been the magnates who, in 1258, had provided for three parliaments a year, "to view the state of the realm, and to treat of the common business of the king and the kingdom". The colloquy or debate might be of a political nature: the judgements, as in Segrave's case[3] might have political overtones due to the fact that his judges included not only legal experts but the leading men of the land. The "equitableness" of the tribunal might at times be attributable to political expediency rather than to theories of discretionary power. Perhaps the ultimate supremacy of the king's high court of parliament would owe as much to these factors as to its judicial omnicompetence.

But in 1893 it was the judicial, the official aspect of parliaments that needed to be emphasized. Stubbs' saving clauses had been generally disregarded, and students of history had to be reminded that in 1305 the "assembly of estates" had not yet become part of the national council, and that the elected representatives were not necessarily called upon to vote taxes—the function which in the long run was to give the full-grown House of Commons the key to parliamentary sovereignty.

mited himself to a view of parliament as a court of justice and that alone." Powicke, cited by G. P. Cuttino in *The Forward Movement of the Fourteenth Century*, ed. F. L. Utley (Ohio State University, 1961), pp. 56-7.

[1] Powicke, *The Thirteenth Century*, p. 343.

[2] Powicke, *The Thirteenth Century*, p. 345. See also J. G. Edwards in the *Bulletin Inst. Hist. Research*, 1954, pp. 35-53.

[3] *Sel. Hist. Ess.*, pp. 85-6; Powicke, *The Thirteenth Century*, pp. 331-3.

V

In a much quoted phrase, Maitland called himself a dissenter from all the churches. One who knew him intimately describes him as a "very Protestant agnostic"; but whatever his personal predilections were, his passion for historical truth and legal exactness made him a papalist when determining an issue long obscured by ecclesiastical controversy. In his lectures on constitutional history (1888) he had given a lucid sketch of the relations of church and state in medieval England; in the *History of English Law* (1895) he had traced the frontiers of Common and Canon Law at length. In the summer of 1895, while working on a course of lectures on Canon Law for law students, his study of Lyndwood's *Provinciale*[1] convinced him that Roman or Papal Law had been authoritative in English church courts and that "any special rules of the Church of England had, in the view of the canonist, hardly a wider scope than the by-laws of London in the eye of the English lawyer". English Canon Law, in fact, "was only English because it was universal".[2] This opinion, expounded fully (1896–7) in the three articles reprinted in the volume *Roman Canon Law in the Church of England* (1898) was "an assault on the established theory". Stubbs had said in 1882 that "in England neither the civil law nor the canon law was ever received as authoritative, except educationally",[3] and had justified this position at length in the historical appendices to the Report of the Royal Commission on Ecclesiastical Courts in 1883. The High Anglican party took this as proving the legal continuity of the modern Church of England from that of the Middle Ages. There had been no revolution in the sixteenth century. As Maitland put it, they held that the Church of England "had been Protestant before the Reformation and Catholic afterwards". In 1888, Maitland had summed up the effects of that revolution in the words "Religion has now become

---

[1] Written in 1430; the leading English authority on medieval canon law.

[2] Pollock and Maitland, *History of English Law* (2nd ed.), I. 115.

[3] *Seventeen Lectures on Medieval and Modern History* (1900 ed.), p. 354. In 1900 Stubbs, without being fully convinced, deferred to Maitland's superior learning. *Ibid.*, p. 335, Maitland is today considered to have proved his case. See Holdsworth, *History of English Law* (1922), I. 582.

an affair of statute".[1] By agreeing to follow up his articles on Canon Law with a chapter on the Elizabethan Settlement in the *Cambridge Modern History* projected by Acton and himself[2] he was drawn further into the controversy. Acton, he said later, had induced him to put his hand far into a very nest of hornets.[3] But he had known from the first that he was "trailing his coat",[4] and his correspondence with Round, a Protestant of a very different kidney, reflects a curious alliance. From 1897 to 1899 Round was fanning the flames of controversy with articles in the *Nineteenth Century* and the *Contemporary Review*, on "The Idolatrous Mass" and kindred sixteenth-century subjects. Maitland wrote to him in December 1897 "I do not wonder that your articles should have won praise in more than one camp. I have lately re-read and admired. My suspicion is that the Anglican legend of the Reformation has seen its best day, and that its popularizers have done it a mischief by their recklessness."[5] One of these popularizers, a Canon of Ripon with a large reading public, published an article[6] in which he sought to prove that the Elizabethan Settlement had been approved by Convocation as well as by parliament. He had gone far out of his depth, and his assault on historical fact evoked a rejoinder written, as Le Bras would say "avec une verve discrètement impertinente".[5] Maitland, who had just offended Round by his review of the *Commune of London*, hoped that his prickly ally might be mollified by this trouncing of a common enemy;[8] but apparently in vain. The insensible Mr. MacColl returned to the attack in *The Reformation Settlement examined in the light of History and Law* in 1900, and the ignorance of Canon Law revealed in it was well and truly exposed by Maitland in a more academic article in the *English Historical Review*.[9]

Maitland's account of the Anglican Settlement and the Scottish

[1] *The Constitutional History of England*, p. 512.

[2] "It will be a very strange book, that *History* of ours," he wrote to H. Jackson in 1900 (Fisher, p. 124).

[3] Letter to Jackson (Fisher, p. 152).

[4] Letter to Poole, 15 August 1895 (*C.H.J.*, 1952, p. 322).

[5] Letter at Girton College.　　　　　　　　[6] *Fortnightly Review*, October 1809.

[7] "Canon MacColl's new convocation"; *Fortnightly Review*, December 1899; *Coll. Pap*. III. 119-36; *Sel. Hist. Ess.*, pp. 247-258.

[8] Letter to Poole, 26 November 1899 (*C.H.J.*, 1952, p. 328).

[9] *E.H.R.* January 1901; *Coll. Pap*. III. 137-156.

Reformation,[1] contributed to the second volume of the *Cambridge Modern History*, was a triumphant incursion into fields remote from medieval legal history. It was his main concern after the completion of *Domesday Book and Beyond* (January 1897) and *Township and Borough* (February 1898), and was being revised in the summer of 1899. "Just at present", he wrote to Round in July, "I keep Elizabeth for Sundays".[2] It was in Acton's hands before Maitland left England for the Canaries in November of that year;[3] it only reached the reading public in 1903. But its by-products, the first four "Elizabethan Gleanings", including the delightful "etc." article, and a close study, clause by clause, of the acts of Supremacy and Uniformity, had appeared in the *English Historical Review* in 1900.[4]

Maitland "liked most centuries better than the sixteenth".[5] He also doubted his own ability to handle narrative; few of his readers will share his doubt. He can re-create an atmosphere from details skilfully selected. He can drive home a point with an epigram, and hit off a character or a situation in a phrase that provokes delighted laughter in the reader. Competent judges have borne witness to the "vast erudition" concealed by this lightness of touch. He treads warily, almost daintily, among the complexities of diplomatic and theological rivalries.[6] His interpretation of the steps by which the two great acts of the parliament of 1559 were reached is not accepted by all; but the latest historian to treat of the Elizabethan religious settlement describes it as still "shrouded in mystery".[7] Nor does Maitland's detachment from the conflict mean lack of sympathy or doubt of the genuineness of opinions he does not share. He is at home with the personalities of the sixteenth century. Elizabeth, he held, was actuated by religious rather than by political motives in

---

[1] *Cambridge Modern History* (1903). II. 550-98; *Sel. Hist. Ess.*, pp. 152-210.
[2] 7 July 1899 (L.U.L. 653).   [3] Letter to Jackson (Fisher, p. 125).
[4] The fifth Gleaning was published in July 1903 in the *E.H.R.*
[5] Letter to Round, 29 December 1898 (L.U.L. 653).
[6] His account of John Knox's restraining influence on the English Puritans—"The Coxian Church of England might be an erring sister, but still was a twin sister of the Church of Scotland"—originally ended "So Cox and Knox were satisfied." *Cambridge Law Journal*, 1923, p. 286.
[7] J. E. Neale, *Elizabeth I and her parliaments* (1953), p. 51.

rejecting Rome; and he wrote to Round in February 1898, "I am among Calvin's letters. I think that he and Elizabeth understood each other."[1]

VI

Between 1888 and 1906 Maitland wrote at least thirty-five learned and suggestive reviews of the publications of English and foreign scholars,[2] and his longer writings, both in the text and in the footnotes, constantly, and often warmly, acknowledge his debt to others.[3] From these reviews, and from his correspondence with R. L. Poole, editor of the *English Historical Review*, 1893 to 1906,[4] we can deduce his code for critics. He could master a book with amazing rapidity, and he knew very well what he thought of it, but in pronouncing on its merits his judgements are most delicately balanced between the demands of scholarship and those of the special character and circumstances of the writer. He is reluctant to offer purely destructive criticism. H. B. Simpson on the Constable is "pretty perverse" but contains "no corrigible mis-statements".[5] Apropos of an error that he is intending to correct, he inquires about the writer. "If he is a young man he might like the opportunity of having a second word about his document, and I should be unwilling to hurt his feelings"; and later, in the same connection, "I don't like to see that document lying about unqueried, but would not make an unnecessary fuss."[6] But he took off the gloves when dealing with the egregious errors of the Dean of Lichfield as to the law of marriage in the Middle Ages,[7] and in his exposure of MacColl's discovery of a non-existent convocation, as we have seen, he could be gaily ruthless, though he admitted to Poole that MacColl was an experienced controversialist and a clever tactician.[8] It is in relation to Round, most learned of scholars and most merciless of critics, that these

---

[1] Letter at Girton College.
[2] See A. L. Smith's bibliography of Maitland in *F. W. Maitland: Two Lectures* (Oxford, 1908).
[3] e.g. Liebermann, Round, Stevenson, Vinogradoff.
[4] Printed in the *C.H.J.*, (1952, pp. 318-51.   [5] 7 June 1895 (*C.H.J.*, p. 319).
[6] 29 August 1898, 3 August 1899 (*C.H.J.*, pp. 325-7).
[7] *E.H.R.*, 1895, pp. 755-9, *Coll. Pap.* III. 21-30.
[8] 30 October 1900 (*C.H.J.*, p. 331).

qualities of Maitland shine out most notably. The two had corresponded since 1888.[1] They had exchanged references on such subjects as early fines, and Maitland had held his hand on Domesday Book until Round's *Feudal England* should appear.[2] Maitland was a keen admirer of Round's work and that the admiration was returned appears not only in Round's many reviews of Maitland's books, but in the eloquent tribute to him which he published after his death.[3] But Maitland, like many other scholars, found Round's passion for controversy over the *minutiae* of history unedifying and wearisome. "Is *the* battle over yet?" he had asked, with some amusement, in June 1894,[4] but Round's "terrific conflict" with Freeman and his followers over the battle of Hastings, opened in 1892, was still raging in 1899 when amusement had long ceased and the object of dispute had become "that infernal palisade".[5]

The controversy between Round and Hubert Hall over the *Red Book of the Exchequer*, however, had had uglier aspects and had caused Maitland acuter discomfort. Hall, the much loved helper of generations of workers at the Public Record Office, had been appointed joint editor with Round of the *Red Book* for the Rolls Series in 1890, but the two differed fundamentally as to the trustworthiness of Swereford, the thirteenth-century compiler of the *Red Book*, and after a few months Round resigned. The *Red Book* was published in April 1897. Round had seen the proofs beforehand, and his mouth should therefore have been closed on the subject,[6] but none the less he attacked the editor's errors savagely in various periodicals and finally in a privately printed pamphlet. The controversy was opened by Hall's review of *Feudal England*[7] which had contained observations about the *Red Book* which "my friend Mr Hall" was editing, and Maitland, knowing both men well, foresaw trouble. "I quite agree", he wrote to Round privately, "that the Quarterly Reviewer has a weak spot

---

[1] See the correspondence in the London University Library.

[2] Letter of 18 July 1894, and letter no. 10, which should follow it (L.U.L. 653); letter to Poole, 15 July 1895 (*C.H.J.*, p. 320); preface to *Domesday Book and Beyond*, p. v.

[3] *Peerage and Pedigree* (1910), I. 145-7.   [4] Letter at Girton College.

[5] Letter to Poole, 26 November 1899 (*C.H.J.*, p. 328). For a bibliography of the whole controversy, see *Sussex Archaeological Collections*, vol. xlii.

[6] C. Johnson in *Trans. R. Hist. Soc.*, 1946, p. 3.   [7] *Quarterly Review*, July 1896.

in his love for Swereford, but I think this is evident enough and will do no harm—certainly not to you, nor I think to any one else, and as there are few people in the world who are of such a right good sort as he is, I am hoping that you will be content with the *status quo*. I am thoroughly convinced that you can "afford" to let the matter be. Pray do not think that I am tendering advice— nothing of the kind! I am pleading for a friend."[1] Maitland's pleadings had no effect and the unedifying conflict continued. Maitland had little doubt that Round was in the right, historically speaking. When he received Round's pamphlet he wrote to him "I shall learn much, though I expect to feel in my proper person some of the blows that you inflict upon H.H. I fear that what I read will be all too true, and yet of the said H.H. I am fond."[2] Both parties appealed to the editor of the *English Historical Review* for a judgement, and Poole asked Maitland to act as umpire. Maitland was "tormented" by the request. He begged Poole to look else- where—"Would not the good Bishop (Stubbs) intervene?"—he had known that "his very good friend" Hall was incapable of sus- taining an argument but had not, when he saw Hall's proofs, suspected the blunders. "If all that R. says is true, I still think that he is using language that should be reserved for cases of a very different sort . . . Poor Hall has a curious fluffy mind, but never scamps work, besides being (but this alas is irrelevant) the most unselfish man I have ever known."[3] So Poole had to under- take the thankless task himself,[4] and Hall retired wounded from the fray. "This, alas, is irrelevant." So Round himself would have said, omitting the "alas"! When in 1899 the *Athenaeum* sent Maitland Round's *Commune of London* for review,[5] Maitland, we are free to believe, was not sorry to have a chance of saying what he thought of Round's methods.

The review is anonymous but unmistakable.[6] It is a learned and appreciative estimate of an important book, but it puts its finger unerringly on Round's weak points—his failure to produce

[1] 7 September 1896 (L.U.L. 653).   [2] 31 August 1898 (L.U.L. 653).
[3] 7 September 1898 (*C.H.J.*, 1952, pp. 325 ff.).   [4] *E.H.R.*, 1899, p. 148.
[5] The editor was Norman MacColl, Maitland's fellow as one of the "Sunday Tramps". The review appeared in the number for 21 October 1899.
[6] Reprinted, for the first time, *Sel. Hist. Ess.*, pp. 259-265.

large-scale constructive work,[1] and his bad manners in writing history. Round did history invaluable service by his devotion to exact scholarship, too often displayed in exposing the errors of others.[2] In this he excelled; but he completely lacked the courtesy and modesty with which Maitland advanced his corrective views. Now at last Maitland unsheathes his rapier to counter Round's battle-axe. Too much of Round's brilliant gifts, he suggests, are devoted to slaughtering his opponents. "Gnawing off the nose of a butchered foe", is not the technique of the good historical critic, "who executes justice, in an appendix, as noiselessly and painlessly as may be." If Round goes out of his way to sneer at Kate Norgate's "lady's Latin" "We do not say that Mr. Round's German is gentlemanly" when he mis-spells the name of a distinguished historian. Did Maitland really find this part of his task unpleasant? We may doubt it. But having sheathed his blade, he gives the greater part of his review to a close and appreciative examination of the valuable contributions to knowledge in Round's non-controversial section.[3] The review appears to have terminated the intimacy of the two. Round, who was as vain as he was learned, wrote a peevish rejoinder in the *Athenaeum*,[4] insinuating that the "erudite critic" was of those who received only with carping comments the results of "the dreary work of exploration"[5] which they were nevertheless ready to use.

"I am sorry", wrote Maitland to Poole, "that Round has taken offence. I tried to do him full justice and thought that by this time he would have lost the taste for unmitigated praise such as is rightly bestowed upon promising young persons."[6] He himself had warmly welcomed Tait's criticisms of *Domesday Book and*

[1] The bibliography of Round's writings by W. Page, in *Family Origins and other Studies, by the late J. Horace Round* (1930), pp. xlix-lxxiv, is the best evidence of the truth of this allegation.

[2] That he sometimes overreached himself as a critic as shown by Powicke, *Modern Historians* (1955), p. 57. For an estimate of Round's positive achievements, see Stenton, *English Feudalism* (1932), pp. 1-6. See also Galbraith, *The Making of Domesday Book* (1961), p. 123.

[3] Subsequent research has borne out his criticism of Round's view of the bull *Laudabiliter*. See A. L. Poole, *Domesday Book to Magna Carta* (1951), p. 300 n. 1.

[4] 28 October 1899.

[5] Contrast Maitland's enjoyment in compiling an Anglo-French grammar for the use of students of the Year Books (Fisher, pp. 166-7).

[6] *C.H.J.*, p. 328. Note 44 on this page misses the allusion.

Beyond in 1897,[1] all the more, because he had, according to Poole, "suffered from too much adulation".[2] But Round lacked both the humour and the generosity of his critic, and six months later Maitland wrote "I foresee that I shall have J. H. R. as an assailant until the end of our joint lives."[3] Round was to outlive Maitland by twenty-one years, and was to pay posthumous tribute to the "great genius" of the historian who had "to prove all things",[4] but he was incapable of valuing justly that combination of absolute intellectual integrity with courtesy, modesty and kindliness in which Maitland the critic has never been excelled.

This modesty is apparent in his obituary notice of Stubbs,[5] worthy of re-reading by a generation that has heard much of that great man's small defects. Maitland writes with the deference, not to say the diffidence, of a pupil. As we have seen, he had upheld a view on the authority of Canon Law diametrically opposed to that of Stubbs. But he "hated to bark at the heels of a great man whom he admired", and was prepared, in 1898, to destroy all or some of the sheets of his *Canon Law in England* if the reappearance of his articles in book form would make Stubbs "more unhappy than a sane man is whenever people dissent from him"[6] As a Cambridge man, and one who had never met Stubbs in person, he only agreed under pressure to write "four or five pages" for Poole.[7] But what he had to say came to nine pages. Full measure of honour could be given where honour was due without any sacrifice of truth.[8]

In the years following the death of Stubbs Maitland had had to write obituary notices of colleagues and friends—Acton, Leslie Stephen, Henry Sidgwick.[9] His last tribute was to a pupil. Schools of graduate study did not exist in England or in Cam-

---

[1] See his letter to Tait printed by Powicke, *Modern Historians*, pp. 55 ff.
[2] *Ibid.*, p. 54.   [3] To Poole, 6 May 1900 (*C.H.J.*, p. 329).
[4] *Peerage and Pedigree* (1910), vol. I, p. 145.
[5] *E.H.R.*, 1901, pp. 418-426. *Coll. Pap.* III. 495-511, *Sel. Hist. Ess.*, pp. 266-276.
[6] Letter to Poole, 12 September 1898 (*C.H.J.*, p. 326).   [7] *C.H.J.*, pp. 331-4.
[8] The same fine discrimination is seen in his private references to Acton, whose obituary notice he wrote for *The Cambridge Review*, 16 October 1902. Acton had given History an established position at Cambridge (Letters to Poole, *C.H.J.*, pp. 337-9), but he was a man "who could not bring to birth the multitude of thoughts that were crowding in his mind". Letter to Jackson (Fisher, p. 135).
[9] *Coll. Pap.* III. 512-540.

bridge when Maitland was professor, but there was one Cambridge scholar of his training whose work had to be appraised in the brief notice that Maitland sent to *The Athenaeum*[1] when the news came of her untimely death. In writing of Mary Bateson he, for once, surrendered some of his characteristic reserve. "I don't feel at all sure that the editor will not suppress what I wrote in a hurry and call it hysterical—and maybe he will be right. I was not very cool."[2]

It was the last thing he wrote; he himself died three weeks later.

vii

If, fifty years after his death, we try to recover the aroma of Maitland—artist and literary craftsman as well as historian—we may begin by clutching at the personal reminiscences of those who knew him; who heard him speaking in the Union or in the Senate House, as in the immortal speech that killed the project of a Queen's University, for ladies only, in March 1897; of those who attended his lectures on English law, given "in a sort of liturgic rhythm, as though he were some sort of monk reciting the miracles of his order—but they sent one away feeling that the study of twelfth-century law was the only thing worth living for";[3] of his fellow-walkers in the Alps; of the correspondents with whom he shared his enjoyment of Spanish grammar and of the many-coloured landscape of the Canaries; of the friend who found him reading a musical score with his feet on the fender; of his children who heard from him the melodies of Mozart and Wagner and saw with him the drawings of Blake. But in the end we come back to his writings; it is in his words and works that we can best recognize Maitland.

The single-minded pursuit of truth of necessity leads to a concern for words. "If we speak, we must speak with words. If we think, we must think with thoughts. Perhaps, as Mr. Gilbert suggested, it is too late to be Early English. Every thought will be too sharp, every word will imply too many contrasts."[4] The

---

[1] *Athenaeum*, 8 Dec. 1906. *Coll. Pap.* III. 540-3, *Sel. Hist. Ess.*, pp. 277-8.

[2] To Poole, 5 December 1906 (*C.H.J.*, p. 351).

[3] J. T. Shotwell, another student, complained that he could take no notes at Maitland's lectures because they were so interesting.   [4] *Township and Borough*, p. 22.

desire, the determination to describe justly the truth that he had perceived or the conception he had grasped made Maitland's ear for gradations in the scale of meaning extraordinarily sensitive, as Mr. Schuyler has said. It made his style at times allusive—only by recalling a series of analogies can the point be made; at times tentative, as Vinogradoff has described. "He feels his way, as it were, like a musician running his fingers over the keys in an improvised prelude towards *leitmotivs* and harmonious combinations." When his children heard him trying out his lectures orally, what they heard was not an orator practising his effects before an imaginary audience, but an explorer eager to communicate his discoveries as he himself had made them. In an undergraduate speech he had gibed at the "Lords of the realm of tautology"; twenty-seven years later he is "struggling with the unnecessary adjective; we must have as many substantives and verbs as possible".[1] It is from this rejection of the superfluous that his lapidary phrases are born. "The very early concentration of justice in this *conquered country*" gives us the long-distance effects of the Norman Conquest in two words. "Of the old belief that all the Middle Ages lived at the same time there remains the disposition to think that all 'Low Latin' is equally low", kills with one stone two very big birds. "I doubt if we Englishmen, who never clean our slates, generally know how clean the French slate was to be", gives us the legal consequences of the French Revolution, but a good deal more. Something has already been said of his use of the concrete, his "tracing of ideas to their embodiment in facts" (Vinogradoff). In the written word this often flowers into metaphor. Praising a younger historian, he will say "one of the virtues which is placing Mr. Tout in the very front rank of our historians is his determination to leave no stone unturned, no thicket unbeaten. Out of the thicket may fly a bird worth powder and shot. Under the stone may lurk a toad with a jewel in its head."[2] But the metaphor can also be used with the "musician's" approach. When describing how Leslie Stephen trained his team of contributors to the Dictionary of National Biography (of whom

[1] Fisher, p. 14; letter to Round, 27 December 1897 (at Girton College).
[2] *E.H.R.*, 1906, p. 783; *Coll. Pap.* II. 488.

Maitland himself was one),[1] largely by personal example, he will say "In course of time the stroke was caught. Many could raise the flower. A school has been established."[2] And, when he reaches the point where words will not serve him, Maitland the poet can still make us share his vision. He is speaking of Leslie Stephen's wife—Virginia Woolf's Mrs. Ramsay. "Her friends Watts and Burne-Jones did their best; Mrs. Cameron her best; Leslie himself said a little in the 'Forgotten Benefactors'; eyes that saw and ears that heard can never be satisfied."[3]

We are in the same case with Maitland himself. Let us say with Powicke, "Maitland is one of the immortals" and leave it at that.

---

[1] Maitland wrote on Le Breton, Fleta, Glanvill and his own father, John Gorham Maitland.

[2] *Life and letters of Leslie Stephen*, p. 372. (The reference is to Tennyson's "The Flower".)

[3] *Ibid.*, p. 312.

Index

Index

Laws of Edward the Confessor, 12, 15, 16, 30, 46, 169
Laws of Teutonic nations, 124
Le Bras, G., 225
Lees, B. A., 75
Leges Henrici, 121, 168
Leicht, P. S., 168 n.
Lennard, R., 74 n.
Levett, A. E., 35 n.
Lewes, Song of, 12, 189
Lewes, Battle of, 137
Lewis, C. S., 181
Liberty *see* Franchise
Liebermann, F., 59 n., 108 n.
Lincoln, Statute of, 152
Livery, 52-4, 58
Lobel, M. D., 35 n.
London, 14, 29, 57, 85-105, 134, 139, 155, 164, 224
   ,,   charter of 1132, 85, 86, 87
   ,,   ,,   ,, 1319, 92,
   ,,   ,,   ,, 1327, 90, 93, 105 n.
   ,,   courts of, 85-94, 105, 108, 118
   ,,   crafts of, 155
   ,,   custom of, 95, 102, 104, 105
   ,,   rents in, 96, 97, 100-5
Lords (feudal and manorial), 15, 26, 28, 30, 32, 37, 46, 47, 48, 51-5, 59, 74, 76, 78, 79, 81, 152
Lords (in parliament), 18, 112-16, 128, 130, 131, 140, 146-8, 154, 166, 187
Lordship, 46, 54-6
Lousse, É, 159-63, 165, 166, 168, 171, 172
Lyon, Bryce, 47 n., 49

MacColl, M., 225, 227
McFarlane, K. B., 55, 57, 58 n., 156, 201, 207
McIlwain, C. H., 135, 179, 196, 218, 220, 221
McKisack, M., 207
Madox, T., 37 n., 73, 78, 79, 107 n., 108 n., 118 n., 119, 125
Magna Carta, 11, 12, 38, 39, 48, 72, 121, 135 f., 139, 143, 150, 164, 194 f.
Maine, H., 22
Maintenance, 52, 58
Maitland, E., 218 n.
Maitland, F. W., 17, 22-7, 31, 35, 40, 44, 45 n., 46, 51, 63, 64, 72 n., 73, 74, 75, 78 n., 79, 81 n., 83, 96 n., 100 n., 101 n., 104 n., 107, 110, 128, 135, 143, 161, 188, 189 n., 190, 192-5, 210, 212-34
Major, J. R., 172-3
Mallum, 108, 123, 124
Manor, The, 30, 45, 57, 63, 71, 74, 76, 81, 216-17
Manorialism, 45-6
Marlborough, Statute of, 89, 90, 137, 143
Marongiu, A., 160
Matthew Paris, 189, 191, 194

Maurer, G. L. von, 193
Maxwell-Lyte, H. C., 219
Mayor, appearance of, 164
Mayor of London, 87, 88, 90-4, 105, 134
Meekings, C. A. F., 39 n.
Merchants, 138-40, 144, 154, 155, 157, 158
Merton, Council of, 136
Miller, E., 29 n., 33, 38 n., 39 n.
Mills, M. H., 191, 194
Milsom, S. F. C., 88 n., 91 n.
Modus tenendi parliamentum, 126 n., 127, 129
Moots, 13, 23, 25, 26, 168. *See* borough, folk moot, halmote, hundred, shire, soke
Morison, S. E., 183
Morris, J. E., 51
Morris, W. A., 26 n., 29 n., 32 n., 119-21, 122, 135
Mortmain, 102, 103
   ,,   Statute of, 151, 163
Myers, A. R., 130 n., 143, 148

Neale, J. E., 58 n., 226 n.
Neilson, N., 61 n., 75
Newgate gaol, 88, 92, 105 n.
Norman Conquest, 27, 30, 44, 66, 85, 163, 194
Normandy, 44, 46
Northampton, Assize of, 71
   ,,   Parliament of, 139, 153
   ,,   Statute of, 153
Novel Disseisin, Assize of, 16, 77, 94, 95-105

Offa, 41, 64
Olivier-Martin, F., 97 n., 100 n.
Ordinances, 132, 133, 134, 138, 139, 140, 141, 142, 150, 151
Ordinances, The, of 1310-11, 110, 111, 150, 203
Oswaldslaw, 28, 45, 64
Otway Ruthven, A. J., 22 n., 42 n., 54
Outlawry, 118, 120, 122

Page, W., 34 n., 86 n.
Painter, S., 31 n., 35
Palatinates, 33-5, 120
Palgrave, F., 190
Parliament, 17-21, 106-31, 132-58 *passim*, 166, 168, 174, 185, 190, 191, 195-9, 204-8, 213, 218-23
Parliament of 1258 (Oxford), 137, 157
   ,,   ,, 1259, 53
   ,,   ,, 1290, 109
   ,,   ,, 1295, 106
   ,,   ,, 1297, 106
   ,,   ,, 1315, 72
   ,,   ,, 1318 (York), 110, 111
   ,,   ,, 1322 (York), 110
   ,,   ,, 1328 (Northampton), 139, 153
   ,,   ,, 1333, 128